MANY VOICES

TRUE TALES

FROM AMERICA'S PAST

MANY VOICES
TRUE TALES
FROM AMERICA'S PAST

The National
Storytelling Association

The National Storytelling Press
Jonesborough, Tennessee

© 1995 by the
National Storytelling Association

Published by the
National Storytelling Press
of the National Storytelling Association
P.O. Box 309 ■ Jonesborough, Tenn. 37659 ■ 800-525-4514

Printed in the United States

99 98 97 96 95   5 4 3 2 1

Director of Publishing: Nell Tsacrios

Editor and Project Director: Mary C. Weaver
Copy Editor: Becky Menn-Hamblin
Art Director: Jane L. Hillhouse
Art Assistant: Martha V. Jones

Library of Congress Cataloging-in-Publication Data

Many Voices: True Tales From America's Past/The National Storytelling Association:
    [project director and editor, Mary C. Weaver].
        p.   cm.
    Includes bibliographical references and index.
    Summary: Includes thirty-six stories, based on facts, describing people and events
from over three hundred years of American history.
    ISBN 1-879991-17-9
    1. United States—History—Anecdotes—Juvenile literature.
    [1. United States—History—Anecdotes. 2. Storytelling—Collections.]
    I. Weaver, Mary C.   II. National Storytelling Association (U.S.)
    E178.3.M32   1995
    973—dc20   95-21310
                                                                         CIP
                                                                          AC

Preface

Many Voices was created to help breathe life into history. Much more than a collection of unrelated facts, names, and dates, our history is indeed our story—our interpretation of past events, a reflection of the way we see ourselves and of what we think really matters.

This collection's 36 stories are essentially true: they describe actual events and people or are based on fictional characters in true-to-life situations. (Each story's introduction indicates any artistic license invoked in the tale that follows.) The stories are arranged chronologically, and each is dated by the year of the plot's conclusion.

Contributed by 36 storytellers from the United States and Canada, the tales illustrate the struggles, joys, and triumphs of people from many ethnic groups and all walks of life. Some of the stories' characters are famous: Abraham Lincoln, Sacagawea, Scott Joplin, and Sitting Bull, to name a few. Others are ordinary citizens who lived during extraordinary times. Many stories include a child's perspective—for after all, it is not only grown-ups who helped shape and build our country.

The tales are meant to be told as well as read both silently and aloud. And although this book is well-suited to classroom use, the stories may be read purely for pleasure. Think of this collection simply as a series of tales, like the bits of calico cloth that make up a vast quilt, gathered to shed light on the North American experience.

This book's companion volume—the *Many Voices Teacher's Guide*—offers helpful teaching tips, learning objectives, questions for discussion, worksheets, and a rich variety of classroom activities. Together the two volumes can be used to enrich the history curriculum and make the subject compelling and relevant to young learners.

The National Storytelling Association

(NSA) is a nonprofit organization dedicated

to promoting the practice and application of storytelling.

Founded in 1975, NSA now counts as members

some 7,000 teachers, librarians, storytellers, therapists,

ministers, and others who have made storytelling

and story-listening part of their

work and life.

Contents

Anne Hutchinson

Jonathan Kruk

Twenty years after the pilgrims celebrated their religious freedom in the New World, Anne Hutchinson was banished. Teaching that the Holy Spirit came to inspire us as a friend, Anne threatened the Puritans' rigid rule. This story— based on accounts of her trial, colonial occurrences, and Native American traditions—reveals this country's early struggles for religious and racial tolerance. The dialogue is an imaginative retelling of events from Anne's life. Banished in 1638, she and her followers left Massachusetts for Rhode Island, only to be asked to leave in 1642. The Hutchinson group sought sanctuary in a remote wilderness claimed by the Dutch yet controlled by the Native Wappinger Confederation. A year before the Hutchinson party arrived, the Dutch Director-General Willem Kieft had massacred hundreds of Wappinger people. Soon thereafter, many native people took revenge. In 1643 European and native fears and misunderstandings clashed at the Hutchinson settlement.

CAPTAIN JOHN UNDERHILL, THE MASSACHUSETTS COLONY'S HERO OF THE Pequot Indian War, felt a strange chill despite the terrific fire roaring from the Hutchinsons' hearth. And the captain liked being the only man in a room with 50 petticoated women. He squirmed and tugged at the corners of his frock coat.

Could it be Mrs. Hutchinson's lively talk about the Holy Spirit's being a person, like a friend standing close by? he wondered. *Does Mrs. Hutchinson know that her description of the Holy Spirit sounds much like the Indian belief in a manitou, or Great Spirit?*

Captain Underhill thought about a Pequot Indian he'd found during the war. The poor man had had a musket ball deep in his chest. Underhill remembered that the man had smiled and said, "My friend the Great Spirit comes and is in me." With his last breath, he said, "We go!"

"Captain Underhill? Captain Underhill!" a woman's voice called.

The captain returned from his daydream. "Forgive me, Anne!" he answered.

"I do pray my talks offer some inspiration, Captain," said Anne Hutchinson.

"Indeed. You are my inspiration! I was merely thinking."

"On what subject, sir?"

"The newly elected colonial governor, Anne. I do hope he will prove as kind to you as our former governor, Henry Vane."

"I daresay Elder John Winthrop is a fair man. No doubt he will govern the Massachusetts Colony well."

"Yea, no doubt." The captain paused and asked, "But how will he look upon your teachings? You have all the ladies of Boston town believing that if they have enough faith, the Holy Spirit will walk right up and embrace them!"

Mrs. Hutchinson smiled. "'Tis what the Good Book says, Captain: 'Know ye not that ye are the temple of God and that the Spirit of God dwelleth in you?'"

"Verily, I know, with thanks to you, dear lady."

Now, many of the ladies who had come to listen to Anne Hutchinson speak gathered to hear what she'd say about the colony's new governor.

Underhill went on. "Mrs. Hutchinson, often you say that good works without faith lead to death. Now, Elder Winthrop claims he follows the advice in Matthew's Gospel and lets his light shine before men, that they may see his good works. That's the Puritan way to get to Heaven! Why, I once heard Winthrop preach: 'An hour spent idle, doing nothing, is as sinful as an hour spent drunk!' The church says we must prove our faith by our works. What, pray tell, will you do?"

Anne's husband stepped forward to answer for his wife. He patted down his high lace collar and explained, "Ever since we arrived here last year, Anne has done good works because of her faith. She patches breeches for poor farmers and gives willow-bark tea to Indians feverish with smallpox. She even comforted a gossip locked in the stocks! For a year now Anne has been a woman of both works and faith."

"Dear husband," Anne said, smiling, "I thank you for your kindly defense, but I thank the Holy Spirit for coming to me with these gifts. And as for Governor Winthrop, he knows I am only preaching to women—and to you, my good captain. Let him send a magistrate for me if he has any doubts."

The ladies giggled and raised their eyebrows at their teacher's little challenge.

It was not long before the governor did call for Anne Hutchinson. She had to appear in court on a dank November morning.

Dressed in a simple black cloak with a painfully sharp white collar, the new colonial governor of Massachusetts Bay boomed, "Mrs. Hutchinson, this tribunal has been assembled for you. We want to help you save your soul. So explain, please, that you did not mean to preach that the Holy

"And as for Governor Winthrop," said Anne, "he knows I am only preaching to women— and to you, my good captain. Let him send a magistrate for me if he has any doubts."

Spirit is a person, uniting only with the faithful."

Anne stood alone before a handful of men. She spent the next 10 hours explaining her teachings and her good works. The tribunal, however, did not care to hear what she had to say in her own defense. They listened, while now and then Winthrop interrupted, asking, "That's all well and good, but will you confess to a heresy about the Holy Spirit?"

"Lord Governor, I cannot in clear conscience confess to any such crime," Anne said. "Will you please let me call in my husband or Captain Underhill or former Governor Vane to help me explain my . . ."

"Cease!" Winthrop barked. "We are here to help you save your soul."

"Well, then, my Lord, please grant a recess so that I might have a little food. I have been standing for more than eight hours without pause and . . ."

"Cease! You will talk until we are satisfied your soul can be saved!"

When night fell, the tribunal reached its decision. "Anne Hutchinson, you have committed a foul heresy. You have lied about the Holy Spirit and acted brazenly by preaching in public. We sentence you to be burned to death at the stake." Winthrop paused.

"Bring Mrs. Hutchinson some water, and revive her from that fainting spell. It will do no good if she cannot hear the rest of our decision."

When Anne came to, Governor Winthrop went on. "Your good works, however, move us to show mercy. You, Anne Hutchinson, and any of those who still follow you are hereby banished forever from the Massachusetts Bay Colony."

The court did show one more bit of "mercy." Anne did not have to leave Massachusetts until winter had passed. She was held in a jail made from a tiny bedroom in the house of Joseph Welde.

In March 1638 Anne Hutchinson, a few loyal followers, her husband, and most of their children journeyed south by horse cart on the Post Road to Rhode Island. They found little acceptance there. The strain of the ordeal aggravated Mr. Hutchinson's consumption, and he later died during a coughing spasm.

One day while in the market, Anne learned that the Dutch Colony of New Netherlands welcomed all kinds of settlers. A Dutch fisherman said, "Why, I have heard Director-General Kieft boast that 18 languages can be heard spoken on the cobblestone streets of New Amsterdam. And that's with just 2,000 inhabitants! See here, my good woman, if settlers leave New England's colonies to join the New Netherlands, it strengthens Kieft's hand against the Indians."

Anne listened. In late summer 1642, with her few followers and her children, she boarded the schooner of John Throckmorton and sailed along the Connecticut coast for the New Netherlands.

Throckmorton explained, "We'll go to settle the necks of land east of the Broncks' farm. It's a dark wilderness, with trees as big around as three men outstretched. I've heard it takes one man a year to clear off an acre there."

Anne wondered aloud, "Why, pray tell, Mr. Throckmorton, are we going to try to settle such an inhospitable land?"

"The Dutch call the wilderness a *Vredeland,* or place of peace. All people, English or French, Quaker or Huguenot, are welcome to live there, free to practice whatever religion their hearts choose."

Throckmorton bid Anne and her tiny band of settlers farewell on a desolate neck of land a few miles northeast of Jonas Bronck's farm. Immediately everyone began to work in preparation for winter. Great trees were felled and stones gathered to make a few houses. These were not homes capable of sheltering 50 ladies, as the Hutchinsons' home in Boston had been. These were structures of rough-cut oak with a dirt-floor kitchen, a sleeping loft, and a roof hole to vent smoke and air. The beams fit together, tongue in groove, and 8-year-old Susannah, Anne's youngest daughter, was given the task of chinking them. She gathered gooey mud from the nearby marsh and mixed it with dry grass. Carefully she stuffed the mixture between the wall boards.

"Mother!" Susannah called. "Come look at my wattle! I've filled in all the chinks. We'll surely stay warm come winter."

Anne smiled and folded her arms over Susannah. Collins, Anne's son-in-law, inspected Susannah's work. "We'll need to leave a few openings."

"Why?" asked Susannah.

"We'll want to look through to see if Indians are about to attack."

"Will they, Mother? Will they attack?"

"We'll pray the Holy Spirit will come to be with us," Anne offered.

"Yea," added Collins. "And I pray that Captain Underhill comes here with us and the Holy Spirit!"

Winter passed uneventfully for Anne Hutchinson's tiny colony. But down on the southern tip of Manhattan Island, tensions were high. Several hundred local Mahican Indians, fleeing Mohawk warriors armed with Dutch-supplied muskets, sought protection from Director-General Kieft. The director kept them safe in a couple of forts—for a while.

But then the Dutch folk living in New Amsterdam cried, "The Mohawks are gone. Get rid of the Mahicans! Why don't they pay a tax for our protection? Listen to their howling and chanting. They're planning to attack us!"

Pressured by a committee of 12 wealthy men, Kieft gathered a well-armed force of about 100 soldiers and attacked the unsuspecting Indians while they slept. Fearing they'd tell other Indians about the attack, Kieft ordered his men to kill every Indian they saw. The Indians' screams woke up all of New Amsterdam several miles away. Children were shot trying to swim across the Hudson River. Only a few survived to tell the terrible tale.

Among those who heard of the massacre was a sachem, or chief, named Wampage. The council fire blazed when Wampage took the talking stick and vowed, "I, Wampage, sachem for the Weckquaskeck people, ask Manitou, the Great Spirit, to be with me as I avenge the deaths of our brothers and sisters at the hands of the white savages!"

Months later Wampage discovered Anne Hutchinson's settlement. He approached respectfully, offering a wampum belt. The little colony got an eyeful in Wampage. He stood half a foot taller than Collins. He sported red dyed hair that looked like quills on top and a horsetail in the back, and he wore only a deerskin loincloth. His lean, tattooed body glistened with bear grease. Anne managed to smile and curtsy like the proper Englishwoman she still was.

"I am Anne Hutchinson," she called.

Wampage, imitating, did the same. "Ann-Hooek?"

Collins frowned; the older children cowered in fear. But little Susannah laughed, delighted with Wampage's gawky curtsy. The girl's joy briefly caught hold of the sachem, and he laughed too. He reached into his deerskin pouch, beaded with colored porcupine quills. Out came a chunk of maple-sugar-sweetened corn mashed with deer meat. "Pemmican?" he said, offering it to the girl. Taking the gift, Susannah curtsied and said thank you. Abruptly Wampage turned and disappeared into the forest. He could not allow himself to become too friendly with the white tribe he thought had massacred his people.

"See, my dear ones," cried Anne, "the Holy Spirit is with us. The native folk will bring us no harm."

Later, during the night, Collins squinted through a chink in Susannah's wattle. "I hear something out in the wilderness . . ."

Hiss! Pop!

The attack took the Hutchinson settlers completely by surprise. Wampage had returned with a war party. Fiery arrows pierced the tiny square houses. Trapped in a tinderbox, Anne's followers and family scarcely had time to scream before the smoke and heat filled their lungs. Only Anne managed to meet the Holy Spirit in the silence of prayer.

Susannah burst outside, thinking the fire pit had gotten out of control. An Indian caught sight and pointed his arrow at her, but Wampage pushed the man aside.

The sachem chased Susannah down and carried her back to his village. Stunned, little Susannah didn't speak for an entire year. But when she did, she spoke only in the Algonquian dialect of Wampage's people. Wampage's name was not spoken anymore either. At the next council fire, he took the talking stick and proclaimed, "I take, with respect, my slain enemy's name. I am now Ann-Hooek."

And that name later appeared on a deed selling Thomas Pell's lands in the Bronx and Westchester County, including the lost settlement of Anne Hutchinson.

When Captain Underhill learned of Anne's death, he left New England to become an officer in the Dutch New Netherlands army. He delivered many more Native Americans to the Great Spirit. One village of 500 souls, near what is now Bedford in Westchester County, New York, met a fiery death at Underhill's hands.

A few years later Kieft drowned in the Atlantic Ocean. The Mahicans died of smallpox or moved farther and farther west. We are reminded of Anne Hutchinson by the name of a scenic parkway. And as for Captain Underhill, may God rest his poor spirit.

Born an army brat in Texas and raised in Westchester County, New York, Jonathan Kruk, M.A., grew up on tall tales and daydreams. Traveling from the forks of Long Island through the Hudson Valley, Kruk offers children a world of participatory tales. Each year he gives more than 350 performances and creative-writing workshops. A National Endowment for the Humanities grant enabled Kruk to work with urban children on a local-history project. He lives in Cold Spring on Hudson, New York.

The Man Who Would Not Change His Name

Judith Kinter

This story describes the flight of Judge Caleb Potter from the wrath of King Charles II of England. It covers the tumultuous period from 1642 to 1680, when the issue of the divine right of kings split royalist Cavaliers from Cromwell's Roundhead Puritans. Escaping to America with other Puritans, Caleb continued to be affected by matters of religious freedom, discontent with English rule, and uneasy relations with Native American tribes. In the end his stubbornness helped him survive the harsh New England wilderness, but it brought disaster to him and all who aided him. Although the story is fictionalized, the facts are accurate according to research done by Millicent Pierce Potter, my grandmother and a descendant of Caleb Potter.

ONE FOGGY LONDON MORNING LONG AGO IN 1660 JUDGE CALEB POTTER WAS sitting at his bench, deciding a difficult dispute over a piece of land. Everyone in the courtroom was tense, waiting for his verdict. On one side sat an arrogant lord with his friends of the royal Cavalier Party. They wore long wigs, red coats, shiny black boots, and fancy hats with broad brims. Glaring at them from the other side was a common Puritan man with his friends, dressed in plain gray clothes. They were Roundheads and had been given that nickname because they cut their hair short.

The Cavalier lord claimed the land was his. The Puritan commoner claimed the lord had stolen the land from him.

The air bristled with hostility. It was a difficult time to be alive in England and a dangerous time to be a judge.

Caleb Potter, a Puritan, was one of the "regicide" judges who had condemned the tyrant King Charles I to death in 1649 because the king refused to grant the people any rights. The Roundheads, led by Oliver Cromwell, had taken over the government to help the people, and Caleb had become one of the richest and most powerful men in all England.

But 10 years had passed. Cromwell was dead. Without their strong leader, the Roundheads were losing power. The Cavaliers were threatening to revolt and make King Charles's son the new ruler.

Caleb stood up to give his verdict. He knew the loser of the case would be angry, but he was a brave man who prided himself on doing what was fair and right, come what may. In a strong voice he announced his decision in favor of the Puritan.

He didn't expect what happened next.

The Cavaliers jumped up, drawing their swords and shouting threats at Caleb, and broke up the court in a riot. Caleb escaped out the back door. He knew he had lost his power and would have to flee for his life.

Not long afterward the Cavaliers took over the government and put King Charles II on the throne. The first thing the new king did was make a vow to execute every last judge who had condemned his father.

Caleb had barely escaped with his wife, Caroline, when King Charles confiscated his mansion and everything in it. And so a battle of wills began. Caleb declared he would never be taken, and he had a stubborn streak that didn't know the meaning of the words *give up*.

But the king was equally stubborn. He sent his soldiers in all directions with the order to pursue Caleb to the ends of the earth if necessary and bring him back alive to feel the king's royal vengeance.

It was the beginning of a lifelong flight, with Caleb never sure whether he was one step ahead or one step behind. Wherever he went, he left a trail of disaster for those who tried to help him.

Tall and dark, with a rugged, stern face, Caleb walked with a tell-tale limp and was terrified that someone would recognize him. He and Caroline sped on horseback far north, beyond Liverpool, to the farm of his cousin Weldon.

"You're welcome to stay here," Weldon told him. "Change your name, and no one will ever know who you are."

Caleb's eyes grew dark with sorrow, and his jaw tightened. "Never!" he cried. "I've lost my position, my home, and all I had—everything but my name. If I lose that, I'll feel as if I'd lost my whole life. Don't ask me to give up my name!"

The first victim of Caleb's stubbornness was his wife. Caroline knew that when Caleb had made a decision, no amount of reasoning or pleading would move him an inch. So she said nothing. But she worried and fretted herself sick, and after two years she died. Then, with hardly time to grieve, Caleb found that the king's soldiers had caught up with him, and he fled with only the clothes on his back and a pouch of money hidden under his shirt.

Weldon was the second victim. He was arrested for aiding a criminal, and he died in prison.

Meanwhile, Caleb headed for Liverpool and boarded the first ship out for America. In those days the Puritans were leaving England in droves for the new land where they could follow their religious beliefs without

Tall and dark, with a rugged, stern face, Caleb walked with a tell-tale limp and was terrified that someone would recognize him.

persecution, so Caleb found himself among friends.

After many weeks the ship landed at Salem, near Boston. Caleb's heart leapt at the sight of what he thought was freedom. He would buy a house and live in peace. But he hadn't counted on the intelligence and quickness of his archenemy, the king. Before he had a chance to set foot on shore, he saw two red-coated Cavalier soldiers waiting to check the boat.

An officer seized Caleb, but his Puritan comrades came to his rescue by starting a fight. In the confusion Caleb left his friends to pay the price for resisting the king and fled into the forest. Caleb headed due west to somewhere, anywhere—to find a settlement so far away that no one would ever find him.

But he hadn't counted on a forest like this. Caleb had entered a wilderness of maple and oak trees, hemlocks and pines, tangled with vines and choked with underbrush so dense that he had to fight for every inch. He had to go through ravines, around granite boulders, and across river after river. His bad knee slowed him down, but he couldn't risk the easier way on established trails. He might meet trappers, Indians—even soldiers.

So Caleb pushed, slashed, and crawled his way through 100 aching miles of what is now Massachusetts. His only food was birds' eggs and watercress. His only companions were mosquitoes and his stubborn will.

One day blurred into the next as he struggled through the Berkshire Hills and headed north into Vermont. The brilliant red and yellow hues of autumn were fading to the stark, icy blue-white of winter, and Caleb knew he had to find a settlement soon. In his hurry he slipped on a frosty granite ledge, struck his knee and head, and fell unconscious.

When he came to, he was lying on the ground. He looked up into a circle of dark faces. The faces belonged to members of an Algonquian tribe. They gave Caleb food, bound up his knee, and made him a slave—for three long years. They also gave him a new name: "Many Deer."

Caleb did as he was told, but all the while he was looking for a chance to escape. One day the chief let Caleb take some boys on a four-day fishing trip. When they arrived at their camping place near Bennington, Vermont, Caleb sent each boy out on a different path—except for the one heading north. As soon as the boys were safely gone, he took the northward path himself and was free once again—and struggling through the wilderness once more.

After walking for four days up and down the Green Mountains of Vermont, Caleb heard a strange sound—a loud horn and a sweet voice calling. He wondered if he was in heaven. He followed the sounds and discovered—at last!—a cabin. A couple named McDaniels lived there with their daughter, Sally. He was near a settlement called Dorset.

Caleb promptly gave the McDanielses his name and told them about his flight from the king. The family was sympathetic. Even though it was only 1664, many settlers were grumbling about the way the king was treating them, and the hard feelings that led to the Revolutionary War a hundred years later were already building up. The settlers were especially unhappy with the way the redcoat soldiers were pouncing on them and carrying them off to fight the French in Canada.

The McDanielses said, "Stay with us, Caleb. Change your name, and we'll tell everyone you're a pioneer. No one will ever know your secret."

But Caleb refused, saying, "My name is all I have. I cannot give up my name."

The McDanielses let him stay anyway, and he helped them on their homestead. He learned how to build, plant crops, hunt, and trap for furs. He learned how to carve bowls from wood and to grind corn.

All went well for a year and a half, until one day a traveling peddler came to the McDaniels homestead. They were overjoyed to see him, and not only because they wanted the cloth and tools he brought. Peddlers were the news media of the day—the people's main connection with the outside world.

The peddler told them, "I saw two English officers in Dorset today. It seems there's a criminal somewhere about who's wanted by the king. They put up a poster at the tavern about a reward. The man is tall and dark and walks with a limp. His name is Caleb Potter."

Instantly Caleb knew he had to leave. The McDanielses knew it too because the penalty for aiding a fugitive from justice was a heavy fine and prison. As soon as the peddler disappeared down the trail, they threw together a few supplies. In minutes Caleb was heading north, and the McDanielses were heading south for the home of a friend who lived 40 miles away. In return for their kindness the McDanielses lost not only the home they loved but also the parents' lives: The mother died of exposure on the wintry trip, and the father was killed by a falling tree.

Caleb made his way to the northernmost settlement in Vermont, the town of Danby. He thought his pursuers would never find him there. He stopped at the settlement's largest cabin, but as soon as he opened the door, his hopes vanished. He found himself in a nest of men wearing long red coats, black boots, and beaver-trimmed hats—Cavaliers!

Only pure luck saved Caleb this time. The Cavaliers were too busy quarreling to think about who he might be. King Charles had rewarded them for outstanding service with a large piece of land, and they were quarreling about how to divide it. Thinking quickly, Caleb offered to settle their argument by surveying the land in exchange for a piece for himself. He gave them his Algonquian name, Many Deer.

The Cavaliers agreed, and Caleb chose the section the farthest from Danby. He built a cabin, then went to find Sally McDaniels and asked her to marry him. She agreed.

During the next 15 years they lived in the cabin, had two sons, and did very well. Caleb could have been happy at last, but he still refused to change his name, so he was always haunted by the fear that red-coated soldiers would suddenly appear and carry him away.

He went to town only when he had to and tried to avoid everyone. He figured that if he had a mill, he could grind his own grain. Then he'd be entirely self-sufficient and would never have to go out among people.

He decided to order some millstones from Bennington. He could almost taste the sweetness of peace at last. That was when he made his fatal mistake: he signed his own name to the order.

The millstones arrived, and Caleb built his mill. Then one fall morning, as the frost turned the maple leaves glorious shades of red and gold among the dark green hemlocks, he took his sons, Arnold and Philip, to school by horseback. He pulled up in the shelter of the forest and helped his sons off the horse. Just as he turned to go, he heard cries from the schoolhouse: "Help! Help!" Philip recognized the schoolmaster's voice.

Caleb did not hesitate for the blink of an eye. Every bit as strong as his stubbornness was his determination to do what was right. He had to help the schoolmaster. He limped straight through the schoolhouse door.

As he did, a strong hand seized his arm, and he heard the terrible words he had dreaded for so long: "In the name of the king I arrest you, Caleb Potter!" His archenemy had tricked him. The red-coated officers bound him and took him away. He never went home again.

But King Charles II never tasted the bittersweet vengeance he had hoped for. Caleb cheated him out of it.

On the way back to England on a prison ship, Caleb died. And all he had left was his name.

Judith Kinter of Sacramento, California, is a writer and a storyteller. A former elementary-school teacher and a mother of three, she writes articles on teaching and parenting, children's stories, and plays. Her poems have been published in the collections Ghosts and Goose Bumps *(Random House, 1991),* Puddle Wonderful *(Random House, 1992), and* Scared Silly! *(Little, Brown, 1994). She specializes in telling tandem tales with her husband, Dick, and she has written a book on tandem storytelling.*

Ticonderoga

Joseph Bruchac _____

This story, which takes place in Scotland and the American colonies during the time of the French and Indian Wars of the mid-1700s, is one that I grew up hearing. After all, Fort Ticonderoga, where the tale comes to its climax, is less than 60 miles from my home. The story paints a picture of a man caught between honor and blood responsibility and also of the turbulent time when the great powers of Europe struggled for control of the gateway to North America—the place now called New York state. Although some may question the supernatural dimension of this story, it is told in a manner completely true to its history and characters. The events are described as they are reported to have happened.

IT BEGAN, AS DO MANY SUCH STORIES OF DEATH AND GHOSTS, ON A DARK NIGHT. In his castle by the banks of the wild Awe River in the western Scottish highlands, Duncan Campbell, the Laird of Inverawe, sat drowsing by the fire, his hounds by his side. Suddenly his dogs lifted up their heads. A knock had sounded at the great door.

Duncan Campbell rose and looked down from the window. The moonlight showed him a man standing below, a man with dark stains on his kilt and his hands that could be only blood. The man lifted up his face, and Duncan Campbell saw that he was a stranger, no one he had ever seen before.

"Inverawe," the man shouted, "I am being followed by men who will kill me. I ask for sanctuary."

"Before I grant any man sanctuary," Duncan Campbell replied, "I must know that he is not guilty of any great crime. Why do those men want your life?"

"I killed a man in a fair fight," the stranger said. "Now his kinsmen seek to do me in. That is the whole of it."

"Swear on your dirk that you speak the truth, and I will grant you sanctuary," Duncan Campbell replied.

Without hesitation the man pulled out his knife and swore his oath. So Duncan Campbell went down and unbarred the door. He brought the man in and led him to a room deep within the castle, where he gave him food and drink and a bed to sleep upon. Then—for a strange restlessness was upon him—Duncan Campbell did not go to his bed but went once more to sit by the fire.

It was not a great deal of time that passed before Duncan Campbell again was roused by the sound of a fist pounding on his door. But this time when he looked out, he saw familiar faces. Below him were men of his own clan.

"Inverawe," they called up to him, "we are following a man who killed your own cousin Donald. Have you seen such a man pass this way?"

Now the Laird of Inverawe was in a terrible position. It was his duty to avenge the death of his cousin. Blood called for blood. Yet sanctuary was a sacred thing, and no man could call himself God-fearing and betray a person who had been given such refuge.

"A terrible thing it is that's been done," Duncan Campbell called back down, "but this night I cannot help you." The men of his clan wheeled their horses and rode off into the night.

Duncan Campbell took a lantern and went to the room where he had taken the man he had given sanctuary. He swung open the door and looked down at him.

"You did not tell me it was my own cousin you killed," he said, his voice filled with anger.

"Indeed, I did not," said the man, "for then there would have been no sanctuary here. But I swore that the fight was fair, and it was indeed. I have heard you are a man of your word. Will you now be the one to betray your own promise?"

"I did not give you up to my clansmen who sought your life," Duncan Campbell said, "but I can allow you to stay no longer under my roof. You must follow me."

Then Duncan Campbell led the man out through a secret door and through the night to a cave in the nearby hills.

"Here you can stay and be safe," said Duncan Campbell. "But be gone by morning. I can do no more for you."

When Duncan Campbell sat down again by his fire it was with a great weight on his mind and his heart. Somehow, though, sleep found him. But as he slept, he heard a voice calling his name.

"Duncan Campbell," the voice said. "Duncan Campbell!"

Opening his eyes, the Laird of Inverawe looked up to see before him the ghost of his murdered cousin. There was a great wound on Donald Campbell's breast and blood upon his face.

"Inverawe," the ghost said. "Inverawe! Blood has been shed. Shield not the murderer!"

Then, as suddenly as it had appeared, the ghost was gone.

Duncan Campbell leaped up and grabbed his sword. He picked up a lantern and took the trail to that cave in the hills. But when he reached it, he found the cave empty. The man who had killed his cousin was gone, and no one ever saw that man again.

But that was not true of the ghost of his cousin. Each night that terrible specter appeared to Duncan Campbell, speaking these words: "Inverawe! Inverawe! Blood has been shed."

Duncan Campbell became a man who no longer slept at night. He was a brave man, a man who had fought without fear in battle, but the weight of having shielded the murderer of his own kinsman was heavy. The guilt he carried was great, and the story of his cousin's ghost became known to all of Scotland.

Then one night the ghost appeared and spoke different words: "Farewell, Inverawe," it said. "Farewell till we meet at Ticonderoga."

Ticonderoga was a name Duncan Campbell had never heard before. He asked others about it, but no one knew of a place or a person by that name. So that mystery too became part of the story of his haunting.

WHEN THE HIGHLANDERS OF THE 42ND REGIMENT, THE FAMED BLACK WATCH, were sent to the American colonies to continue the great conflict against the French that was known in Europe as the Seven Years War and in America as the French and Indian Wars, Duncan Campbell and the tale of his ghost went along as well. He had joined the Black Watch, the elite regiment of Highlanders who went into battle with bagpipes skirling, and had become a major.

They would fight in New York, the colony whose rivers were the gateway into the heart of the huge continent. He traveled with the other Scots up the Hudson River from New York to Albany. There orders were given for them to proceed up to the long body of water the French called Lac St. Sacrement and the British, who sought to drive the French from North America, called Lake George, after their king. They would rendezvous at the site of the ruins of Fort William Henry, whose wooden ramparts General Monro had vainly defended. There a great army would be found to go up the lake and attack the French at Fort Carillon in July 1758.

The army that gathered at the southern edge of Lake George was the largest ever seen in North America. More than 15,000 men, a combination of American settlers and troops brought from the British Isles, would go up the lake in a huge flotilla to strike the French stone fort, built to command the narrows between Lake George and the even larger

Duncan Campbell leaped up and grabbed his sword. He picked up a lantern and took the trail to that cave in the hills. But when he reached it, he found the cave empty.

lake the French had named Champlain. Whoever could travel that route up the lakes would have an easy road to Montreal, the heart of France's colonial empire in North America.

With them went Sir William Johnson and a group of Mohawk warriors who had pledged their loyalty to this white man they called War-rahiyagcy—"He Who Does Much Good Business"—a man who had always dealt with them honorably. Those Mohawks were much needed, for they knew the ways through the hills and valleys around the lakes better than anyone else and understood better than the British that the rules of war were different in this new land.

The commander of those troops was a man who, we are told, was at best a second-rate soldier. A friend of the king and a political appointee to his post, General James Abercromby was called "Old Lady Nabby-cromby" behind his back. But neither Abercromby nor his troops were worried, for their real leader was one of the greatest of England's soldiers, a man respected by every man in the army—from the brave Scots of the Black Watch to the greenest colonial recruit. That man was Brigadier Lord Howe. Only 34 years old, he was described by General James Wolfe as "the noblest Englishman that has appeared in my time and the best soldier in the British army."

As they began their journey up the lake, the officers and troops of the Black Watch kept a close watch on Duncan Campbell. He was a well-loved man, brave and generous, and he was pitied for the sad circumstances that had led to his haunting. His cousin's ghost had not visited him since his long voyage to the Americas, and it was with a lighter heart than he'd had in years that he set forth on the lake toward the great battle that they would surely win.

They would not only surprise the French but also greatly outnumber the French general, the Marquis de Montcalm, and his men. The great fleet of more than a thousand boats covered a full three miles of the surface of Lake George as it set out on its triumphant way. The only cause the Black Watch had for foreboding had come when a member was talking with one of Sir William Johnson's Mohawk warriors.

"French call that place Carillon," the Mohawk said. "We remember it by another name—Ticonderoga."

At last, it seemed, Duncan Campbell was about to come to the place prophesied by his cousin's ghost. But the other men of the Black Watch, seeing how light his spirits were, decided not to tell him. They feared that if he heard he was close to Ticonderoga, he would go into battle with a heavy heart and be at greater risk of injury or death.

That day the weather was good and the lake waters calm. The huge flotilla went swiftly along, and the men camped the first night 25 miles down the lake at Sabbath Day Point. Lord Howe spread out his great bear rug and talked with the officers about how the attack would go. All was proceeding according to plan.

By morning of the next day they reached the shore just below the French fort. But before their attack, Howe decided to send out a scouting party. And it was then that everything began to go wrong. Lord Howe accompanied the party, led by the ranger Robert Rogers. By chance, as they came through the thick woods, they surprised a small party of French from the fort. Shots were exchanged before the French were routed, and 50 of them were taken prisoner. There were few British casualties, aside from the first man to fall, who was struck in the breast and died on the spot. But that man was Lord Howe, the heart of the British army.

The scouting party hurried back to tell the sad news to General Abercromby. Not only had they lost Lord Howe—now Montcalm knew they had arrived. Still, since they outnumbered the French by more than three to one, victory would certainly be theirs. But disheartened and confused by the loss of Lord Howe and faced with the greatest decision of his life, Abercromby was about to make the worst possible mistake.

Two things happened that night. Camped on the shore below the fort and the outnumbered French, the English army heard the sound of woodchoppers cutting, cutting, all through the night. And in the middle of that night Duncan Campbell came wide-eyed from his tent.

"I have seen the ghost of my cousin," he said. "He told me I've come to Ticonderoga."

When the sun rose in the morning, the army saw why the sound of axes had filled the night. The forest around the fort had been cut down, and the logs now formed an added breastwork in front of the fort. Montcalm, a general known for his craftiness, had made his weak position much stronger.

Abercromby surveyed the battlefield. Then he gave his orders. The men were to attack. But they were not to wait for the arrival of cannon, which could have cleared their way. Nor would they attack the fort's more vulnerable flank. Instead the foolish general ordered them to attack the fort head-on. Sir William and his Mohawks turned away in disgust. They climbed to the top of nearby Rattlesnake Hill, where English cannons could easily have raked the fort, and watched the sad spectacle from above the field.

The Scots of the Black Watch were among the first in that disastrous frontal attack. They fell like wheat before the scythe, but some, Duncan

Campbell among them, bravely fought their way through the hell of trees and cannon fire and musket shot and almost reached the great stone walls. But they were driven back. Carrying their wounded, they retreated—only to be told by Abercromby to attack again in the same place. Scots and colonials and British troops attacked the front of Ticonderoga three times and three times were driven back. Their losses were so great that their last retreat became a rout when General Abercromby took fright and ran. Many men left their boots stuck in the mud of the lakeshore as they scrambled for the boats.

Having suffered almost 2,000 casualties, the British made their way south while the wily Montcalm and his French, who had lost only 377 men, celebrated their great victory. Duncan Campbell was with those battered British troops. He had suffered a great wound, and a surgeon had removed his arm. He died and was buried near Fort Edward, south of the lake.

So it was that the ghost of his cousin saw Duncan Campbell for the final time, but that is not the end of the story. Far off in Scotland on the day of the battle, figures were seen in the sky, struggling among the clouds over the castle of Inverawe, and it was said by the local people to be an omen of the death of their laird.

An old man, a kinsman of Laird Duncan Campbell, told the story of how that night, when he was just a boy, a ghostly figure had appeared, dressed in full Highland regimentals. It bent over and spoke to his father. The next morning the boy asked his father what had happened.

"Och," said his father, "that was Macdonnochie.[1] It was Duncan Campbell, telling me his spirit is at last at rest.

"He finally came to Ticonderoga."

Joseph Bruchac is a writer and a storyteller who lives in the same house in the Adirondack foothills town of Greenfield Center, New York, where he was raised by his maternal grandparents. The dual focus of his work is the Adirondack region of New York and the stories of his Native American (Abenaki) heritage. His books include Dawn Land *(Fulcrum, 1993), a historical novel about the Abenaki, and the five-volume* Keepers of the Earth *series, also published by Fulcrum.*

1. Duncan Campbell's Gaelic patronymic

Lydia Darragh

Jack Briggs

This story of a woman who spied for the Continental Army during the American Revolution comes to us from her daughter, to whom Lydia Darragh revealed her secret after the war. Like other Quaker families of the time, the Darraghs struggled with conscience, torn between following the Peace Testimony of the Society of Friends and supporting the patriots' struggle for liberty. The time is December 1777, in and around Philadelphia, just before Washington withdrew to Valley Forge. Although conflicting versions of the tale exist, my story's elements are generally agreed on. Details about the delivery of the message, however, are disputed. The conversations are imagined. After a telling in Philadelphia, I was approached by a man who told me that the story was pretty much the way he had heard it in his family when he was growing up. His name was John Darragh.

IN 1777 GENERAL HOWE AND THE BRITISH ARMY WHIPPED THE AMERICANS AT the Battle of the Brandywine in September. Then they licked them again at Germantown in October. The beaten American Army retreated to Whitemarsh, where it camped on the present site of Fort Washington. The British army moved into the city of Philadelphia for the winter.

General Howe set up his headquarters on Second Street. And there he began to plan the final battle, a surprise attack that would defeat Washington once and for all and end the rebellion. But he hadn't counted on his neighbor across the street.

At number 177 lived Mistress Lydia Darragh. Now, Lydia Darragh was a small woman and somewhat frail-looking. She wore the old-fashioned gray bonnet and dress that marked her as a member of the Society of Friends. She was a Quaker—very religious, God-fearing, and devout. She was also a good wife and mother. And Lydia Darragh was a spy.

It was well known in Philadelphia at that time that the Quakers as a group were opposed to all warfare. Pacifists by conviction, they refused to take sides during the Revolution, thus earning the displeasure of both sides from time to time.

But there was a small group among the Society of Friends whose members were known as the Free Quakers. They believed that the patriot cause was right and just, and they were willing to support it by force of arms if need be. The Darraghs' son Charles was one such Quaker, and he had secretly joined the American Army. Even now he was camped with Washington at Whitemarsh.

The family supported their son, but they kept their sympathies secret from their neighbors. That was why Lydia Darragh began to spy for the Continental Army.

Lydia's bedroom window looked right out on British headquarters, and she could see the officers coming and going. When she went shopping, she would stop and chat with them. They liked her and trusted her, and why not? They all knew the Quakers did not take sides in the war. They did not suspect her.

When Lydia learned an interesting piece of information, she would go home and tell her husband, William. William had created a special secret code, and he would write the information in code on a tiny slip of paper. Lydia would take that paper, fold it up tightly, and stuff it inside a hollow wooden button mold. She'd cover the button mold with fabric and sew the button to the coat of her younger son, John.

John was 14 years old—too young to bear arms but not too young to take a long walk into the country. He would go out the Germantown Pike until he came to the Bethlehem Pike, and near Whitemarsh he would meet his brother, Charles. Charles would cut the buttons off the coat, take out the slips of paper, and return with them to American headquarters. This went on for some time.

Then near the end of November, the Darragh family were told that they would have to move. The British army had selected their house for its use.

With indignation flashing in her eyes and fire in her tongue, Lydia stormed across the street. What was the meaning of this? It was outrageous! Who was responsible for this order?

She gave 'em quite a piece of her mind, I can tell you. For although Lydia was a small woman, she could be powerful and persuasive when she got riled. The outcome was, the Darraghs were allowed to remain in their home on one condition: that at any time General Howe could use the house for staff meetings.

A few days later there came a knocking at the Darraghs' door. There stood a young British officer, an aide to General Howe. He told Lydia, "The general wishes to use your house for a meeting tonight. You are to see to it that all your family are asleep by seven o'clock. When the meeting has ended, I will knock at your bedroom door. Then you may get up, put out the lights, and lock the front door."

She gave 'em quite a piece of her mind, I can tell you. For although Lydia was a small woman, she could be powerful and persuasive when she got riled.

Lydia did as she was told, and her family were all in bed by seven. William was snoring away beside her, but Lydia could not sleep. She lay wide awake, weighed down, she later said, by a great sense of evil.

She heard the British officers come into the house and go into the room selected for the meeting, but she couldn't hear clearly what they were saying. So she got out of bed and slipped on her dressing gown.

The floor was icy cold. She tiptoed out of the bedroom and down the hall, slowly, slowly . . . The floorboard squeaked! Had they heard? The penalty for spying was death. No . . .

She went on until she came to a closet beside the meeting room. She went in, and there only a thin partition separated her from the British general's staff.

She overheard clearly their plans for a surprise attack on the American Army. General Howe's troops would leave at midnight two days hence. Lydia memorized the details: so many infantry, so many artillery. Then she heard the chairs scraping on the floor as the meeting ended.

She scurried back down the hall and into her bedroom and lay down on top of the covers, not daring to move.

Shortly there came a knocking on the bedroom door. "Mistress Darragh? Mistress Darragh?" Lydia said nothing.

Again the aide knocked. "Mistress Darragh? Mistress Darragh!" She held her breath. He knocked again.

Then she heard his boots retreating down the hall. The front door opened and closed. They were gone.

Lydia lay awake the rest of the night, wondering what she should do. By dawn she had decided that she herself would take this information to the American Army. It was too important to be entrusted to John and his buttons.

When William awoke, she told him, "Tomorrow morning early I'm going out of the city for some flour."

"In this weather?" he said. "There's several inches of snow on the ground. Are thee daft?"

"William, there's a great deal of baking to be done, and we're nearly out of flour."

"Well, 'tis not safe. I cannot let thee go. There has been fighting on the edge of the city."

"William, no one will harm a woman as harmless-looking as myself."

"The British sentries will stop thee."

"William, are thee forgetting that I have a pass signed by General Howe himself? I may come and go as I please." William knew enough at this point to hold his peace.

...out on foot, carrying an

... heading northeast. There

... and soon her shoes were

...d her greetings at the British

...on. After all, she wore the

...ociety of Friends, and they

...ot. It was about five miles to

...he empty sack to the miller.

...ck for it later. I've got some

..., she headed west. It was

...ow and cold air. Finally she

...ortant crossroads, where the

...use of its location it was a

...pproaching the tavern, Lydia

...een.

...r eyes became accustomed

...ted at a table. Walking up to

...ge. Without saying a word,

The officer happened to be the chief of George Washington's secret service. He opened the package and inside found a tightly rolled piece of paper. Upon reading it, he stood up and left the tavern in a great hurry.

Lydia, meanwhile, was returning through the ice and snow to the flour mill. When she got there, she put the heavy sack of flour on her shoulders, and as the light of day was failing, she started back to Philadelphia.

It was dark that December day when at last she reached home, exhausted. But although she was tired, she could not sleep. She watched from her bedroom window at midnight as the British army marched out of the city, on its way to launch a surprise attack against the Americans.

At dawn the following morning the British reached Whitemarsh, and they found—to their surprise—that the Americans were wide awake and waiting for them behind earthworks. The two armies settled down to watch each other for the day. There was some skirmishing, but there was no battle.

At last General Howe decided that his army should return to Philadelphia. The soldiers marched back, feeling outsmarted, like a parcel of fools. General Howe, much to his surprise, had been surprised by George Washington.

Later that day there came a knocking at Lydia Darragh's door. It was that British officer, General Howe's aide.

"I must ask you some questions, Mistress Darragh," he said.

"Yes, friend?"

"Tell me, the other night when we had our staff meeting here, was anyone else in your family awake?"

"Why, no," she said. "They were all asleep as thee ordered."

"Well, someone knew of our meeting," he said. "The Americans knew we were coming. Our surprise attack failed.

"I know," he went on, "that you were asleep. I tried three times to rouse you with my knocking. You didn't even lock your front door that night. Good day to you, Mistress Darragh."

"And good day to thee, friend."

Lydia Darragh was never caught, and it was a great comfort to her that that young man phrased his question the way he did.

"Had he done otherwise," she said, "why, as a God-fearing woman, I would have had to tell him the truth."

Jack Briggs has been an elementary-school teacher for more than 20 years at Friends' Central School near Philadelphia. As "The History Teller" he performs both living history and storytelling programs. A member of the National Storytelling Association and Patchwork, a Philadelphia-area storytelling guild, Briggs has served as a consultant on historical storytelling to Independence National Historical Park and contributed to a book on teaching the history of flight produced for the National Air and Space Museum.

Gone to War

Lucinda Flodin

This story is about the events surrounding the muster at Sycamore Shoals in Elizabethton, Tennessee; the march to Kings Mountain, North Carolina; and the Battle of Kings Mountain, fought October 7, 1780. Although the events and chronicle of the times are true, the story is seen through the eyes of a fictitious 12-year-old girl. It focuses on a community's preparation to go to war and the events of the muster, but it also tells the tale of the people left behind to carry on with their lives and do the work of a whole family despite the men's absence.

I'VE HEARD ENOUGH TALK OF HANGIN' AND RETRIBUTION FOR ONE NIGHT," she'd said. "Enough of that talk in front of the little ones. And Josiah, you're my eldest, and you're full of your war talk, but you're still my child, and I shouldn't need to remind you—every man and boy there was some mother's son. In spite of all these good causes, there's part of my heart breaking for all the women—all the wives and mothers tonight."

With that, she'd sent us all to bed, and though I was bone weary, I heard her and Pa talking late into the night. I lay on my bed in the loft above—too tired to sleep, thoughts of the past month galloping through my head.

It was the 20th of September that the news had come to our farm on the Old Fields at Sycamore Shoals—the word from Colonel Isaac Shelby from Sapling Grove: there's to be muster on William Lyles's land at Sycamore Shoals on September 25 to march across the mountain and fight that Ferguson.[1]

Papa, Josiah, Mathew, and Benjamin, patriots all, were willing to march with them. For days we all did as much work as we could, and before dawn on the 26th we went with Papa and the boys to join those at the muster.

We arrived just as Reverend Doak began to preach. His words inspired us: "Your brethren across the mountain are crying like Macedonia unto your help. God forbid that you shall refuse to hear and answer their call.

---

1. Major Patrick Ferguson, who led the Loyalist force

But the call of your brethren is not all. The enemy is marching hither to destroy your homes." I feared that they were just around the bend. That Ferguson had been haunting my dreams.

But then he said, "Thou knowest the dangers and snares that surround us on march and in battle. Thou knowest the dangers that constantly threaten the humble but well-loved homes which thy servants have left behind them. O Lord, in thy mercy, save us from the cruel hand of the savage and tyrant. Save the unprotected homes while fathers and husbands and sons are far away, fighting for freedom." Those words scared me to the bone as I thought about the dangers that those of us left at home might face.

When they had the draft, they drafted to see who would stay home. Everyone lined up, and they counted off: "One, two, three, four, five, six, step out . . . one, two, three, four, five, six, step out . . ."

Every seventh man was drafted to stay at home to defend our community. Pa and the boys, anxious to be with the militia, were thankful to miss that draft. I saw Mama scowl, but she said nothing.

After Reverend Doak preached, they all got on their horses and rode away, driving the cattle that were to be their food. Eleven hundred boys and men left the Watauga that Sunday morning, heading up Bright's Trace into the mountains. Mama and I and the little children walked home.

The men who stayed at home were there to defend us, not to do our work, so on our farm, which was 640 acres, there was Mama; her mama; me (I was 12 and suddenly the oldest); Jacob, age 11; Patience, age 9; Mary, age 7; and Elizabeth, who was only 4. We were already doing a full day of work anyhow, but with the men gone, we had to do our work and theirs too.

Before they left, we'd slaughtered a mess of cattle and deer because they'd enlisted for six months, and who knew how long it'd go on. So there was drying racks and the smokehouse to attend to; there was skins to tan; and there was lard to cook down. It bein' late September, there was still much of the food to be harvested, roots to dig, leaves and berries to pull and dry.

And then there was the live animals to tend, the wood to haul and split, the spinning, weaving, and mending to keep up with, and the house to tend. Everyone's work doubled, tripled—even the baby had chores to do that we couldn't do without.

On the first night, Mama got called. A baby was comin' to a young woman whose husband had marched off that morning. Mama said, "You'll have to be in charge till I come back. This could take a while. You make sure the cattle stay and the fire's stoked—there's bread to bake in the mornin'. God bless you, Daughter." And she left.

I lay awake a long while, so afraid I's shivering. I worried that Dragging Canoe would come to kill us, knowing our men were gone. I worried how I'd get everyone to the fort. I moved a flintlock to right next to my bed and relived the weeks that we'd been in the fort when Old Abrams had attacked it in the summer of '76. I'd been 8 then.

In the morning Mama came home—the child had come quicker than they thought it would. Without even a rest, she went out, bridled the horse, and went out to skid wood down the hill for firewood. As she finished her work that evening, I remember she said, "I always knew I could do the work of two men, but I prayed I'd never have to prove it."

Every day went like that. We'd work—work hard—through every minute of daylight and as late into the night as we could see by firelight or stay awake. Several nights Mama woke me where I'd sat spinning so I could go to bed. We thought it might be like that forever.

The Overmountain men

THE TERM *OVERMOUNTAIN MEN* WAS USED TO DEscribe the first colonists to settle the area directly beyond the crest of the Appalachians. A regiment of 900 mounted Overmountain men and Carolinians led by colonels William Campbell, Isaac Shelby, and John Sevier pursued and on October 7, 1780, engaged a Loyalist force of 1,100 in the Battle of Kings Mountain, North Carolina.

Using the "war whoop" they had learned from Indian fighters, the colonists won a devastating victory in what turned out to be one of the decisive battles of the Revolutionary War, leading directly to British General Cornwallis's retreat from the South and, a year later, his surrender at Yorktown.

Although the Overmountain men easily defeated the Loyalist force, they had more to fear from the Cherokee led by Tsu-gun-sili, or Dragging Canoe, who vehemently opposed the idea of white settlement on Cherokee hunting land.

To Richard Henderson, who came in 1775 to persuade the Cherokee chiefs to sign a treaty entitling his settlement company to all of "Kaintuckee" and Middle Tennessee, he said, "You have bought a fair land, but you will find its settlement dark and bloody." Dragging Canoe set up a sort of truce with the British in exchange for ammunition, and the British representative Robert Coleman used this to his advantage and persuaded Dragging Canoe to attack the Watauga settlement (on the Holston River in what is now East Tennessee) while most of the settlement's fighting force was pursuing the Loyalists.

Cherokee warriors did go to attack the Watauga settlement, but the Overmountain men, having won the Battle of Kings Mountain handily, were able to reach home before the Cherokee and forestall the invasion with a counterattack at Boyd's Creek on December 8, 1780.

—David Rhoden

It was the sound of horses moving fast that brought us to the cabin door the night of October 16. Mama grabbed the flintlock and was prepared to fire it when the shouts caught her ear. It was Pa and all three of my brothers flying toward the cabin on their horses. It was over, thank the Lord, it was over.

Lying in bed late that night, it was hard to remember all the stories that Pa and the boys had shared around. Over the mountain they'd been joined by the Carolina militia at Quaker Meadows, forming an army 1,500 to 1,800 strong. About 900 men on horseback went on to Kings Mountain. It was there that they met Ferguson.

He had called them "backwater men," but those men surrounded the foot of the mountain before he even knew they were there. Within an hour of the start of battle, Ferguson was dead, and so were hundreds of his men. They started back again that very night because they were worried some would come after them, but they didn't. They marched 800 prisoners along with them. It was a decisive victory.

It was during the stories of the killin' of prisoners and the hanging tree that Mama sent everyone off to bed.

I lay there late into the night, thanking God that our Pa and brothers had come home—not a scratch on 'em. As I started to drift off, I heard the crackle of the fire and Mama saying, "I can't help it, Jacob. I have to cry for the mothers, for the widows. I cry for all the boys, I cry."

Lucinda Flodin of Hampton, Tennessee, is half of the storytelling duo known as the Storyweavers. She and partner Dennis Frederick tell in tandem style and perform nationally at schools, festivals, and libraries. They have produced two tapes, Strawberries in the Snow *(self-published, 1989) and* Mountain Spirits *(self-published, 1991), and will publish their third in late 1995. The Storyweavers were chosen as Artists on the Road by the Tennessee Arts Commission.*

Sacagawea's Story

Michael Carney

When Thomas Jefferson was elected president in 1800, he immediately began planning an expedition that would cross the continent and end at the Pacific Ocean. The president knew that the explorers would encounter many dangers, so he insisted that only hardy, unmarried men make the trip. He never could have guessed that a 16-year-old woman with a newborn baby would be part of the exploration. This is the story of that woman, Sacagawea, who joined the Lewis and Clark Expedition in 1805 in the Great Plains and traveled thousands of miles with the company. She and her baby suffered many hardships along with the men before returning a year and a half later, safe and sound. This story is based on information from Lewis and Clark's journals. The author has expanded their brief accounts of Sacagawea, and the tale is told from the viewpoint of Captain William Clark.

I'LL NEVER FORGET THE FIRST TIME I SAW JANEY. I HAD REJOINED THE ARMY TO help Meriwether Lewis command an expedition up the Missouri River and over the mountains. When the first winter came, we stopped to build ourselves some cabins by an Indian village near the Knife River. We were working on the cabins one day—it was snowing a little bit— when up walked the strangest-looking family I'd ever seen.

First there was this old French trapper who looked like he hadn't had a bath in 20 years. He came swaggering up and said, *"Je m'appelle Charbonneau.* I am Charbonneau. I will be your guide and interpreter. I have been to many places and speak many languages. I know all of the Indians. Just hire me, and I will take you anywhere."

Then came his two young Indian wives. The older one looked to be about 18 and had a baby on her back. The younger one was probably about 16, and she was pregnant. We couldn't help but stare at the old trapper and his beautiful young wives. Then Charbonneau turned to the women and snarled, "Lazy women, go make the camp. Now!"

The first one, she walked off without any reaction at all. But the second wife—you could see a flash of anger in her eyes. You could tell she didn't like the way he talked to her.

We didn't think too much more about Charbonneau and his family until we had our cabins all done and were spending some time in the Indian village. There were some Frenchmen there who could interpret for us, and we asked a lot of questions about what lay ahead. The Indians

This map, drawn by Captain Clark, depicts a stretch of the Missouri River and its Great Falls in what is now central Montana.

told us that crossing the Stony Mountains[1] was going to be much more difficult than we had expected. We really didn't have any chance of making it on foot. Our only hope was to get some horses, and the only people who might have horses to trade us were the Shoshones.

We did some checking around, and it turned out that Charbonneau's second wife, the younger one, was a Shoshone. So we approached him and offered to hire him on the condition that he bring her along. Charbonneau agreed, and the two of them moved into our fort. Her name was Sacagawea (pronounced Suh-kahj-uh-*we*-uh), which meant "Bird Woman." Our men had a lot of trouble pronouncing that name, and somehow we just started calling her Janey.

Janey had her baby in February, but by the time the ice broke up in the spring, she was ready to travel. I admired the way she kept up with the men, carrying her baby on her back. We set off up the river and didn't see a single person all summer long.

After a while we came to some huge, beautiful waterfalls. They were wonderful to look at, but we had to get around them. It turned out to be 20 miles across the plains to get up above those waterfalls. And what looked like grassy plains turned out to have lots of prickly pear cactus down on the ground.

By that time we'd worn out the boots we'd brought from home and were wearing handmade moccasins. Those cactus spines cut right through the moccasins, which made moving our equipment very hard. It took us a whole month to carry everything around the falls.

Finally we got the boats loaded again and set out upstream. Soon we came to a place where the river divided into three forks. To be certain which was the right way, I took a few men and went off to explore the branches. We went up each fork about eight or 10 miles and then climbed up the biggest hill I could find, to get a better look at what lay ahead. There in the distance were the Stony Mountains, their peaks covered with snow in midsummer.

As we made our way back down to Three Forks, where we were going to camp, I started to feel weak and dizzy. By the time we got to camp, I

1. An early name for the Rockies

had terrible chills and fever. Captain Lewis dosed me with some pills, the ones the men called Doctor Rush's Thunderbolts, and I sat shivering in front of the fire with my feet in a kettle of warm water.

I was in such a bad state that I barely noticed when Janey sat down beside me and started talking. She hardly ever said anything. She didn't speak either English or French. What little conversation she had with Charbonneau was in Minnetaree. But now she was talking to me, like she was telling a story. I called Charbonneau over to interpret, and this is what Janey said:

"My people, the Shoshones, are a weak nation. We cannot stand up against the stronger tribes of the plains: the Crow, the Blackfeet, and the Minnetaree. We live high in the mountains where the winters are long and cold and the hunting is poor, but at least we are safe. My people have many horses, and every fall we bring our horses down to the plains, make a camp, and hunt all the buffalo that we can. We dry and smoke the meat, which we place on the horses and take back up to our home in the safety of the mountains.

Captain William Clark

"When I was still a girl, I came with my people on such a trip. We were camped right here, in this very place, at the Three Forks. One day when most of our warriors were out hunting, the Minnetarees attacked. They had guns. They killed our few remaining warriors. The women and children fled for safety, but most of us did not escape.

"I was captured and made a slave, the property of the chief of the Minnetarees. He did what he liked with me. One evening he sat me on a blanket in a game and gambled me away to the French trapper Charbonneau. That was how I got my husband."

Janey's story made me angry as I could be. I wished I could help her get free, but before I could do anything about it, we set off again up the river. Janey was getting more and more excited. She started recognizing places she remembered from her childhood.

But Charbonneau was getting more and more agitated. One night he yelled at her in camp and struck her. We grabbed him and pulled him away. We could see he was getting desperate. The closer Janey got to her people, the more he could feel her slipping away from him.

We were starting to get desperate too. For us it was the summer that was slipping away. Even in August the nights were cold, and there was frost on the ground. We knew we'd never be able to survive a winter in those mountains. If we couldn't find the Shoshones and buy some horses, we'd have to turn around and go back. Finally we decided that Captain Lewis would take three men and go ahead on foot to locate the

Shoshones. The rest of us would continue upstream with the boats.

After he'd been gone a week, we began to feel a little concerned. One morning I was walking alongshore, with Janey ahead of me. Suddenly I saw her raise her hands and start to dance with joy. She looked back at me and then up ahead: there were Indians. Janey raced up the trail and embraced one of the women. I'd never seen her so excited, and I knew right away that she'd found her people.

When we got to Janey's village, we found Captain Lewis and the rest of our men. While she was with her family, meeting children she'd never seen before, we got down to the business of trading for some horses. Captain Lewis had been trying to talk to the Shoshones with signs, but he found it very difficult, so we called Janey over to interpret. This was

Sacagawea: Fact and myth

SACAGAWEA WAS A TEENAGE GIRL WITH A NEWBORN baby when she and her husband, trapper Toussaint Charbonneau, joined the expedition of Meriwether Lewis and William Clark. Her chief work was as an interpreter with the Shoshones, her native tribe, and her presence was invaluable as a sign to Indians met along the way that the expedition was not a war party. The company also valued her knowledge of medicinal and food plants.

Sacagawea's exact whereabouts after the expedition are hard to pin down, but enough references exist to give a general idea. Charbonneau and Sacagawea were discharged from the expedition on August 17, 1806, when they left the region where their interpretive talents were needed. Charbonneau was paid $500.33. Sacagawea was not paid for her services, as she was considered Charbonneau's wife but not a member of the expedition herself. Charbonneau declined Clark's offer to adopt their son and transport them to Illinois, so he and Sacagawea stayed where they were, near Fort Mandan in what is now North Dakota. They did spend some time in the more urban areas of the West, where she was recognized as a member of the famous expedition. When traveler Henry Brackenridge saw Sacagawea in St. Louis in 1811, he wrote that she was "a good creature, of a mild and gentle disposition, greatly attached to the whites, whose manners and dress she tries to imitate, but she had become sickly, and longed to revisit her native country. . . ."

Though Grace Hebard's best-selling book *Sacajawea* (Clark, 1957) put forward the often-believed claim that she lived to be 100, Sacagawea would not live very long after the expedition. A fur trader at Fort Manuel (in present-day South Dakota) named John Luttig wrote in his diary, "This evening the wife of Charbonneau, a Snake [Shoshone] squaw, died of a putrid fever. She was . . . the best woman in the fort, aged about 25 years. She left a fine infant girl." She died on December 20, 1812.

She was survived by a son, Jean-Baptiste, who went on to become an adventurer in his own right, and a daughter, Lisette, about whom no more is known. Clark adopted both children.

—David Rhoden

against the customs of the Shoshones, for in their nation women did not speak in council. But we felt our lives depended on it, so we insisted.

We sat with their leaders under an arbor, smoking a pipe together. Captain Lewis stood and spoke to the Indians, telling them of our friendly intentions. He said we were exploring the country and that if they helped us, traders would follow who would bring them metal axes and knives and cook pots. But we needed them to help us by trading us some horses.

Then Private Labiche said the speech in French, and Charbonneau said the speech in Minnetaree, and Janey said it in Shoshone. When the chiefs finally heard it in a language they could understand, they withdrew for a few minutes. When they came back, they gave their speech in return, which Janey translated into Minnetaree, Charbonneau into French, and Labiche into English. They told us how glad they were to see us, that we were welcome to stay as long as we wanted, but they were not interested in trading their horses. They needed them for their own survival.

Statue of Sacagawea and her baby

We were persistent, however, and day after day we went back and forth through this cumbersome chain of interpreters. I'm sure that without Janey we'd never have had a chance of getting any horses. We were grateful for all the work she did as our interpreter, and because of her connection with the Shoshones, they finally agreed to trade us a few horses. Then it was a few more and a few more, until at last we had almost 30 horses, and we felt that was enough.

So we set to work. We took every skin we had and began to make saddles and bridles and saddlebags. We unpacked all our gear. What we were taking with us we packed into the saddlebags. For the rest, we dug deep pits in the earth, stowed the gear inside, and replaced the grass on top so perfectly that you couldn't even see where the caches were. We pulled our boats up above the waterline and put rocks in them so they wouldn't wash away.

We were so busy with these preparations that I didn't even think about Janey. At the last moment I realized that she probably wouldn't continue with us. She was back with her people, and it was a perfect chance for her to get away from her miserable husband. I realized then how difficult it was going to be to say goodbye to her.

Finally the day came for our departure. The horses were packed, and we had a guide. We were saying goodbye to the Shoshones when Janey walked up with her baby on her back. She looked at me and said the first two words I'd ever heard her say in French: "*La mer*." The ocean.

And she went with us, as we made our way across the mountains and down to the Pacific Ocean.

When Michael Carney first moved to Point Reyes Station, California, he spent hours telling stories to the young children he worked with. Now he enjoys adult audiences as well, especially when telling his tales of history. Carney is devoted to the idea that history can be exciting and fun—a chance to meet interesting characters from the past. He hopes that students will be inspired by his work to create their own stories.

A Love Story

Ruth Stotter

This story occurs at a time of dynamic exploration, when countries were eagerly claiming land around the world. Spain had dominated California for approximately 350 years but for the first half of that period was occupied with colonies richer and closer to home. When Catherine II came to the Russian throne in 1762, she encouraged exploration, and Russia soon established territorial claims north of the Spanish land in California. Now, the Spanish were afraid that the Russians would decide to expand south. They also feared that the Americans would want to expand west. As a result Spain accelerated its plans to install settlements, establishing the San Francisco Presidio in 1776. It remained in use as a fort until 1993, when many U.S. military installations were closed.

WHEN TWO YOUNG PEOPLE FALL IN LOVE AND THEIR WHOLE LIVES BECOME A sad but beautiful story, it isn't easy to forget them. Do you remember Gabriel and Evangeline? Romeo and Juliet? Their stories linger in our memory . . . haunting and unforgettable.

The girl in the story I'm going to tell you now was just about Juliet's age, and as in the story of Romeo and Juliet, there was an obstacle to her marriage. But unlike Juliet, the girl in this story doesn't die. She *lives*, like Longfellow's Evangeline, with the memory of her love.

The story begins in 1806 in San Francisco, which at that time was called Yerba Buena. In Spanish that means "the good herb." The girl this story's about, Concepción Arguello, had just turned 16. She lived in a fort called the Presidio, which had been established by the Spanish 30 years earlier, and her father was the commandant.

Concepción often stood on the hillside at the edge of the Presidio and gazed down at the sea. She loved to watch the waves rise and fall, to see the white foam and the sun sparkling on the blue water.

When she looked to the right, she saw an island bay and two jewel-like islands, today known as Angel Island and Alcatraz. Across the water she saw oak and redwood forests. Ships would sail across the bay to bring back wood and water.

A narrow opening separated the inland bay from the ocean, and submerged rocks and strong tides made it dangerous for ships to pass through the gateway. It became even more treacherous when the fog rolled in and reduced visibility. Today the Golden Gate Bridge stretches across the gateway.

Concepción, or Concha, as she was nicknamed, spent a lot of time by herself. Her father, the commandant, was a busy man, preoccupied with the responsibilities of an administrator and soldier. Her brother, who had spent a lot of time with her when they were younger, now spent his days hunting or exploring the regions around the bay. Her mother was busy with overseeing servants.

Then on April 6, 1806, something happened that was to change her life forever. It began when a strange ship was sighted, sailing right up to the little dock near the Presidio. Now, this was unusual because foreign vessels weren't allowed in the bay: the government had given strict orders to keep them out. But there it came, bold as anything.

The men on the ship's deck called out, but the people on the dock couldn't understand what they were saying. They didn't even recognize the language. But the men on the ship looked friendly, so permission was granted for them to come ashore. As they walked down the ship's plank onto the pier, everyone stared at their clothing—no one had seen anything like their shirts or pants or fur hats.

Since the strangers didn't speak or understand Spanish, communication could take place only through gestures and smiles. Someone suggested finding Father Uria, who spoke a little English, so he was sent for. But when Father Uria arrived, he discovered that the strangers did not speak or understand English.

In desperation Father Uria tried speaking Latin, and one of the ship's men stepped forward and answered him. But since neither man spoke fluent Latin, it took some time to unravel the mystery.

The newcomers were Russian. They said they had come in friendship from a place called Sitka, to the north. Now, it's important to know that on the day the ship arrived, both the governor and the commandant were away. If they'd been present, the strangers would never have been allowed ashore. But when the governor and the commandant were gone, Concepción's brother was in charge. He enjoyed playing the role of host, and he invited the Russians to have dinner with them that evening. He was young and curious, Mexico was far away, and he didn't feel bound by political considerations.

During dinner the story of the Russians unfolded. The man who knew Latin said his name was Langsdorff and that he was a scientist and engineer. He introduced the Russians' leader—young, handsome, courteous

Count Nikolai Petrovich Rezanoff. Langsdorff told them Rezanoff had been sent to Sitka as overseer for the Russian fur trade. But when he'd arrived in Sitka, Count Rezanoff had found the people in the Russian settlement sick with scurvy. The supply ship that had been sent from Siberia had never arrived. People were facing starvation, and some had died. Rezanoff hadn't seen any prospect of finding food in that barren place, so, knowing there were settlements to the south, he decided to set sail, hoping to find provisions down the coast that he could bring back to the village. Concha felt sorry for the people in Russian Alaska, and she was glad they had such a caring young man as their protector.

Despite the language difficulties, the dinner went well enough. Rezanoff smiled and nodded to everyone, but he couldn't seem to stop looking at the beautiful young woman. Although Concha kept her eyes lowered, she could feel him looking at her. She felt excited and self-conscious as she listened intently to the conversation.

Concha's brother tried to explain to the Russians the difficulty of giving them food to take back to Sitka: "We have plenty of meat and grain, but it's not for sale. Spanish law forbids our selling any supplies to foreigners." Father Uria translated the message, but the Russians didn't seem to comprehend it. They kept repeating their request to buy food.

Toward the end of the meal it was discovered that several of the Russians spoke French, so a French-speaking priest living in Santa Clara was sent for. His arrival the next morning improved communication considerably. But communication couldn't solve the political problem. The Russians did not—or could not—seem to understand that although food was abundant, it could not be given or sold to them. Later that day, when the governor and the commandant returned to the fort, they emphatically told the Russians that although they liked them, they could not assist them or provide food.

If this sounds cruel, keep in mind that the Spanish were worried about invasion from both Americans and Russians. The Spanish didn't want American or Russian outposts on the West Coast. They believed the Russian fur trade was a threat, so it would be foolish to do anything that would help the Russians expand.

Rezanoff, however, was not a man to accept defeat easily. He asked to be taught Spanish, and in an amazingly short time he was able to talk to the commandant and Concha's mother and brother—and of course, with Concha. He had his men bring from the ship wonderful Russian gifts—including magnificent furs for Concha—which he presented to the Arguello family.

That first night at dinner, Concha had known she was falling in love

The Spanish didn't want American or Russian outposts on the West Coast. They believed the Russian fur trade was a threat, so it would be foolish to do anything that would help the Russians expand.

with the intelligent, handsome foreigner. She knew that, desperate for supplies, he might be paying attention to her as a ploy in order to get what his people needed. She was aware that he was older than she, a man of the world, and she suspected that he had probably broken a few hearts at the czar's court. Still, she felt that he too was falling in love.

It's possible that Rezanoff did fall in love with the beautiful Concha. There are those who say his love was real. And there are those who maintain that he was only pretending so that he could get the food he needed.

Concha and Count Rezanoff spent a great deal of time together, and at first they were properly chaperoned, as was the custom. But they found ways to get around this old-fashioned convention. They would go for long walks and tire out whoever had been sent along with them. Then, in a most honorable way, Count Nikolai Petrovich Rezanoff asked Concepción Arguello's parents for her hand.

They told him, "We admire you and like you, Count Rezanoff. We would be pleased for Concha to have so fine a man as her husband. But marriage is impossible. Concha is a Roman Catholic, and she must marry someone of our faith." Rezanoff was of the Eastern Orthodox faith. Concha's parents were adamant: "We would need permission from the pope. We are sorry, Rezanoff, but she cannot marry you."

Concha pleaded. Rezanoff persisted. Finally, when Rezanoff said he would become a Catholic, her parents relented and gave their approval, on one condition: Rezanoff must obtain permission from the czar to marry Concha. The lovers were disappointed because they wanted to be married immediately. But a promise was better than nothing. For the next three weeks, before the ship was to leave, Concha and Nikolai happily held hands, kissed, and planned their future.

Meanwhile, because Rezanoff was now about to become a member of the family, his ship was being filled with the food he so desperately needed. On May 21, 1806, six weeks after Rezanoff had arrived at the Presidio, the Russian ship set sail for Sitka. Rezanoff's plan was to go to Sitka, cross the Bering Sea to Kamchatka, cross Siberia, and report to the czar. Then he would return.

Concha stood on the hill, watching as his ship sailed out through the narrow gateway into the sea. She watched it turn to the north and disappear behind the headlands. She stayed on that hillside for a long time, praying for his safe return.

Weeks and weeks, then months and months went by without a word. Then the time came when they thought Rezanoff would surely have completed his journey. Still no news came. Had he reached Sitka safely?

Had his ship been wrecked? Had he reached the czar but failed to get permission for the marriage? Had he forgotten Concha and turned his attention to another woman?

No one knew. But Concha felt that he would come back.

A few years later the Russians established a settlement at Fort Ross, not far up the coast from Yerba Buena. Concha wrote to the fort and asked about Rezanoff, but there was no reply. She had heard a rumor that a man named Rezanoff was there with his wife. Perhaps he was a relative of the count . . . Perhaps Rezanoff had married someone else and couldn't own up to it . . .

Her letter was not answered. But Concha never lost faith that her lover would come back to her if he could. Several years slipped by, and still Concha waited.

Every day, with hope riding high in her heart, she would stand on the hillside, looking out at the sea and straining her eyes for the sight of a sail—longing for the ship that would bring back her lover. She wasn't interested in any of the other young men who came to call on her.

Then one day she didn't go out to look at the sea. Nor did she go the next day or the next. Soon after that she stopped her daily praying for the ship that never came.

Gradually she turned her prayers to other things. Her prayers and love, no longer focused on this earth, were for God, and eventually Concepción Arguello took vows and became a nun. She went to live in Benicia, north of Yerba Buena, where she helped establish a girls' school.

What ever happened to Rezanoff? Was he a cad? Had Concha been deceived? It wasn't until 11 years after Rezanoff's departure that Concepción Arguello may have learned the truth—the answer to all the various possibilities.

Historians have found a letter, sent in 1817 to Concepción's father, José Darío Arguello, from an Alexander Baranov, informing him of Rezanoff's death and the circumstances under which it occurred.

Nikolai Rezanoff had indeed reached Sitka with the food and gone on to Kamchatka. Then, traveling across Siberia to reach the czar, he had gotten sick. And at a place called Yakutsk he had died. All those years while Concha waited, Rezanoff's body had lain in a lonely grave in the frozen earth of northeast Russia.

Some historians maintain that Concepción was not told about the letter and didn't learn of Rezanoff's death until 35 years after he set sail. A British man, Sir George Simpson, came to California in 1841, planning to buy the then-abandoned Fort Ross. Many people believe that it was from Sir George that Concha heard what had happened.

All her life Concha remembered the powerful feelings of earthly love she had known in those few short weeks when she was a girl of 16. But she knew now that her heart hadn't deceived her. *Life works in strange ways*, she thought. *Perhaps God intended me for a different purpose.*

She knew her love for Nikolai had remained pure. She had never stopped loving him.

But there was no question that her life had been worthwhile. She touched the lives of hundreds of young women who went to her school in Benicia. Historians have found in the diaries of girls who attended that school many references to the inspiring effect of her devotion.

Concepción Arguello died peacefully in her early fifties. And that is California's own true and hauntingly sad love story.

Ruth Stotter of Tiburon, California, is the director of the Dominican College Certificate-in-Storytelling Program and teaches storytelling and folklore at Sonoma State University. She has master's degrees in speech pathology and storytelling. A professional storyteller, Stotter produces the multicultural annual Storyteller's Calendar *and in 1994 published* About Story: A Collection of Articles About Stories and Storytelling *(Stotter Press). She is a consultant to the Puppeteers of America on storytelling with puppets and is listed in* Who's Who Among American Women *and* Who's Who in American Education.

Tsali: Cherokee Hero Of the Smoky Mountains

Duncan Sings-Alone

The story of Tsali takes place against the backdrop of the Cherokee removal and the Trail of Tears, which occurred in 1838 and 1839. From the time the early Southeastern white settlements were created, pressure began building to remove the Cherokee (and also the Choctaw, Chickasaw, Creek, and Seminole) tribe to the Indian Territories now known as Oklahoma. Ultimately a few subchiefs signed a bogus treaty against the express will of the Cherokee nation, and General Winfield Scott was sent to oversee the removal. Tsali, a Cherokee hero and martyr, is a symbol of Cherokee determination to maintain identity and culture within the dominant American society. Many variations of the Tsali story exist, and all testify to his unconquerable spirit and the martyrdom he accepted so that a remnant of 2,000 Cherokees could remain in the East. One-fourth of the Cherokee nation died of disease, exposure, and malnutrition on the Trail of Tears.

IN 1837 AND 1838 THE LEGISLATURES OF GEORGIA, NORTH CAROLINA, AND Tennessee conspired with the U.S. Congress and President Andrew Jackson to rob the Cherokees of their lands and force them onto the infamous Trail of Tears. It was an evil time in American history.

The Cherokee were prosperous people. Sequoya had developed a syllabary for written Cherokee. Old and young alike could learn to read their language in a week. The Cherokee had a literacy rate higher than that of the white settlers nearby. The Cherokee nation had its own schools, court system, and legislature. Many Cherokees owned fine farms and plantations with fertile land in the states of Georgia, Tennessee, and North Carolina. But in Georgia there was something else in the land: gold.

The white settlers of Georgia had long coveted Cherokee land. In time the Georgians were joined by North Carolinians, Tennesseans, and populists in Congress to remove the tribe by legislative fiat.

The Cherokee nation, with its lawyers, headmen, and Principal Chief John Ross, fought valiantly against the proposed removal.

But Congress, after prolonged and passionate debate, favored removal by one vote. The decision was appealed to the Supreme Court under

Chief Justice John Marshall, who ruled in favor of the Cherokees' right to remain in their homeland. Then President Andrew Jackson, may he live in infamy, said, "John Marshall made his decision. Let him enforce it." Those words sealed the doom of the proud Cherokee nation. The Trail of Tears had begun.

The Army erected concentration camps up and down the main roadways throughout the Cherokee lands. Militiamen began to appear without warning at the farms, abducting the people at gunpoint, forcing them to leave all their possessions behind, and marching them to the nearest camp, where the Cherokee people languished, sometimes for months, before embarking on the journey west.

The stockades were awful. Accustomed to living well, the Cherokee people were now thrown together with minimal shelter, meager food, and totally inadequate sanitation. A pervasive stench permeated the camps. Disease and death were rampant. One-quarter of the Cherokees who were interned died in the stockades or on the trail to Oklahoma.

Eager to strip the farms of furniture, livestock, and all personal possessions, the white rabble dogged the heels of the militia. The Cherokee farms had already been allotted to new owners by raffle. Sometimes the new owners fought the rabble over the spoils of removal. It was an ugly scene repeated over and over throughout the Cherokee nation.

It is against this backdrop that we lovingly retell the story of Tsali, who, with his simple life and heroic death, calls forth the very best from his Cherokee descendants. As we tell his story, we pray that we, his grandchildren, are worthy of him.

The old man, Tsali, lived with his crippled wife and two sons in the mountains of northern Georgia. News of the removal hung like a pall over the mountains, but it was too horrible to think about. Indeed, what could one do?

An older son of Tsali had come home to visit the folks. He was worried about his mother, who was painfully arthritic, but he could not stay long because his wife was near term in her pregnancy. The family was at dinner one night when the dog's furious barking warned of trouble. By the time Tsali reached the door, the militia was in the yard. Hell had come.

Tsali, his wife, and their three sons were herded from their cabin, past the leering, jeering faces of human vultures, down to the road, where they joined the long, tragic passage of a proud people into captivity.

A young red-haired, freckle-faced Georgia militiaman was in charge of Tsali's family. Without regard for the crippled old woman, he appeared to take particular pleasure in prodding the family along. When the old woman stumbled or slowed, he would push her with his bayonet. Inwardly Tsali and his sons raged. Although they were deeply grieved over losing their land, this mistreatment of the old woman was intolerable. The young Georgian marched along, blissfully unaware that his wards were plotting vengeance.

The road turned sharply, and for a moment the militiaman was out of his comrades' sight. The young Georgian never made the turn . . . alive. By the time his comrades stumbled on his dead body, Tsali and his family had melted into the woods and were making their way into the high mountains. There they joined some 2,000 Cherokee who had chosen to return to the caves and a primitive lifestyle rather than be moved like cattle to an unknown land.

General Winfield Scott was in charge of the removal, and although he did not like his assignment, he was a professional soldier who followed orders. He was not willing to let one of his soldiers be killed without exacting retribution. General Scott, however, was realistic. He knew that he had no chance of prying Tsali out of those mountains. Scott sent Will Thomas, a Scottish trader and a friend of the Cherokees, into the mountains with a message: If Tsali and his sons surrendered, Scott would ignore the other Cherokee refugees hiding in the mountains and would report to President Jackson that all the Cherokees had been removed.

If Tsali and his sons surrendered, Scott would ignore the other Cherokee refugees hiding in the mountains and would report to President Jackson that all the Cherokees had been removed.

Tsali and his sons considered the offer. Sorrowful as they felt, they could give only one response. Notice was sent to General Scott that on a given day Tsali and his boys would turn themselves in. Fellow refugees formed an honor guard to accompany Tsali out of the hills.

The fate of Tsali and his sons had already been decided. The youngest son would be spared. Tsali and the two older sons would be executed immediately. The general decreed that the Cherokee honor guard must carry out the death sentence because then, according to his warped way of thinking, the Cherokee people would not claim Tsali as a martyr. But when those shots rang out and Tsali and his sons crumpled onto Grandmother Earth, the Cherokee people took the three as heroes to live permanently in their hearts.

Each spring we Cherokees tell the story of Tsali to our children so that we will always remember the price of freedom in our homeland. We are here because Tsali and others like him were willing to die for the people.

May the Cherokee never forget—and may the American people never forget—the story of Tsali, hero of the Smoky Mountains.

Note

The story of Tsali is found in many forms and has achieved mythological status. This version of the story has been retold by Duncan Sings-Alone, a storyteller of Cherokee descent.

Duncan Sings-Alone is a writer, a storyteller, and a psychologist. Of Cherokee descent, Sings-Alone tells traditional and modern Native American stories in settings ranging from art galleries to powwows. Sings-Alone is an elder and a chief among the Free Cherokees. His recent book, The Fractured Mirror: Healing Multiple Personality Disorder *(Health Communications Press, 1994), includes stories for child alter-personalities. Sings-Alone lives in Mechanicsville, Maryland.*

Tom Stowe

Paul Leone _____

Tom Stowe's escape from slavery occurred in the decade after the passage of the Fugitive Slave Law (1850). This story is adapted from a reminiscence published by a Fredonia, New York, newspaper in the 1870s. The author, Eber Petit, a well-to-do and respected physician of that village, had been active in the workings of the Underground Railroad, both locally and nationally. Petit contributed a number of articles to the Fredonia Censor *describing the system that aided fugitive slaves and the personalities who participated in it. His home in Fredonia was one of the final stops along the route to Canada. Most of his accounts, including that of Tom Stowe, are retellings of the stories he heard from the slaves he helped find freedom. The details of Stowe's escape are taken from Petit's accounts. The dialogue and the name of the storekeeper in Morgantown—Mr. Burgess—come from my imagination.*

MR. HENRY STOWE WAS A GAMBLING MAN. HE KEPT A BARNFUL OF THOR-oughbred racehorses on his plantation outside of Vicksburg in the state of Mississippi. He had a fine collection of fighting cocks too. And dogs. Loved to gamble, Mr. Henry Stowe did. And he generally won.

Every year in the spring, when the season came round, he'd load up his horses on the steamship at Vicksburg and head north up the Mississippi River. He'd stop at Memphis first, then move east on the Ohio River to Louisville and Cincinnati. That's where the big races were. You can imagine him on that steamship, dressed in fancy clothes, smoking a cigar, hanging onto his cane with the silver head.

Tom Stowe would go along to tend the horses. Now, Tom Stowe wasn't his blood kin, you understand. Tom was his property—his slave. Slaves didn't generally have names, except what their masters had given them. So folks generally called slaves by their masters' names.

Tom was a first-rate horse trainer. He was gentle and firm with the horses, and they seemed to want to do just what he wanted them to. Mr. Henry Stowe thought mighty highly of Tom. More than once he'd been offered $3,000 for him. Wouldn't think of selling Tom, though. Henry Stowe kept Tom happy and well-fed, gave him pocket money to spend on the trips. Of course, Tom—he loved the horses. Loved the traveling too.

So year after year they went off. Tom got himself an education, talking to white folks, buying feed at their stores, showing them the horses. Sometimes folks'd whisper to him, "You ought to cross that river. Ye'll be a free man. The Railroad'll take care of ye."

Tom knew what they meant. The Ohio River separated the free states from the slave states. Cross into Ohio or Indiana, and you were on free soil. It wasn't a real railroad, of course. It was invisible. But there were folks who'd help you if you ran. You'd need it. If you ran, they'd chase you.

Tom never considered it, even after Mr. Burgess started encouraging him. Mr. Burgess ran the feed store in Morgantown. That's West Virginia now, but in those days it was still Virginia. Weren't a lot of slaveholders in that part of the state. When the war came, folks up there elected to stay with the Union.

First time Mr. Burgess mentioned it—runnin', I mean—he looked straight at Tom. Mr. Henry Stowe was gone—he always left Tom alone in Morgantown and went off to New York.

"Only six miles to Pennsylvania," Mr. Burgess said. "You're a smart boy. You could make it." Tom grinned a shy grin and looked at the floor. Slaves knew how to disguise their feelings when they talked to whites.

Such talk made Tom nervous. Why was this white man telling him to run? Wouldn't be no time before Mr. Henry would get out a search. Call out the bloodhounds. Put a reward on him.

He was a valuable slave, Tom knew that. Might even be that Mr. Burgess would set the law after him and claim the reward himself. Besides, Tom couldn't run. He had a wife who worked in the big house back on the plantation. A beautiful woman called Lucy. They had a little boy too.

When Mr. Henry Stowe purchased some new horses in Texas, he sent Tom to round them up. When Tom returned, his little boy was gone—sold out of state, Tom didn't know where. Lucy told him that while Tom had been gone, Mr. Henry Stowe had wanted to take her to bed. She had refused and fought him. He'd sold the child in anger.

Then Lucy got sick. Mr. Henry Stowe sent for the doctor, but she couldn't be saved. She died.

After that Mr. Henry Stowe kept a watchful eye on Tom. Maybe Tom wasn't cheerful, but he continued to do his work and do it well. For two more years the gambling trips continued. One year Mr. Burgess told him how to get to Canada.

"It's just six miles to Pennsylvania. When you get there, follow the ridge of the mountains west. You can't miss Pittsburgh. There's three rivers there. The Allegheny'll take you to Canada." Mr. Burgess was mistaken. The Allegheny River doesn't reach Canada.

But this time Tom made up his mind. He decided to run.

He made it to Pennsylvania all right, up into the hills. But Mr. Henry Stowe had notified all the newspapers. He'd printed up posters describing Tom and had them hung up everywhere. He offered a $2,000 reward, and that brought out the bounty hunters.

Tom followed that ridge just like Mr. Burgess said. He didn't have nothing much with him except the clothes on his back. He cut a stout hickory walking stick and tried to keep out of sight. He ate what he could find in the woods and what he managed to steal from farms. He slept under the stars.

It's 50 or 60 miles from Morgantown to Pittsburgh the way the crow flies. Wouldn't take long to get there if you didn't have to hide. Tom was out three days when he ran up on a camp of white men. Six of them. They saw him before he could get out of the way. They knew who he was right off—must've thought it was their lucky day. Right away they were on their feet, pointin' and hollerin'. Tom was close enough to hear what they said: "That's the $2,000 nigger!"

They came after him, but Tom had the high ground. First one to reach him wished he hadn't. Tom just cracked him with that hickory walking stick. Laid him out. Second one too. That one came swinging a hatchet. The others decided to regroup and think about it, and it gave Tom the chance to slip off.

He walked right through Pittsburgh, bold as brass. You've got to remember, though, he was tired and hungry. He sure wasn't safe yet. He found the Allegheny all right and began to follow it.

His belly was gnawing at him. You've probably never been that hungry. Finally he came upon a black man and asked him for food. That man looked at him, must've known he was a runaway. Took him to a farmhouse on a country road. Folks there, white folks, gave him a hot meal and a bed to sleep in. Kept him in a secret room behind a false fireplace.

Tom stayed there two days and rested up. Then the folks put him on a wagon at night, rode him five, 10 miles up the road, and left him at another farm. That's how he came to Mr. Petit's house. One farm at a time. That was the Railroad.

Mr. Petit delivered him up to Black Rock on the Niagara River. Canada's on the other side. Mr. Petit watched him get into the boat and get rowed across. Last thing Tom Stowe did before he shoved off, he gave Mr. Petit that stout hickory walking stick.

Tom followed that ridge just like Mr. Burgess said. He didn't have nothing much with him except the clothes on his back.

Paul Leone teaches local history for the Feneon Historical Museum in Jamestown, New York. As a roster artist for the Chautauqua County Arts in Education program, he conducts residencies and performances in area school systems. He has twice been awarded grants for storytelling by the New York State Council on the Arts, and in 1992 he received a Chautauqua County Fund for the Arts fellowship. Leone has a special interest in the 19th century and lives in a Victorian house with his wife, son, and two cats.

Westward Migration: Nancy Robbins's Story

Katherine Lesperance

Nancy Robbins's story is based on the journey made by 54-year-old Nancy and three generations of her Illinois family in 1851. On the trail her family suffered numerous hardships, including the death of several relatives, hunger, thirst, and fear of Indians. Native Americans along the trail, however, turned out to be friendly and helpful, often supplying the family with food. This story is a fictional re-creation of the journey through Nancy's eyes. The family members who accompanied Nancy are present in the story, which presents a true account of the death of her daughter Mahala. In 1993 Barbara Stinger, Nancy's great-great-great-granddaughter, retraced her ancestors' footsteps along the Oregon Trail with the Sesquicentennial Wagon Train Celebration. During the journey Barbara, also 54, shared her family's experiences from diaries passed down to her.

THE DAY NATHANIEL TOLD ME ABOUT MOVING WEST TO OREGON, I COULDN'T believe my ears. Move west! How could we leave behind our beautiful home, our comfortable life forged out of the Illinois forest?

Nathaniel smiled at me, explaining that we would do exactly what our ancestors did: carve out a new life for our 11 children and their children, a sweet life in a land blessed with abundance. Then he lifted me into the air and swung me around, shouting, "Nathaniel and Nancy Robbins of Oregon Territory!"

Nathaniel's Oregon fever caught on: William, our eldest, and his wife, Melvina, decided to travel along with their nine children; our daughter Bethia and her husband, Absalom Barnes, couldn't wait to get started; and the others—our children and grandchildren—filled our home for weeks with excited chatter and westward dreams.

Everyone agreed: 1852 would see three generations of the Robbins family in a new territory. I confess I began dreaming about walking across Oregon's black, rich soil as a bright sun warmed my back and our children and grandchildren grew straight and tall.

It's five months later now, and Oregon fever still burns inside me. But the journey hasn't been easy. We loaded our possessions in 22 large wagons that Nathaniel and the other men built from fallen oak trees. We hitched the finest teams of oxen to the wagons to take us to Missouri, where we joined a wagon train going to Oregon.

The day we left, Nathaniel spoke with a blazing intensity I'd never heard before: "The Robbins family is beginning the greatest adventure ever!" Then Nathaniel shook the reins, and the oxen lumbered toward our destiny: Oregon.

The journey has worn everyone out. We've seen plenty of nights without a decent supper and felt a raging thirst that closes the throat up tight. My legs ache like the dickens from walking as much as 20 miles a day. We've lost 19 of our wagons along the way, losing so many special possessions: my grandmother's organ, trunks of fine clothes, even my daughter Mahala's dowry.

But I don't fret about all those worries. I try to look on the positive side: all the new sights, the new friends we have made, and the wonderful opportunity awaiting us in Oregon. Nathaniel says my outlook has spread through the wagon train.

Perhaps so. But most of the women have wanted to give up—to just lie down on the prairie because of their terrible weariness. Instead they find their way to me. We walk awhile, and soon their worries pour out like floodwaters.

Every one of them says, "Nancy, don't you ever fret?" I laugh and look them straight in the eye.

"I do. But only when fretting will do some good."

This past week I've had reason to fret. Mahala took sick a few days back, and she isn't getting better. Absalom says it's the water tainted with alkali; Mrs. Andrews thinks the journey did her in. I don't know what's caused her sickness; I do know that she is so weak she rides in the wagon now, her coughing echoing inside my head. Nathaniel told me earlier this morning that Mahala may have cholera. He's read about it and claims she has the symptoms. I told him not to think such things. Mahala has a cold, that's all.

The sun overhead causes me to think, *If we hadn't left home, Doc Stearns could tend to Mahala.* Here in the wild? I have only the Good Lord to ask for help. As I walk, I silently ask him to deliver my whole family to Oregon. I don't know if he hears me in this big country. So every time I hear Mahala cough, I pray a little longer and a little harder.

Two nights ago, after tending to Mahala, I suggested we turn back. You should have seen the look on Nathaniel's face! Bone weary from the weeks of travel, he looked at me with his eyes narrowed and his mouth set firm. "We aren't going back, Nan. She'll pull through. You'll see."

But I don't see Mahala getting better. Every day that passes sees her a little more pale, a little weaker. The others disagree, but wouldn't I know? Shouldn't a mama know her own children?

The dust kicks up something fierce out here. I pull my kerchief over my face and close my eyes. Lately I've found that if I squeeze my eyes closed, I can see Mahala running outside our Illinois home, the wind whipping her reddish hair. It soothes me.

Reverend Jackson used to say, "The Lord rewards the struggle with precious rewards." These days I keep repeating his words over and over.

Nathaniel also recalls the good Reverend's words. He reminds us that this journey will bless everyone. At night, after a campfire supper of biscuits and soup, Nathaniel reads to our children and grandchildren from Dr. John Townsend's narrative. A doctor and naturalist, Townsend traveled the same route, noting descriptions of the wildlife and plants. After the reading Nathaniel asks each of the children what they discovered during the day. It especially pleases him when one of the children finds a plant Townsend described.

The nightly discussions never stay on the book, however. Without fail, Nathaniel begins spinning his own stories of the Oregon Territory, weaving a spell on the children. With his strapping arms, Nathaniel gestures and describes the abundance in Oregon. He's so good with stories that I confess more than a few adults listen as well.

Nathaniel talks of gushing rivers, green pastures as far as the eye can see, and crops that jump out of the earth, bursting with plenty. My children, filled from supper, lick their lips, imagining juicy fruits squirting into their open mouths and stalks of plump yellow corn begging for creamy butter.

Last night Nathaniel told a story of building Oregon cities that will welcome all new immigrants. "Wagon trains just like ours will roll into town," Nathaniel whispered, "and families will stand in awe of Oregon's prosperity: beautiful homes, wealthy merchants, schools, churches. . . ." I stood on the outside of the circle of listeners, holding my breath with the children.

In my mind I saw our spacious home and rich fields. Tears welled up in my eyes, and I cried myself to sleep. I longed so for Oregon! Nathaniel says it's exhaustion, and he's right. But Nathaniel's dream hasn't left me, and I spend each day walking and thinking about arriving in Oregon.

The children also dream of arriving, but the journey keeps them occupied. Every morning the wagon master sits on his horse, shouting, "Wagons ho!" The children then hear the jostling of yokes and reins against the waking prairie. The animals snort and grunt as they lift their hooves for another day's journey.

Nathaniel talks of gushing rivers, green pastures as far as the eye can see, and crops that jump out of the earth, bursting with plenty.

My grandson Nathaniel Norval says those sounds are far more exciting than the bell atop the old schoolhouse at home. Such a rascal! I have to remind him that schooling will continue in Oregon, which brings a frown to his face. In the meantime, every day excites the children: during our journey we've seen large, furry buffalo, snakes that seem as long as our wagons, and scorching heat that causes the prairie to shimmer, not to mention some peculiar plants.

That isn't all, either.

One scorching afternoon, as we passed near the Snake River, Nathaniel Norval ran up to me and tugged on my skirt. He didn't say anything, and when I looked into his face, I saw pale spots of terror dotting his cheeks.

"What is it, child?" I asked. All he could do was point.

Following his outstretched hand, I saw what had frightened him. Off in the distance, outlined against the hills, sat shadowy figures on horseback. Those figures weren't other immigrants: the men held long spears and wore bonnets covered with feathers. Indians! My blood ran cold, and my breath caught in my throat.

We had heard chilling stories in Missouri before we left, as grizzled mountain men described terrible tragedies out West. Whole families butchered in their beds! The men covered the grandchildren's ears, but not before the stories had seeped through.

They'd looked at Nathaniel and me with wide eyes. "Will Indians scalp us in our beds?"

We had told them no, but we weren't certain. And that day as Nathaniel Norval clung to my skirt, shaking like a leaf, I still wasn't certain.

Nathaniel had seen them too. He pulled our wagon alongside Nathaniel Norval and me, and he shushed me before the scream could rip loose from my throat. I was glad for his wisdom. Screaming wouldn't have helped and could've scared everyone.

As it was, the Indians did nothing! There were no war whoops or scalpings. They just watched as we rolled past, the dust clouds swirling in the heat.

That night wagon master Steed, a good man, came to our campfire to talk to the families. Nathaniel, Absalom, and William stood beside Mr. Steed as he told everyone to remain calm. The savages, Mr. Steed explained, mean us no harm. He also explained that the Indians feel displaced by our presence.

"They have lived on this land for thousands of years. Now, as we follow our manifest destiny west, they find themselves strangers in their own land. We must prove ourselves trustworthy. Part of trust is to lay down our weapons and to make peace."

Who could argue with such logic? I wondered.

Mrs. McGibney did. Shouting to Mr. Steed from the back of the group, she said we shouldn't trust them. "They are, after all, uncivilized heathens, are they not?"

Mr. Steed took a deep breath before responding. Then he walked around the campfire and stood close to Mrs. McGibney. He spoke in a patient tone.

"Mrs. McGibney, not everyone in this big beautiful land has had the privilege that we have," he told her. "We must show them Christian charity. That is our duty, is it not?"

No one spoke. Any of the others who also doubted the Indians' intentions said nothing. Those shadowy figures on horseback had shown us no ill will. No one could say they had.

This day will make five days without sight of any Indians. This day is especially hot and tiresome. Looking down the trail, I can see Bethia waving and pointing to me. She is speaking to Absalom, who's riding today. Could we be stopping so soon? He's pulled her onto his horse, and they are riding back to me. Why such a hurry?

She arrives flushed and breathless. "Mama? You'd better hurry back to the wagon. Mahala's much worse. Mr. Steed is stopping the wagons."

Picking up my skirt, I quickly follow Absalom's horse back to the wagon. I'm frightened, and I can't stop my tears. I should have stayed with Mahala today. I just knew it! But Mrs. Ransom needed to rest in our wagon. I took pity on her swollen feet and the Ransoms' overloaded wagon. Was I wrong to do so?

Running now as I haven't since I was a girl, I pray out loud, "Dear Lord, don't take my girl from me!"

Wiping the tears from my face, I stop. Mrs. Ransom and Mrs. Tanner approach from our wagon. They grab my arms to stop me, but I will not stop.

"Let me pass! I must get to her!"

Mrs. Ransom's gentle voice has an uncharacteristic firmness.

"Stop, Nancy. She's gone. I saw her pass myself."

"No! No! She's . . . she's just asleep. Weakened is what she is! She's weak from the trail and not having a decent meal in so long! She's . . . she cannot be . . ."

I collapse onto the prairie, my head buried in my skirts. I cannot bear such grief. My girl! My baby girl! Tears flow from my eyes, as my sobs mingle with the dust to close my throat.

Sensible Mrs. Tanner lifts me off the ground.

"Come, Nancy. Nathaniel is waiting for you at the wagon. Your family needs you now."

I cannot stand without support. The hot sun spins the horizon around before my eyes, and the pain in my heart splits my chest in two.

Gone. My girl Mahala gone to her Maker years before her natural time.

"Easy, Nan . . . Thank you, ladies, I'll take her." Nathaniel stands beside me now, supporting me. I cling to his jacket, my breathing uneven.

"Come on, honey. We have to give her a proper burial. The men have started tearing apart the Steeds' second wagon. It'll have to do."

I turn to him, and my words come haltingly. "My baby . . . will lie in an open wagon?"

"Stop it, now. We have to do it this way." He looks away. "Mahala isn't the first person to die on our wagon train. Mrs. Vickers lost her son, and poor Mrs. Henderson is without her son and her husband. We have to be strong, Nan. Find something to cover her properly."

Barbara Stinger, Nancy Robbins's great-great-great-grand-daughter, at Nancy's grave in 1993

I look up into my Nathaniel's face. The broad brim of his felt hat shields the sun's rays. I can see the glistening tears in his eyes. But he will not shed them. He knows other lives depend upon the wagons' continuing west.

Taking a deep breath, I try to stop crying.

I cannot.

An hour has passed, and clouds gather now on the horizon as we lay Mahala to rest. They signal a welcome storm to replenish our water barrels and cool the land. Mr. Steed speaks a few words, reading from Ecclesiastes. As his steady voice reads a passage, I can hear the barrels on the side of the wagons being opened to receive the rain. Most of the members of the wagon train stand with us, but some do not watch.

Superstition, Nathaniel calls it. "They want to stay as far from death's chokehold as they can."

I understand such fear. I stare at the fresh grave where my girl sleeps. She's covered with her favorite quilt, made from calico cloth so long ago. I tremble, remembering her bright face when her sisters and I finished the quilt.

How will I go on? The tears just won't stop. How can I move another step? Perhaps this is where we should stay . . .

As Mr. Steed closes his well-worn Bible, horses approach in the distance. Nathaniel and the men leave the graveside, but I can't. One by one the other women also drift away, yet still I don't move. Mahala needs me. She's my baby, and she's all alone.

Closing my eyes, I see the wind whipping through her red hair . . .

A noise startles me, and I turn. A young Indian woman stands behind me, her dark eyes peering into mine. I stare back. Where did she come from? I look for Nathaniel, and I see him standing with Mr. Steed and some Indian men. He nods to me silently.

I look back at the young woman's gentle face. What does she want? I start to wipe my tears, and she reaches forward. I flinch from fear, but she means no harm: she wipes a tear from my cheek, touches my blond hair, and points to Mahala's grave. Fresh tears well in my eyes.

She knows I grieve, yet she doesn't speak. Instead she lifts her other arm to show me a bowl and stone. I watch as she points again to Mahala's grave. Then, kneeling on the prairie, she begins grinding the stone into the bowl.

I don't understand—there's no corn in the bowl. Why does she grind? She does not look up; she just keeps grinding and grinding.

Slowly understanding washes over me as a light rainfall begins. This woman is showing me the way through my grief: I must keep moving and working; it is the only way. Everyone needs me.

My tears drying, I touch her shoulder in thanks. She smiles up at me, placing her hand over mine.

Epilogue

Nancy Robbins and her family endured many more tragedies on the Oregon Trail, but they made it to Oregon City in 1852. More than 140 years later, in 1993, her great-great-great-granddaughter Barbara Stinger re-created part of Nancy's journey with the Sesquicentennial Wagon Train Celebration. Her family lives near Portland, Oregon.

Katherine Lesperance is a freelance writer and a journalist living in Los Osos, California. She taught American history in junior high school for several years before becoming a writer and has retained her love for the American experience. She sees history as the perfect opportunity for imaginative storytelling: "Part of history's allure is that it allows the imagination to roam backward in time," says Lesperance. "Students can then grasp the emotional similarities of past experiences to modern ones."

Willie the Handcart Boy

John L. Beach

Perhaps the worst group disaster during the entire Western migration oc-curred in 1856 when two Mormon handcart companies were caught in a terrible winter storm. More than 200 people died in the storms that trapped these pioneers on the plains. Handcart travel was unique and took place for only four years. The courage and long-suffering endurance shown by the Latter-day Saints at this time of trial make the experience unique as well. All this story's characters, except Captain Edward Martin, are fictional represen-tatives of those who undertook the journey. Hope, faith, and charity were the values these pioneers stood for and lived up to during their harrowing days on the Wyoming plains.

IT WAS A MORNING UNLIKE ALL THE MORNINGS SO FAR ON THIS TRIP. WILLIE Madison woke up shivering. Even though when he went to bed he'd worn all his clothes, including his coat, and he'd slept next to his little sister, he was cold! As Willie got up from the cold ground, he wrapped his arms around his body and began to hop up and down to try to get the blood flowing.

Willie looked at the slate-colored sky. The wind was whistling out of the Northwest, and the mountains that had been so far away in August and September now towered over him. They looked cold and forbidding. Willie remembered that his father had called them the Rocky Mountains. He had never seen anything like them.

Back in England, piles of coal slag were the tallest things Willie had ever seen, and now he had to tip his head to see all of the mountains that marched ahead of the company. Snow covered the tops of all the highest peaks, and nothing about them looked inviting. Yet Willie knew that they had to go over them to reach Salt Lake City, where his parents had told him Zion was.

Willie looked around at the handcart camp. Many people were slowly rising from their makeshift beds. Others were just lying in place, too exhausted to rise. Some were preparing what little food they had, and Willie knew that breakfast would be only a part of a biscuit cooked the night before. He walked over to the spot where the Blair family had camped the previous night and spoke softly to his friend, Helen.

"Helen, it's morning. Come and see the mountains. They're so tall."

Little Helen didn't stir, although her mother and father began to move under the worn quilt that offered them their only protection against the night's chill.

"Willie, is that you?" came the voice of Sister Blair. "Help me get to my feet. They're a little numb this morning from the cold."

Willie held out his hand and helped Helen's mother to her feet. She in turn helped her husband up from the cold ground. Both of them then bent over Helen's supine form and slowly uncovered the blond hair that identified her.

"Helen." Brother Blair's deep voice carried over the sagebrush flat to the other carts. "Helen—come girl; let's get up. It's time to go on."

But the small figure under the quilt did not stir. Helen's mother knelt by her side and placed her hands on Helen's face. After a few moments she rose and quietly announced, "She's gone. Helen's not with us anymore. She must have gone during the night. I didn't even get to say goodbye."

Brother Blair put his arm around his good wife and consoled her over the loss of their only child. While the couple stood together in the wind, others in the company came and gently took the body of Helen Blair to a place where three others lay. The company had lost four during the night. And the weather was getting colder.

Willie slowly walked back to his mother, father, and little sister, who were getting ready to start the day's trek.

"Helen's gone, Ma. She's just gone. She died during the night. Sister Blair didn't even get to say goodbye."

Willie's mother put her arm around him, and he took comfort in her touch.

"I know, son; but we must go on. Helen's suffering is over, and now she is with others who love her."

Captain Martin, the company's leader, began to go from cart to cart and round up the survivors while several of the men finished scratching out a shallow grave for those who would be left behind. He came to Willie's cart, and he too put an arm around the young boy.

"I know that you'll miss Helen. We all will, but we need your help to finish this journey. Can we count on you?"

Willie Madison squared his shoulders under the older man's arm and looked up at him.

"Of course you can, Captain. What shall I do first?"

"Well, Willie, I know your folks need your help, but during the day, could you see how Helen's parents are getting along? I'm worried about them."

"Yes, Captain, I'll do it."

Before leaving the night's camping spot, the handcart pioneers gathered at the gravesite, held a brief service, and sang the song that was becoming the anthem for all Mormons crossing the plains. "Come, Come, Ye Saints" rang out across the windswept plains and lingered in the sage surrounding the spot where their loved ones lay buried.

Within the first hour of pushing and pulling the handcarts along the trail that had long been established by wagons and earlier handcart companies, a woman's anguished voice rang out: "Snow! It's snowing again."

The snow had begun to fall in great wet flakes. A strong northwest wind drove into the pioneers' faces, making every step more difficult than the one before it.

Later that day the pioneers had to ford the Sweetwater River. There was a thin film of ice along the edges of the river, and chunks of ice and slush flowed along in the current. The men and older boys tried to help as many children and women as they could, and some made several trips back and forth in the icy water. They didn't have time to dry off before the company moved on.

Willie was pushing his parent's cart with his little sister when he looked over his shoulder and saw Helen's parents struggling with their cart. He leaned over to his sister, Nancy, and whispered, "Can you do this by yourself? Helen's daddy is sick, and her mother is doing most of the work. I need to help them. Can you, please, Nancy?"

His sister looked at him and nodded her head. He hated to leave, but Brother Blair had spent considerable time in the icy river and was beginning to stagger through the ruts in the road. The cart lurched from side to side. Willie quickly dropped back to the Blairs' cart, which Helen's mother was trying to pull mostly by herself.

"Here, let me help, Brother Blair," said the young boy.

The older man was too far spent to object as Willie slipped under the handle of the cart and began to pull. Then, because there wasn't enough room for all three of them, Brother Blair stooped down and moved out from under the handle. He waited until the back of the cart passed and fell in behind, attempting to help by pushing. His strength was not sufficient even for that, and it was all he could do to hang on and let the cart help him along. Up front Willie and Sister Blair could feel the extra drag, but neither said anything. They simply renewed their efforts.

Soon the snowstorm closed in around the little band, and it was impossible to see more than 50 yards in any direction. Captain Martin began to range back and forth along the line, encouraging all and giving a hand where he could. But the line started to falter and slow, until the pioneers were making only a few feet at a time. It wasn't long before the lead cart pulled over to the side and let the rest of the train go past. The next cart did the same, each family trying for a brief rest before struggling again through the white world around them.

Time for a break came and went, and Captain Martin kept moving the group along the trail. No one complained or murmured during the day's struggle, but at times the sounds of subdued groans and wheezing from lungs too long in the cold and wet could be heard. Each hour was like the one before it. Each was dark and cold. Sounds were muffled in the falling snow, and the groaning of the handcarts' wheels echoed the company itself.

The snow grew deeper and deeper, and soon it was all that anyone could do just to move the carts over the small rises in the snow-covered trail. Just then Willie heard Captain Martin cry out.

The Saints bury one of their own in this painting, The Martin Handcart Company, Bitter Creek, Wyoming, 1856, *by Clark Kelley Price. Handcarts can be seen in the background.*

"Stop! Stop here. There's a small cove over there in that hill. It will give us some shelter from the wind. We'll stop there for the night."

Willie and the others turned their carts in the direction the captain had indicated, and soon all were out of the wind a little. Those with tents quickly erected them, and the others sought the leeward side of the carts to make their beds.

Willie helped the Blairs make their shelter beside the cart because Brother Blair had gotten worse and worse all afternoon. He was coughing constantly and barely able to stagger to the shelter of the cart before slumping to the ground. His wife and Willie bundled him up in all that they had for cover, and Sister Blair started a small fire to heat water to warm them. Willie adjusted a borrowed tarp over Brother Blair and noticed that Sister Blair was nearly blue from the cold herself.

"Go along, Willie. Your mother and father will be worried about you. Thank you for all your help today. We couldn't have made it without you." After she had spoken, Sister Blair bent over the fire in a way that didn't allow Willie to debate the issue.

No one in the camp seemed to have any strength that night. As Willie looked for his family's resting spot, he saw pioneers retiring quickly to their shelter for the night as if it might be the safety they so desperately needed. Willie also heard the murmuring of nightly prayers from those who were still strong enough to utter them. In their own ways, all sought the comfort of their Maker, even in such dire circumstances.

It snowed throughout that late-October night. As the temperature dropped, winter blew its icy breath on the high plains of Wyoming. By morning the deadly snow was so deep that the company could go no farther.

Willie and Captain Martin walked around the camp to encourage the pioneers and remind them that help would come from Salt Lake as soon as the advance party reached the city. Brother Blair had died that night, and more and more died each night following. Many others were unable to walk because their feet and legs were frozen.

Three days later, Willie heard one of the sisters' voice: "Angels! I see them! They're coming! They must be angels!"

Willie and the rest of the company looked to the west, and advancing across the plains were several men on horseback, followed by a wagon.

A hard road to Zion

IN THE WINTER OF 1846–47 THE MIGRATION OF "SAINTS" (AS CONVERTS TO MORMONISM WERE called) to "Zion," their settlement in the Great Salt Lake valley, began in earnest. Parties of 10 required a wagon with two yoke (pairs) of oxen, two milk cows, and a tent. Each year the Saints formed trains of several hundred wagons to make the journey across the Great Plains and the Rocky Mountains.

Beginning in 1856, however, travel funds provided by the church were running low, and impoverished converts, many of whom had immigrated to America from Scandinavia, sought a cheaper method of travel. Their solution was handcarts. Ox-drawn wagons were still used to carry the heaviest items, and handcarts bore food and personal belongings.

A handcart consisted of nothing more than a wooden box attached to two wheels, some with iron tires, an axle, and shafts for pulling. They usually weighed about 60 pounds and could carry a 500-pound load when drawn by two people (though they certainly could not be so heavily loaded when moving up or down steep hills). Under normal conditions it took nine weeks to make the trip from the embarkation point at Iowa City.

In that first season nearly 1,900 people set out for Zion in this way, with a cart to every four or five people and a wagon to every hundred. Those who left in June arrived without serious mishap, but two large parties totaling 1,076 people that started in July met with disaster. Heavy snows stopped them before they reached the Rockies, and weather and starvation killed more than 200 members of the expedition.

Still, Saints continued to carry their belongings by hand, and from 1856 to 1860, nearly 3,000 handcart pioneers made the journey to Zion.

—David Rhoden

The wagon was loaded high with supplies, and they did appear to be angels coming to rescue Martin's Handcart Company.

It would be another month before the company was taken into the Salt Lake valley, and even then the suffering would not end. Of the 500 who had left Florence, Nebraska, in August, nearly 150 would die, either on the plains or later from complications of the journey.

But now Willie looked across the valley as the pioneers struggled down Emigration Canyon. There was snow on all the mountains surrounding him and snow on the mountains across the valley, reminding him once again of the mountains where Helen had been left. He wondered if he would ever be warm again. As they came into the valley, the other Saints came to meet them, and Willie and his family were taken into a home for the rest of that winter.

In the spring the Madison family started their own home, and it wasn't far from the land where Helen's mother began a garden to grow fresh vegetables to sell for her income. Each pioneer helped the others, and in time the memories of the terrible winter of 1856 were dimmed. But none of the handcart pioneers would ever forget the snowbound plains of Wyoming and the loved ones they had left behind.

John L. Beach has more than 25 years' experience as an English teacher in Rock Springs, Wyoming, and is listed in Who's Who in American Education, 1989–90. *He is a freelance storyteller as well as a teacher and a writer. Weaving music into his stories, Beach works primarily with Western historical stories, family stories, and tall tales set in the West. He strives for a deeper understanding of the past and believes we have an obligation to remember our predecessors and their contributions.*

Pioneering Spirit: The Story Of Julia Archibald Holmes

John Stansfield

When Julia Archibald Holmes set out in a wagon on the Santa Fe Trail for Pikes Peak in June 1858, she was 20 years old, married just eight months, and "young, handsome, and intelligent," as one of her companions described her. She was a pioneer in every sense of the word. She was also a fine writer. Much of the following story is told in Julia's own words, taken from letters to her family and to a women's rights magazine. She also kept a daily journal, most of which has been lost. Her words clearly—and sometimes willfully— express her beliefs about sexual equality and personal responsibility as well as her fascination with nature and the experience of the moment. Without Holmes's writings we would never have known of her adventures or the pioneering spirit that shines so brightly through her words.

IN JULY 1854, 16-YEAR-OLD JULIA ARCHIBALD STOOD IN THE BOSTON RAILWAY station singing a newly written hymn. In harmony with her family and many others leaving Massachusetts that day, she sang:

> We cross the prairies as of old
> The pilgrims crossed the sea,
> To make the West, as they the East,
> The homestead of the free!
>
> We go to rear a wall of men
> On Freedom's southern line,
> And plant beside the cotton tree
> The rugged Northern pine!
>
> We're flowing from our native hills
> As our free rivers flow;
> The blessing of our Motherland
> Is on us as we go.

We'll tread the prairie as of old
Our fathers sailed the sea,
And make the West, as they the East,
The homestead of the free!

Both the singers and their hymn were called "The Kansas Emigrants." The hymn was written in their honor by the famed poet and abolitionist John Greenleaf Whittier.

When the singing was over, Julia helped her parents and seven sisters and brothers board the train heading west. They were going to be pioneers in the brand-new Kansas Territory.

The Archibalds and the other Kansas emigrants were pioneers with a purpose. For soon a vote was to be taken in the territory: would it be slave or free? Should slavery be legal in Kansas? Julia, her parents, and the other emigrants from New England believed strongly that slavery was evil and should be illegal. They hoped to make the West "the homestead of the free."

Julia's father, John, was the only one in the family eligible to vote. Her mother, Jane, was not free to cast a ballot against slavery though she desperately wanted to. In many places at that time women did not have the right to vote.

Julia Archibald Holmes

From her parents Julia learned many important things, including the importance of freedom and equality for all, for both men and women, regardless of race. She also learned the importance of responsibly acting upon her beliefs.

The Archibalds were a founding family of Lawrence, Kansas. Their home became a meeting place for abolitionists (Free-Staters, as they were called) and a "station" on the Underground Railroad for slaves escaping from the South. Battles were fought between those for and against slavery. In December 1854 Lawrence was besieged by proslavery men. For Julia they were exciting and dangerous times.

At her parents' house Julia met James Henry Holmes, the bold captain of the Free-State militia. In October 1857 she married James, and they settled down on his homestead near Emporia.

But the adventurous young couple did not let the prairie grass grow under their feet. The next spring they heard of a wagon train heading west from Lawrence on the Santa Fe Trail. They decided to join it. As Julia wrote later in one of her letters:

We were on our farm on the Neosho River, in Kansas, when news reached us that a company was fitting out in Lawrence for a gold adventure to Pikes Peak. Animated more by a desire to cross the plains and behold the great mountain chain of North America than by any expectation of realizing the floating gold stories, we hastily laid a supply of provisions in the covered wagon, and two days later, the second of June 1858, were on the road to join the Lawrence company.

With Julia in the wagon, drawn by a team of oxen, were James and her 18-year-old brother, Albert. After three days' travel they joined the wagon train camped at Cottonwood Creek.

Finding that we were to have all day to rest, we took our large cooking stove out of the wagon and cooked up provisions for two or three days. Nearly all the men were entire strangers to me, and as I was cooking our dinner, some of them crowded around our wagon, gazing sometimes at the stove, which with its smoke pipe looked quite out of place, but oftener on my dress, which did not surprise me, for, I presume, some of them had never seen such a costume before. I wore a calico dress reaching a little below the knee, pants of the same, Indian moccasins on my feet, and on my head a hat. However much it lacked in taste, I found it to be beyond value in comfort and convenience, as it gave me freedom to roam at pleasure in search of flowers and other curiosities, while the cattle continued their slow and measured pace.

And so the journey of 500 miles and five weeks' time was begun. Wagon-train travel was slow at best. Making 20 miles was a good day's travel on the rugged Santa Fe Trail. In hot weather parties often drove early, stopped to "noon it" during the heat of the day, and continued on in the cool of the evening. The wagons usually rolled on through rainy weather, but in mud they often stopped—and stuck—until extra teams of oxen or mules could pull them out. Waiting for the water to drop in creeks that flooded across the trail was common, for there were no bridges. Fresh food, firewood, and clean water were often scarce. Wagons broke. Animals ran off. Patience was required of all the travelers.

The Lawrence company was made up of 12 wagons with almost 50 men, two women, and one child. Julia's first meeting with the other woman, Mrs. Robert Middleton, was not too friendly.

I was much pleased to learn on my arrival that the company contained a lady and rejoiced at the prospect of having a female companion on such a long journey. But my hopes were disappointed. I soon found that there could be no congeniality between us. She proved to be a woman unable to appreciate freedom or reform, affected that her sphere denied her the liberty to rove at pleasure, and confined herself the long days to feminine impotence in the hot covered wagon. After we had become somewhat acquainted, she in great kindness gave me her advice.

"If you have a long dress with you, do put it on for the rest of the trip; the men talk so much about you."

"What do they say?" I inquired.

"Oh, nothing, only you look so queer with that dress on."

"I cannot afford to dress to please their taste," I replied. "I could not positively enjoy a moment's happiness with long skirts on to confine me to the wagon."

The clothes Julia wore, so practical to her and so curious and radical to others, were called the "reform dress," or "bloomer." For Julia and many other women of her time, the reform dress was a symbol of independence and ability. It also enabled her to discover the simple pleasure and freedom of walking.

The clothes Julia wore, so practical to her and so curious and radical to others, were called the "reform dress," or "bloomer."

I commenced the journey with the firm determination to learn to walk. At first I could not walk over three or four miles without feeling quite weary, but by persevering and walking as far as I could every day, my capacity increased gradually, and in the course of a few weeks I could walk 10 miles in the most sultry weather without being exhausted.

Believing, as I do, in the right of woman to equal privileges with man, I think that when it is in our power, we should, in order to promote our own independence, at least be willing to share the hardships which commonly fall to the lot of man. Accordingly, I signified to the guardmaster that I desired to take my turn with the others in the duty of guarding the camp and requested to have my watch assigned with my husband. The captain of the guard was of the opinion that it would be a disgrace to the gentlemen of the company for them to permit a woman to stand on guard.

As Julia's walks grew in length, so did her appreciation of the wildflowers and wildlife of the prairie. She heard "music wild and thrilling as only a band of prairie wolves can make." She discovered "many new varieties of wildflowers, some of them of exceeding beauty." And she was the first in the Lawrence company to see the wild bison.

When camped on the Little Arkansas River, as I was searching for different flowers a few rods from the camp, I cast my eyes across the river, and there within 40 yards of me stood a venerable buffalo bull, his eyes in seeming wonder fixed upon me. He had approached me unobserved, behind the trees which lined the bank. His gaze was returned with equal astonishment and earnestness. Much as I had heard and read of the buffalo, I had never formed an adequate idea of their huge appearance. He was larger and heavier than a large ox; his head and shoulders being so disproportionate, he seemed far larger than he really was. He looked the impersonation of a prairie god—the grand emperor of the plain.

His presence soon became known in camp, and in a few seconds he was coursing westward with our fleetest horses in pursuit. He was overtaken and shot within three or four miles. Buffalo now began to be a common object.

My husband went out buffalo hunting and returned bringing with him a buffalo calf apparently but a week old. It was a great curiosity to all, and in the fullness of my compassion for the poor little thing, I mixed up a mess of flour and water, which I hoped to make it drink. I approached it with these charitable intentions, when the savage little animal advanced toward me and gave me such a blow with its head as to destroy my center of gravity.

I learned that the mother of the captured calf made a heroic stand. She was in a herd of many hundred buffaloes, fleeing wildly over the plain before the hunter. After a few miles' chase the calf gave signs of fatigue. At its faint cry she would turn and come to the calf, but at sight of the hunter bounded off to the herd. This she did two or three times, the calf falling behind more and more, and his mother wavering between fear for his life and her own. At last her decision was made, and she determined to defend her offspring alone on the prairie. She died in his defense.

Later in the journey Julia had a friendly meeting with two pronghorn:

We were passing over an uneven road today, and getting a mile or two in advance of wagons, we came upon a pair of antelope grazing. Immediately dropping upon the ground that we might not frighten them, we had a fine opportunity to examine their beautiful form and motion. They advanced toward us until they were scarcely 10 rods off, with eyes riveted upon us perhaps a minute, when sudden as lightning they started and bounded away as like the wind. Their smooth form, with slender, tapering legs, glossy hair, bright, large eyes, their graceful, lofty, and intelligent motion, left a deep impress of their beauty.

I felt that I possessed an ownership in all that was good or beautiful in nature and an interest in any curiosities we might find on the journey as much as if I had been one of the favored lords of creation.

Though Julia greatly enjoyed her walks, getting out and away from the wagon train sometimes had its dangers. Once Julia and Albert were driving their wagon ahead of the rest when they were stopped by a party of Indians. They were not sure what the men intended. This caused brother and sister a few minutes of real fear. Then some of their Lawrence company companions rode up, and the Indians rode away.

The rest of the company's encounters with the Cheyenne and Arapaho people they met along the trail were much more friendly—almost too friendly for Julia!

We passed, on the 14th of June, a large number of Cheyenne and Arapaho Indians. Fifty men armed with Sharp's rifles and revolvers were afraid to allow the Indians to know that the company contained any women, in consequence of something which the carriers of the Santa Fe mail told them when they passed a few days previous. I was, therefore, confined to the wagon while we passed many places of interest which I wished very much to visit. Notwithstanding this care to be unobserved, my presence became known. At one time by opening the front of the wagon for ventilation, at another by leaping from it to see something curious which two or three Indians had brought, not knowing that we were very near a village.

It was of no use to hide now, for every Indian within a mile knew of my whereabouts. My husband received several flattering offers for me. One Indian wanted to trade two squaws, who could probably perform four times the physical labor that I could. Others, not quite so timid, approaching the wagon made signs for me to jump behind them on their ponies, but I declined the honor in the most respectful language I knew of their dialect—a decided shake of the head.

The company moved up the trail, following the Arkansas River, without serious mishap. They made a stop at Bent's New Fort, a trading post for Indians and travelers, and then pushed on west. Finally their goal was in sight.

After leaving Bent's Fort, we began to look anxiously for a glimpse of Pikes Peak. On the evening of July third, after camping, a sudden rain and hail storm came upon us, penetrating more or less every wagon cover and blowing down most of the tents. Traveling but 15 miles today, the train camped early this evening in order to celebrate the "glorious fourth." This was done by consuming what little whiskey remained among the members. This day we obtained the first view of the summit of the Peak, now some 70 miles away. As all expected to find precious treasure near this wonderful peak, it is not strange that our eyes were often strained by gazing on it. The summit appeared majestic in the distance, crowned with glistening white.

When she first viewed Pikes Peak on Independence Day 1858, Julia could not know that her life story and the history of that great mountain would soon be entwined forever. On July 8 the company arrived "as near as the wagons could approach the mountains." Here they remained camped for more than a month. Occasionally parties of men would venture out, seeking gold and hunting. They had little success with either activity. No one became rich.

From the camp, Julia wrote to her family on July 12:

Dear Mother and Father and all the loved ones:
Greetings to you from across the plains in sight of the Rocky Mountains. About three days ago we arrived at Pikes Peak. The search for gold hitherto has been unsuccessful. Some are discouraged and talk of going home along with the company which has just overtaken us and with whom this letter is to be sent. We have been very well indeed and enjoyed the journey very much. No danger on the road, the Indians all very friendly, but awful beggars.

We may start for home in the course of two weeks, that is, if we are obliged to go empty. I wish we were not obliged to go at all; this fall I would like to travel through to the Pacific.

The mountains are very beautiful. Pikes Peak looks sublime. I have seen a great deal of beautiful scenery, have not been lonesome, and the journey has not seemed very tedious. I am forgetting how to spell right. My love to all the dear ones, Allie, Jane, Freddy, Clara, Nancy, Ebenezer. Albert is very well; he would probably write, but this is his turn to guard the cattle. He sends his love.

On July 9 Augustus Voorhees, F. M. Cobb, and John C. Miller set out from the Lawrence company camp to climb Pikes Peak. The following day they reached the rocky summit of the 14,110-foot-high mountain. The climbers added stones to the small pile, built as a summit marker from the time of Pikes Peak's first recorded ascent in 1820. They left a piece of wood, carved with their names and the date, in the center of the pile. The stories of the climbers and the sight of the magnificent peak before them each day awakened the mountaineering spirit within Julia and James. With Miller as their guide, they began their climb.

August 1, 1858. After an early breakfast this morning, my husband and I adjusted our packs to our backs and started for the ascent of Pikes Peak. My own pack weighed 17 pounds, nine of which were bread, the remainder a quilt and clothing. James's pack weighed 35 pounds and was composed as follows: 10 pounds bread, one pound hog meat, three-fourths pound coffee, one pound sugar, a tin plate, knife and fork, half-gallon canteen, half-gallon tin pail and a tin cup, five quilts, clothing, a volume of Emerson's *Essays*, and writing material made up the remainder. We calculate on this amount of food to subsist six days.

The climbers made a base camp just above the timberline, where wind and cold stop a forest's growth and only alpine plants survive.

August 2, 1858. Dear Mother: I write this to you sitting in our little house among the rocks, about one hour's walk from the summit of Pikes Peak. It is a curious little nook which we have selected as our temporary home, formed by two very large overhanging rocks and enclosed by a number of smaller ones, while close beside it is a large snow bank which we can reach with ease.

Two days of very hard climbing has brought me here—if you could only know how hard, you would be surprised that I have been able to accomplish it. My strength and capacity for enduring fatigue have been very much increased by constant exercise in the open air since leaving home, or I never could have succeeded in climbing the rugged sides of this mountain.

But I shall not write anymore now, for I mean to finish this on top of the mountain.

With James, on the morning of August 5, Julia reached the high point of her journey at the summit of Pikes Peak. Using a flat rock for a writing desk, she finished the letter to her mother:

I have accomplished the task I marked out for myself, and now I feel amply repaid for all my toil and fatigue. Nearly everyone tried to discourage me from attempting it, but I believed that I should succeed; and now here I am, and I feel that I would not have missed this glorious sight for anything at all. In all probability I am the first woman who has ever stood upon the summit of this mountain and gazed upon this wondrous scene. How I sigh for the poet's power of description so that I might give you some faint idea of the grandeur and beauty of this scene. Extending as far as the eye can

"My strength and capacity for enduring fatigue have been very much increased by constant exercise in the open air since leaving home, or I never could have succeeded in climbing the rugged sides of this mountain."

reach lie the great level plains, stretched out in all their verdure and beauty, while the winding of the great Arkansas is visible for many miles. Then the rugged rocks all around, and the almost endless succession of mountains and rocks below, the broad blue sky over our heads, and seemingly so very near; all, and everything, on which the eye can rest fills the mind with infinitude and sends the soul to God.

Julia Archibald Holmes was the first woman known to have gazed at the world from the top of Pikes Peak. Given her pioneering spirit, it seems fitting that she be first.

In 1893 another woman, Katharine Lee Bates, also admired the view from Pikes Peak's summit. She was moved to write just as Julia had been. Bates's well-known words express the "poet's power of description" that Julia desired. Although Julia never heard them, they are words she would have appreciated. Bates wrote:

O beautiful for spacious skies,
For amber waves of grain,
For purple mountain majesties
Above the fruited plain.
America! America!
God shed his grace on thee,
And crown thy good with brotherhood
From sea to shining sea!

Storyteller and writer John Stansfield loves the American West and sharing stories about its diverse lands, wildlife, and people. His audiotape Song of the Mountains, Song of the Plains *(self-published, 1990) is a collection of factual Western narratives and ballads. Stansfield also enjoys sharing world folklore and literature with audiences of all ages—especially young people. He and his wife, Carol, live in Monument, Colorado, near Pikes Peak and the Santa Fe Trail.*

Why Lincoln Grew a Beard

Lucille Breneman ─────────────────────────

This human-interest story provides a warm and intimate portrait of Abe Lincoln as seen by an 11-year-old girl, who had suggested in a letter that he grow his famous beard. Lincoln himself enjoyed telling this story, and we know he was a master storyteller. The history books preserve many stories about Abe Lincoln, the 16th president of the United States—tales about his early life as a pioneer child on a Kentucky farm, his career as a lawyer, his efforts to hold the nation together during the Civil War, and his assassination. This story focuses on Lincoln's great love and respect for children and their love for him. The following version, with minor editing, was told by Hideko Asou, a student in storytelling at the University of Hawaii. Her full story may be found in Once Upon a Time: A Storytelling Handbook *by Lucille and Bren Breneman (Nelson-Hall, 1983).*

IT WAS AN OCTOBER EVENING IN 1860 IN THE TOWN OF WESTFIELD, NEW YORK. Grace Bedell, an 11-year-old girl, was in her room, looking at a campaign poster featuring Abraham Lincoln and his running mate, Hannibal Hamlin, that her father had just given her.

Her lamp threw shadows about Lincoln's face and covered the hollow cheeks. *Whiskers!* she thought.

"How becoming it would be," she said to herself. "Somebody should tell him. All the ladies like whiskers. They would tell their husbands to vote for him, and he would become president. I must tell him!"

She reached for a pen and began to write the following letter:

Dear Sir:

. . . I am a little girl only 11 years old, but [I] want you to be president of the United States very much so I hope you won't think me very bold to write to such a great man as you are.

Have you any little girls about as large as I am? If so, give them my love, and tell her to write to me if you cannot answer this letter. I have got four brothers, and part of them will vote for you anyway, and if you will let your whiskers grow, I will try and get the rest of them to vote for you. You would look a good deal better, for your face is so thin. All the ladies like whiskers, and they would tease their husbands to vote for you, and then you would be president. . . .

Grace Bedell

At that time about 50 letters a day arrived at the Lincoln campaign headquarters. Lincoln saw only those from friends and very important people. His two secretaries, John Nicolay and John Hay, considered all other mail unimportant and usually did not give it to Lincoln. Grace's letter was picked up by John Hay, and he was intrigued by her original idea. But John Nicolay was not impressed and suggested that Grace's letter be tossed into the wastebasket. The two secretaries began to argue, and neither of them would give in.

Just then Lincoln walked into the room. Now, Abe Lincoln liked little girls. No little girl's letter should be tossed into the wastebasket. He took the letter and began to read it. Soon a pleased expression came to his face.

A few days later Grace received this letter from Springfield, Illinois, dated October 19, 1860:

My dear little Miss,

Your very agreeable letter of the 15th is received. I regret the necessity of saying I have no daughters. I have three sons—one 17, one 9, and one 7 years of age. They, with their mother, constitute my whole family.

As to the whiskers, having never worn any, do you not think people would call it a piece of silly affect[at]ion if I were to begin it now?

Your very sincere well-wisher,
A. Lincoln

The beardless Mr. Lincoln in 1857

You can imagine the thrill Grace felt when she read this reply.

In February of the following year a special train carried the newly elected President Lincoln to the White House. The people of Westfield learned that the train would stop briefly at a station near their town. The Bedell family also heard the news, and on that day they took Grace and went to the station. As they approached, they saw a huge banner, which read HAIL TO THE CHIEF, and the Stars and Stripes flying from the roof of the station.

As Grace looked around at the many strange faces, there was a sudden silence. A thousand people were straining to hear. "Here comes the train!" someone shouted.

Grace raised her eyes as high as she could and saw the top of the black railway engine pass slowly beyond the heads of the people in front of her. Then she saw the top of a flat railway car, and another, and a third with the Stars and Stripes waving from the back.

Then she saw a tall black hat a little higher than a lot of other hats—but that was all she could see. Some of the people were shouting, "Speech! Speech!" Grace held her breath. Everyone around her became quiet.

"Ladies and gentlemen," she heard, "I have no speech to make, nor do I have the time to make one. I appear before you so that I may see you and you may see me."

Grace was ice-cold. That was Lincoln—that was his voice. He was up on the platform. She tried hard to catch a glimpse of him, but all she could see was the tall black hat.

Lincoln spoke again. "I have but one question, standing here beside the flag: Will you give me the support a man needs to be president of our country?"

The people threw their hats into the air, waved their arms, and shouted, "We will, Abe, we will!" And then they were quiet again because Lincoln had something else to say.

"I have a little correspondent in this place. She wrote me what I should do to improve my appearance. I want to thank her. If she is present, I would like to speak to her. Her name is Grace Bedell."

The paper trail

THE STORY OF ABRAHAM LINCOLN'S MEETING WITH Grace Bedell is found in newspaper accounts of the day. Lincoln stopped in several towns on his way from Springfield, Illinois, to Washington, D.C., where he was inaugurated president March 4, 1861. Other crowds were not as friendly as the one that greeted Lincoln in Westfield, however; warned in Baltimore of a plot on his life, Lincoln took an earlier train and arrived in Washington incognito 12 hours earlier than scheduled.

The actual correspondence regarding Lincoln's whiskers still exists. Grace Bedell's letter is in the Burton Historical Collection of the Detroit Public Library (it was donated by a Michigan congressman who collected Lincolniana), and the president's reply is in private hands.

—David Rhoden

Grace's father took her hand and led her toward the platform. People made a path for them as they went. Then her father lifted her up to the platform, up high, where she saw a pair of huge feet.

Somewhere above her she heard a slow chuckle. "She wrote me that I would look better if I wore whiskers."

Then Grace felt strong hands under her arms. She was lifted high in the air, kissed on both cheeks, and gently set down again.

She forgot all about the people. Grace looked up and laughed happily, for up there on the rugged face, she saw the whiskers.

"You see, Grace, I let them grow just for you."

All Grace could do was stand there and look at this great, tall, wonderful man. She felt as though she could have stayed there forever. But Lincoln took her hand, and she heard him say, "I hope to see you again sometime, my little friend." Then she knew the moment had to end. Lincoln helped her down the railway steps, and she obediently went back to her proud father.

She heard the train whistle, the noise of the engine as it started on its way again. People waved and cheered after the train until it was far down the tracks, but Grace heard only three words—three words repeated over and over in her mind: "My little friend."

Lucille Breneman is a professor emeritus of the University of Hawaii. She and her late husband, Bren, co-wrote Once Upon a Time: A Storytelling Handbook *(Nelson-Hall, 1983). The couple performed stories in tandem until Bren's death in 1989. Her recent awards include the 1993 California Traditional Music Society Storytelling Award and the 1993 Bay Area Festival Storytelling Award. She and retired lawyer Richard Koproske were married in 1993. They live in San Diego, and Breneman continues to tell stories and lead workshops.*

A Cold Night

R. Craig Roney

Storytelling enables students to interact with culture (past and present) through narrative—the major means by which children make sense of the world around them. As such, storytelling is a natural way for students to explore the historical past, the belief systems of varied societies, and diverse factual information as well. This story, an adaptation of a ghost story originally written by Ambrose Bierce, provides an example. The scene is a broad, frozen, cadaver-strewn plain spanning the Stones River near Murfreesboro, Tennessee—the aftermath of one of the Civil War's bloodiest days of fighting. The fight for survival continues through the night as the men contend with bitter cold and the persistent fear that they may be killed during the next day's fighting. In the midst of this numbing carnage, a simple act of kindness and respect is acknowledged in a rather eerie fashion.

LATE IN 1862 THE UNION FORCES WERE DIVIDED INTO THREE ARMIES. THE ARMY of the Cumberland, 45,000 strong, under the command of Major General William S. Rosecrans, was situated just south of Nashville. The general's main objective was to march on Chattanooga and take that city, which served as a major railroad supply hub for the Confederacy.

Standing between Rosecrans and Chattanooga were General Braxton Bragg and 38,000 seasoned Confederate soldiers, encamped just north and west of Murfreesboro, all up and down the Stones River.

The Battle of Stones River (Murfreesboro, if you favor the Confederate cause) began on December 31, 1862. Rosecrans' men had marched from the north and west. Bragg and his troops defended from the south and east. The strategy favored by both armies was identical: hold with the right line of forces; attack with the left line. Had both plans been carried out simultaneously, the armies would have swung around like a huge revolving door. But as was typical of most early Civil War battles, the Confederates struck first and drove the Union troops back and in on themselves so that by day's end the Union position was shaped like a giant jackknife with the blade partly exposed.

Perhaps as a result of the confusion, the Confederates were unable to drive the Union forces from the field. Still, the fighting had been fierce.

The volleys of musket fire alone had been so loud that soldiers on both sides of the line had plucked cotton bolls right from the plants and stuffed them in their ears to stave off the awful noise.

Now, for some unexplained reason, Bragg failed to capitalize on his victory that first day. His army sat idle on January 1 and the morning of January 2, but he took up the fight again on the afternoon of January 2 and was repelled by savage cannon fire. Fifty-eight Union cannons lined up in a row tore Bragg's line to shreds—one of the few instances during the war when cannon fire played a significant role in turning the tide of a battle.

Two days later Bragg retreated to Tullahoma, Tennessee, 36 miles to the south, and Rosecrans walked into Murfreesboro. The Battle of Stones River was over.

Both armies would be immobilized for several months. And it is an axiom of war that if you cannot fight, you cannot win. And the casualties? The dead and the wounded? Thirteen thousand for the Union, 10,000 for the Confederates—well over a quarter of the strength of both armies.

Now, one of the Union soldiers still alive at the end of the first day's fighting was Ambrose Bierce, the noted Civil War chronicler and a captain in an Indiana regiment. That day Bierce and his companions had taken refuge behind a railroad embankment that served as a breastwork, staving off the repeated charges of Confederate infantry. Before the embankment lay the dead of both armies, piled two or three deep. Behind the embankment the ground was flat, broad, open, and strewn with sizable boulders. Next to nearly every boulder were dead Union soldiers who had been dragged out of the way during the battle.

When the fighting subsided, the heat of the day was replaced with piercing cold—a crystal-clear night despite the clouds of gun smoke created earlier that day, a night frozen and unyielding.

Among the dead lay one whom no one seemed to know, a sergeant, flat on his back, his limbs outstretched, rigid as steel. He had died on the spot where he lay . . . or so it seemed.

He had been shot squarely in the center of the forehead. One of the Union surgeons (perhaps out of idle curiosity, perhaps to amuse the still-living soldiers gathered nearby) had pressed a probe clean through the sergeant's head until it struck dirt at the base of the skull.

The night had grown so frigid that frost had formed on the grass around the sergeant, on his ashen face, his hair, and his beard. Some Christian soul had covered him with a blanket, but as the night turned colder and unrelenting, one of Bierce's companions approached the body, took hold of that blanket, and said in a solemn voice, "Please forgive me, sir. But I fear I'll be needing this more than you tonight." He took the blanket, and then both he and Bierce wrapped themselves in it and suffered through the night.

That night every man lay still and silent. Pickets had been posted well out in front of the railroad embankment. These soldiers were permitted to move to ensure the security of the army, but movement by all others was prohibited. Conversation was strictly forbidden. There was to be no movement, no sound, no light, no heat. Even lighting a match would have been a grave offense.

Stamping horses, moaning wounded, anything that made noise had been sent well to the rear. All the living suffered the bitter cold in silence, contemplating the friends they had lost that day or perhaps the imminence of their own demise on the morrow. I tell you this to suggest that it was not a scene for a ghastly (or perhaps I should say *ghostly*) practical joke.

When the dawn broke, it broke clear. "It's likely we shall have a warm day of it—the fighting and all," remarked Bierce's companion. "I'd best return the poor devil's blanket."

He rose and approached the sergeant's body. It was in the same place but not in the same attitude. Instead of lying on its back, it was on its side, the chin tucked to the collarbone, the knees pulled up tight to the chest. The collar of its coat was turned upward, the shoulders hunched, the head retracted into the collar, and the hands were thrust to the wrists into its coat. This was the posture of someone who had died of extreme cold, not a gunshot wound. And yet there was the unmistakable evidence, the bullet hole through the head. But within arm's reach of that young dead sergeant, etched in the frost on the grass were written the words YOU ARE FORGIVEN.

R. Craig Roney is an associate professor of teacher education at Wayne State University in Detroit. He specializes in children's literature, storytelling, and the language arts and frequently conducts workshops, school demonstrations, lectures, and seminars on the uses of storytelling in the classroom. He has written numerous publications on the topic and is an active member of both national and local storytelling organizations.

Reprinted by permission of the publisher from Blatt, Gloria, *Once Upon a Folktale* (New York: Teachers College Press, copyright 1993 by Teachers College, Columbia University. All rights reserved), chapter 1 (pages 10–13).

The Story of Wilmer McLean

Mike T. Mullen

The story of Wilmer McLean came to me as I traveled across the battlefields of Gettysburg. I had heard about him while watching the PBS television series The Civil War, *but not much information is available about this man. Wilmer's story takes place between the first Battle of Bull Run (July 21, 1861) and Lee's surrender at Appomattox Court House (April 8, 1865). Although Wilmer was a real person, and the Civil War did more or less begin in his front yard and end in his front parlor, the rest of the story is a fictional account of what might have transpired in his life. This story focuses not on the well-known figures of the worst war in our history but rather on an everyday person who was affected by it. The events described as part of the battle are realistic in that such events occurred at various battles; they may not, however, have taken place at the Battle of Bull Run.*

SOMETIMES A TRUE STORY CAN BE AS INTERESTING AS A MADE-UP ONE. MY grandfather used to sit on his porch and tell me all sorts of tales. Some were true, and others were not so true. He used to tell me the story of Wilmer McLean, and I thought it was a made-up one until I read it in my history book at school.

Wilmer McLean lived in Manassas, Virginia, during the 1800s. The War Between the States was very close to becoming a reality. In April 1861 Fort Sumter, near Charleston, South Carolina, was attacked, and although no one was hurt, people were on edge about the issue of states' rights and the possibility of war.

It was a warm and humid July morning in 1861, and Wilmer McLean sat on his porch, drinking a glass of freshly squeezed lemonade. He sensed something troubling in the air, but he couldn't tell exactly what it was. So he sat back and enjoyed his refreshing drink.

A little later his wife joined him, and they chatted about the weather and their three children. Suddenly Wilmer sat upright in his chair and stared into the woods to the southeast.

"What is it, dear?" his wife asked.

"Something strange is going on in the woods over yonder," Wilmer said as he motioned that way.

Quickly he turned his head to scan the opposite direction. He saw a soldier dressed in a blue uniform and riding a brown and white horse. The soldier was staring at the woods to the southeast. Wilmer quietly stood and walked to the edge of his porch. The soldier, unaware of Wilmer, turned and galloped into the dark Virginia woods.

"What did he want?" Wilmer's wife asked in a frightened voice.

"He's a Union soldier. Probably a scout looking for Confederate troops, although I don't know what he's doing down in this part of the country," Wilmer whispered to his wife as he stared into the woods.

"Maybe he's lost," Mrs. McLean reasoned.

"No, I don't think so . . . he shot out of here too quickly for that!"

Wilmer told his wife to get the children and go inside. He had a sinking feeling in his gut. There was something in the air, and he didn't like it. He continued to watch both directions, trying to catch a glimpse of something, but he didn't know what.

Wilmer didn't have to wait long for another sign. After a while several carriages came from the west and stopped on the hill near the McLeans' farm. The people sat down on the chairs they'd brought with them and began to look down at Wilmer's pasture. Wilmer glanced at his watch. It was nine o'clock on a Sunday morning.

Before he could inquire about what the people were doing on the hill, Wilmer heard a strange noise from the southeast—a noise he had never heard before. Then he realized what it was, as a huge line of Confederate soldiers began to emerge from the woods. They stopped just beyond Wilmer's pasture fence and crouched, staring into the woods directly in front of them—the same woods the Union soldier had ridden into!

Wilmer knew what was coming: the first land battle of the War Between the States was about to begin in his front yard! At 9:32 a trumpet sounded from the northwestern woods. Thousands of blue-uniformed men rushed out to the sounds of guns and cannons. The Civil War had started.

The battle was a fierce one, but the crowd of onlookers gazed onto the battlefield as if they were watching a football game.

The battle was a fierce one, but the crowd of onlookers gazed onto the battlefield as if they were watching a football game. Wilmer looked on too—not as an idle spectator of war but as a farmer concerned about his family, crops, and property.

About three in the afternoon a Union cannonball sailed too far to the right and landed in the McLeans' kitchen. Startled but not injured, the family took refuge in the basement. Wilmer, however, stayed aboveground to watch the Rebel counterattack on the Union Army.

The Confederate cavalry rode briskly from the woods and caught the Union Army off guard. Carrying sabers, the Rebs quickly gained control of the battlefield. In a panic, the Union officers called for a retreat. And the Confederate soldiers followed them into the northwestern woods.

It was just about dusk when Wilmer McLean walked from his house onto the site of what was later called the first Battle of Bull Run. He glanced over the smoky hillside and could see the spectators packing up their belongings and heading for home. Wilmer took a deep breath and coughed because of the gun powder lingering in the air. He turned to see a few Confederate soldiers helping their wounded back into the woods.

Wilmer stood silently and bowed his head in prayer. Although he was a Southerner, he shed a tear for all the men who had lost their lives. He shook his head, wiped his eyes, and headed back into the house.

A few weeks later Wilmer decided to move his family to keep them away from another battle. He studied several areas and chose a small dusty town called Appomattox Court House. The family moved there and settled in a brick house with a small farm. McLean felt that his family was now safe from the terrible war raging in other parts of the South.

For nearly four years the family lived in their new home in peace. It was now April 1865, and the Confederacy was on its last legs.

General Robert E. Lee, the commander of the Confederate army, was forced to abandon Petersburg and Richmond and retreated South. He knew that the time had come to surrender to the Union commander, General Ulysses S. Grant. So General Lee, being a proud soldier, wore his finest dress uniform and sword to the meeting.

Grant waited for Lee in the parlor of a brick house, pleased to have beaten one of the greatest generals who had ever lived but somber out of respect for his defeated opponent. Wilmer McLean, meanwhile, was happy that the war was finally over. He did not agree with the senseless killing over states' rights.

When the day of the surrender came, he shook his head in amazement, but not because the war was finally over. You see, General Lee and General Grant signed the surrender papers in Wilmer's living room!

A flicker of a smile twitched at the corners of Wilmer's mouth. He had watched the Civil War start in his front pasture with the Battle of Bull Run and then end in his living room in Appomattox Court House.

Mike T. Mullen has been spinning yarns for six years. He teaches second grade in Lafayette, California, and travels across the country, telling his tales to children of all ages. He has published two audiotapes, Storytellin' Hat *(1993) and* Hoppy the Frog *(1994). At 27, Mullen brings a youthful touch to the age-old tradition of storytelling. His unique tales of childhood adventures make listeners laugh, cry, and think about the world around them.*

The Cardiff Giant

Martha Hamilton and Mitch Weiss

Our interest in the Cardiff Giant was aroused when we saw the large stone man lying in his open grave at the Farmers' Museum in Cooperstown, New York. We learned that in 1869 he was the centerpiece of one of the greatest hoaxes in American history. The United States was still a frontier country at that time, and fantastic discoveries were not uncommon. As a result, people were gullible and ripe for the uncovering of a man from ancient times.

IN OCTOBER 1869 IN THE SLEEPY LITTLE TOWN OF CARDIFF, NEW YORK, NOT FAR from Syracuse, there lived a farmer named Stub Newell. Stub needed a new well, so he hired his friends Gid and Hank to dig it. He showed them the wet, marshy spot behind the barn where he said he was sure they'd eventually hit water. They set to work, and when they had dug a hole about three feet deep, Gid's shovel suddenly hit something hard.

At first they thought it was just a rock, but they kept digging and digging until they saw what looked like a foot, then a hand—and at last, they had uncovered a giant man at least 10 feet tall! Although he had a peaceful expression on his face, his body looked sort of contorted, as if he had died in agony. His right arm was bent and rested on his belly, and the back of his hand was more than 10 inches across.

The strangest thing about him was not his size but that he was as hard as stone. But when they looked closely, they could see tiny pores on what would have been his skin. They ran and got Stub, and he got pretty excited about it. By the next morning most of the people nearby had heard about it and come by to see the stone man. Stub decided to charge everyone 50 cents to look at him since they were keeping him from getting any work done. He had a huge sign made that said A FANTASTIC DISCOVERY! A NEW WONDER! THE PETRIFIED GIANT!

They raised a big tent over the giant and turned the cow shed into a little store that sold cider, gingerbread, and apples. The little town of Cardiff began to boom. New businesses sprang up to feed and house all the visitors. Horses were tied to the fences on both sides of the road for half a mile. Before long Stub Newell was taking in more than $25 an hour—more than $250 a day! (That's a lot of money even today. Think how much it must have seemed in 1869!) Stub even had to hire a night watchman to protect the giant—it seemed that everybody wanted to chip just a little piece of stone from the giant man.

Right from the start everyone had theories about where the giant man had come from and what he was made of. Stub Newell said he thought it was a giant man who had lived here long, long ago and become petrified after he died. Others were convinced that it was an amazing sculpture that some prehistoric people had chiseled from a huge block of stone.

Some people said they remembered hearing Native American legends about stone giants who had lived around the area long ago and made war on the Onondagas. To defend themselves, the Onondagas used to dig huge pits and cover them with branches—and when a stone giant fell in, they'd cover the pit with dirt as fast as they could. One Onondaga said he thought the stone man must have been killed that way and lain there in the pit ever since.

The people went back and forth and round and round about the stone giant. Everyone had a different opinion, and every opinion had a whole group of experts backing it up.

Some of the most famous people in the world traveled hundreds of miles to get a look at the stone man. Ralph Waldo Emerson, one of our most beloved poets, examined the giant and said that without doubt he was thousands of years old. Oliver Wendell Holmes, a Supreme Court justice at the time, drilled a little hole behind the giant's left ear and declared that it was indeed a statue from ancient times.

Despite all of those opinions, many thought there was something a little fishy about the whole situation. The scientists who visited agreed on one thing: no stone like the giant was made of could be found anywhere else in the state of New York. Beyond that, there was much disagreement. One geologist examined the giant with his magnifying glass and proclaimed, "This is the most remarkable object yet brought to light in this country!" But a paleontologist who studied the stone man declared, "There can be but one opinion. This is a statue cut in gypsum stone and of recent origin."

People didn't seem to care that many of the scientists said the giant was a fake. The crowds had become so big that they were hard to handle, and of course, the money just kept pouring in. The State Geological Museum in Albany, New York, invited Stub to display the giant in its main hall. Stub was delighted because he knew even bigger crowds would be able to see the stone man there, and that meant more money. The problem was getting him there. First they tried picking the giant up. Twenty strong men grabbed hold of him and heaved with all their strength. He didn't budge. Eventually they had to use a whole series of ropes and pulleys to lift the giant out of his hole. The fact that the giant was so heavy, almost 3,000 pounds, persuaded many people that he was real. How, they argued, could anyone have transported the giant to Cardiff and buried him without the whole town's knowing it?

The giant was a huge success in Albany. It wasn't long before P. T. Barnum of the famous Barnum and Bailey Circus showed up and offered to buy the giant for $150,000. Stub refused to sell him, but that didn't stop Barnum. He hired someone to make a copy of the stone man in plaster and called it "the only original giant." He set his statue up in a museum in New York City, and the crowds started pouring in there as well to see the copy.

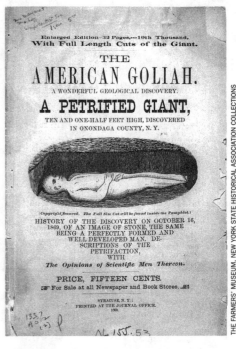

Stub was really mad about this so he floated his giant on a big barge down the Hudson River to a museum in New York that was just two blocks from the museum where Barnum's giant was on display. Both Stub and Barnum hired barkers to stand outside and try to outshout each other.

Mr. Barnum's man shouted, "Step right up, ladies and gentlemen, and learn how you can earn $1,000. That's right, $1,000! It's yours if you can prove that ours is not the only original giant. Don't be fooled by the bumpkins from upstate New York. The scientific facts are on our side. Come right in! Intelligent Americans will take one look and know that ours is, without a shadow of a doubt, the original!"

This pamphlet was used to stir up interest in the amazing stone giant.

But Stub's barker yelled, "Ladies and gentlemen, don't let yourselves be deceived by the giant created by the circus man! Enter, and you will be astounded by what you see. A giant so natural, you'd think he was alive. Arms and legs and body all turned to stone. If you want to see the authentic giant, step right up, and ignore the ludicrous claims of our competitors."

Eventually Barnum found himself in court defending his giant. He argued, "I'm simply exhibiting a hoax of a hoax." The judge agreed.

By now many others were also suspicious of the giant's origins even though word had spread across the country, and people were arriving from everywhere to see him. One scientist who had examined the giant on the day he was discovered and declared it a fake was determined to learn the truth. After several weeks of investigation, he uncovered quite a few facts that led to only one conclusion: the giant was not authentic. The scientist brought all the information to Stub Newell, and Stub finally confessed the true story of the Cardiff Giant.

Turns out, the real brains behind the hoax was Stub's brother-in-law George Hull, who lived in Binghamton. George had traveled out to Iowa, where he had bought a block of gypsum stone and had it sent by train to Chicago. There George hired a sculptor and his two assistants to carve

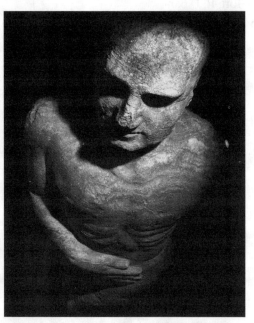

the giant man. When they had finished, they poked tiny holes all over the stone with metal spikes to make the statue look like its skin had pores. Then they poured sulfuric acid on it to make it look old.

George had the giant shipped to a train station near Binghamton. They brought it to Cardiff on a wagon drawn by four horses and buried it in the middle of the night. Then they waited a whole year before Stub had the two men dig his well right where he knew they'd discover the giant man.

But when people heard that the giant was definitely a fake, they didn't stop going to see him. In fact, Stub's giant became more popular than ever. Everybody wanted to see him, so Stub had him taken on a trip all over the United States. Despite all the evidence, many still believed that the Cardiff Giant was real.

The Cardiff Giant:
an elaborate hoax
of 1869

The giant finally came to rest at the Farmers' Museum in Cooperstown, New York, and if you don't believe this story, you can take a trip to the museum and see him. He's there to this day.

George Hull and Stub Newell probably never imagined that 125 years later people would still be fascinated by the stone man and that thousands of people every year would still be paying money to see him.

Martha Hamilton and Mitch Weiss perform professionally as Beauty and the Beast Storytellers throughout the United States, Canada, and Europe. Known for their lively tandem style, they are the authors of Children Tell Stories: A Teaching Guide *(Richard C. Owen, 1990), which won an Anne Izard Storytellers' Choice Award in 1992. Awards-committee members praised the book as "infectiously enthusiastic . . . imaginative, inspiring, easy to read, and tremendously engaging." Weiss and Hamilton live in Ithaca, New York.*

Wild Bill Hickok in Springfield

Richard Alan Young and Judy Dockrey Young _____

James Butler "Wild Bill" Hickok was a frontier scout, a lawman, a prospector, a gambler, and a Pony Express rider—one of the most colorful characters of the American West. In his biographies the years 1872 to 1873 are considered "lost" because there seemed to be no documentation of his whereabouts. This story fills the gap and illustrates changing times as the Middle Border (the western edge of the United States, which changed almost yearly) expanded outward and lawless, fun-oriented frontier attitudes began to give way to the mores of a modern urban society. Springfield, Missouri, had been a lawless town in 1865, but within a few years life was quite settled and proper. In 1872 Alanson Haswell, a schoolboy, apparently witnessed all or part of this story's events. He wrote about them in his newspaper column 50 years later. His great-grandson gave us a copy of the newspaper clipping.

ONE OF THE MOST COLORFUL CHARACTERS IN THE AMERICAN WEST WAS JAMES Butler "Wild Bill" Hickok. Although he gained his fame as a scout, a lawman, and a Pony Express rider in Kansas, his status as a legend began in Springfield, Missouri, in 1865.

Hickok was the fastest draw with a pistol at the time, but he didn't use the low-slung leather holsters you see in cowboy movies. Those were invented in 1940s Hollywood for use in Westerns. Hickok carried his 1851 Colt Navy model pistol high and in front, above his waist, tucked down into a red sash like those worn by officers in the War Between the States. Yet he could pull out that pistol, cock it, aim, and shoot in less time than most men could draw from their pocket or belt.

In an 1865 poker game in Springfield, Hickok lost a family heirloom gold watch to a personal enemy named Davis Tutt. When Hickok tried to redeem the watch for cash the next day, Tutt refused. Later Tutt bragged that he would cross the town square wearing that watch, and he threatened that if Wild Bill tried to take it, he would kill him. At the appointed hour, three o'clock, Hickok was standing at the edge of the square as Tutt walked across it. Without warning, and presumably afraid to have his back to Hickok, Tutt spun around and fired. Before Davis Tutt got one shot off, Hickok drew, cocked his Colt, aimed, and shot Tutt dead with a single bullet. Tutt's shot went wild. Hickok walked out on the square, bent down, and redeemed his watch from Tutt's pocket. This was the first shootout in the history of the West.

A coroner's jury found Hickok to have acted in self-defense, and he was exonerated. One winter years later he returned to Springfield, during a time when most books about Hickok's life are unable to pinpoint his whereabouts.

James Butler "Wild Bill" Hickok around 1870

During the winter of 1872–73 Bill was back in Missouri, enjoying the admiration of the local folks. He and some of his friends had been out in the new part of town, drinking in a tavern on Commercial Street. When they came out after the tavern had closed, the new kerosene streetlights were lit. Hickok, having had too much to drink, began to take potshots at the glass globes of the streetlights. After he had shot his five bullets and shattered five lights, he heard a voice behind him that said, "Here, Bill, give me that gun."

It was John B. Stokes, the town marshal of North Springfield, and he laid a hand on the taller man's shoulder. Wild Bill's companions scattered, thinking there would be a fight.

"Say, old man," said Hickok, "who are you?"

"I'm the city marshal," came the reply. "Now, give me that gun, and do it quickly." The officer's old pistol was suddenly poked into Wild Bill's ribs.

"Well, I'll be . . ." Hickok said, and he gave Stokes his gun.

At that time the inside of the North Springfield jail measured just six feet by eight feet. The jail was built of solid oak joists—two-by-eights laid flat on each other, locked at the corners, and fastened with iron spikes. Marshal Stokes escorted Wild Bill to the tiny "log" structure.

On seeing the jail, Hickok thrust his hand into a vest pocket. The crowd that had followed him scattered, expecting him to draw a derringer. Marshal Stokes seemed to be of the same opinion, for he thrust his rusty old pistol into Hickok's ribs again.

But it was a fat wallet, not a pistol, that Bill drew from his breast pocket. He handed the wallet to Stokes and said, "Here, Uncle, there's $200 in that wallet. Just hold it until morning, and I'll come up and pay my fine." Stokes let Hickok go on his own recognizance, and the next morning the new town justice of the peace, J. J. Barnard, made Bill Hickok pay $30 for each of the five streetlights he had spoiled and a $50 fine for disturbing the peace.

Hickok laughed and said, "Well, Judge, you sure set your fine by the size of my wallet. You can bet I'll stay in Springfield's Old Town the next time I get out on a spree!"

It was the only time anyone ever got the drop on Wild Bill Hickok.

Richard Alan Young and Judy Dockrey Young have nine books and 10 audiotapes to their credit. They are known for their storytelling appearances on national television; in schools, libraries, museums, and universities; and at festivals. A former high-school teacher, Richard retired to do storytelling and character acting at Silver Dollar City, Missouri. After teaching dramatics for two years, Judy began a full-time character-acting and storytelling position at Silver Dollar City, where the couple met.

Inspector Walsh and Sitting Bull

Marie Anne McLean

Canada was formed through conference rather than revolution, and discussion is a cornerstone of Canadian history. Events like the ones described in this story helped develop the Canadian fondness for negotiation. This story comes from Canada's early years, and its historical characters are Inspector Walsh, Sitting Bull, and assorted people associated with them. The setting is southern Saskatchewan and Alberta from May 1873 through 1881. The fiction of the two-man Sitting Bull escort is a well-known piece of Royal Canadian Mounted Police lore. In The Law Marches West (J.M. Dent & Sons, 1972) Sir Cecil Denny tells of the astonishment of the American generals Terry and McNeill that a mere handful of men (about 60 total in Fort Walsh) could handle thousands of "the most warlike Indians on the continent." The idea of the Sitting Bull escort probably came from such quotations and the many anecdotes told about two-man patrols.

THE STORY OF WALSH IN THE WEST STARTED IN 1866, WHEN AN AMERICAN-based pro-Irish, anti-British group known as the Fenian Brotherhood made a series of raids into Upper Canada. (That's the part of Canada you know as Ontario.) The Fenian raids were like what we think of as terrorist attacks nowadays, and they scared the living daylights out of the other settlers of Upper Canada. The colonial government and citizens formed militia. One of the men who joined was James Walsh.

The training he received as a young fellow preparing to fight the Fenians made him ready for the great adventure of his life eight years later.

In the early 1870s the area around Cypress Hills in what we now call southern Alberta and Saskatchewan was Canada's wild frontier. People were living in small remote outposts there for the sole purpose of trading liquor to the native people and cheating them out of their furs and buffalo hides. The worst of the frontier adventurers were the Wolfers. They were wild men, hated on both sides of the border, who poisoned buffalo carcasses to kill wolves for their pelts. They were lawless, violent, and dangerous.

A bunch of American Wolfers got into a dispute over horses with a band of Assiniboine on the Canadian side of the border. The Wolfers killed everyone in the village, about 30 people.

The Canadian government was shocked and indignant, and it immediately created a police force of 300 men to protect the citizens of the territories. It was named the North-West Mounted Police, or NWMP for short. James Walsh was one of the recruits.

Everyone who joined had to be young, healthy, and tough, so most of the recruits were in their early twenties. Anyone over 30 or who had any army experience was considered officer material. That was Walsh. He was 37 and had militia experience from the Fenian raids. On the day he joined, he was given the rank of inspector. He used the title of major.

In the summer of 1874 the force made the march west, and it was an ordeal. Many of the men were city boys, and they had to learn horsemanship as they crossed the plains. They suffered through raging prairie thunderstorms and horse stampedes. They sweated through hot prairie days in wool serge uniforms and slept through the cold nights on the ground. They got lost and sometimes ran out of food. In spite of all that, they hardened into strong horsemen and arrived at their destination. Each company was sent to a trouble spot to build an outpost and enforce the law.

Walsh and his men were sent with a small force to build an outpost and police the border in the Cypress Hills. They built their fort in an area west of where the town of Maple Creek, Saskatchewan, now stands.

Walsh was a vain man, so of course he named the fort after himself. He loved the dress uniform with its scarlet jacket and gold trim. He expected his men to get dressed up in full dress uniform as he did every Sunday afternoon for church parade.[1] His men found it hard to keep everything as clean as Walsh liked it. They complained that he was hard on everyone. But they respected him. Walsh judged all men according to the law and NWMP regulations and was scrupulously fair. In later years when his men talked about their time in the force, they were happy to say that they had served with Walsh.

In the long run the fussiness and fairness paid off.

In 1876, across the border at the Battle of Little Bighorn—which you may know as Custer's Last Stand—the Sioux people fought and killed the

ROYAL CANADIAN MOUNTED POLICE

Sitting Bull, or Tatanka Iyotake, a great Sioux leader who helped defeat General George Custer at the Little Bighorn

1. A traditional term used in British military organizations. It means a full turnout of a military company in walking-out or day dress uniform for a regularly scheduled church service.

American General George Custer and all his men. The Sioux knew that the Army was going to be after them, so they began to drift north into Canada to safety.

There were a lot of worried people in the Canadian towns back East. The stories of the American Indian wars were terrifying. In 1877 Sitting Bull himself brought his people into Canada, and the Canadian government was really sweating because people were sure something terrible was going to happen.

But it never did, and the main reason the violence did not come to Canada was Walsh and the cool style of the men of the force. You see, these men had to police an area that was hundreds of square miles in size, and there were only 300 of them in the whole territory. They just didn't have the men to go out on patrol in companies like an army did. A patrol might be one man on horseback, traveling a hundred miles or more alone. When a really important occasion came—such as a visit of Major Walsh to Sitting Bull's village—how many would he take as an escort? Two or three! That's all.

They would ride into a village of armed warriors who had fought at the Little Bighorn and were raging at the army that had chased them from the south. Walsh and his men would stay calm. Walsh would explain quite reasonably that he was there to uphold the law. The law was the law for everyone. Everybody obeys, and nobody gets into trouble. Then he proved his point by impartially arresting anyone at all who broke the law of the queen. When Sitting Bull saw Walsh, he thought, *There is a brave man.*

The other thing that worked for Walsh and his men was the red coat. The scarlet coat of the NWMP was different from the blue coats of the army that had fought with and chased the Sioux people from the American territory.

The men in scarlet traveled alone and visited many villages. Even the important redcoats traveled with only two or three men. To the Sioux it looked as though these men wanted to talk instead of fight.

Sitting Bull and Walsh became good friends. Walsh delighted in putting on his full dress uniform and going to visit Sitting Bull. The great Sioux chief liked Walsh's romantic costumes and his confidence, and he respected the courage and fairness of Walsh and his men.

Then the Canadian government began to worry because there wasn't enough food in the land for all the people. The buffalo were disappearing, and there would not be enough food for the Indian people who already lived in Canada. The government wanted Sitting Bull and his people to go back home.

Sitting Bull was concerned that if they went back, they would suffer because the American government was still angry about Little Bighorn. So he asked for Walsh's help. Walsh went back East to seek protection for his friends. He explained why they were worried and asked the Canadian government to go to the American government and speak for the Sioux people.

But officials of the Canadian government said, "You're a policeman. You're not supposed to interfere in politics." As punishment they gave him a desk job in Ottawa and wouldn't let him go back out West for a while. This was sad for Walsh because when his friend Sitting Bull left in 1881, Walsh did not get to say goodbye.

A couple of other members of the force were given the job of escorting the Sioux. They got dressed up in their full dress uniforms and accompanied Sitting Bull's people to the border. They set up a camp in the valley at the border and waited for the American cavalry detail to come to escort the Sioux to their reservations.

Early on the designated morning a lone member of the North-West Mounted Police and a delegation of Sioux warriors and chiefs went down to the meeting place at the border. In the hollow of the hills behind them, the great body of Sioux people were camped, and the smoke of their fires scented the air. Soon the cavalry arrived. It was a good-sized company, well-armed and with flags flying, a very businesslike group of soldiers.

The cavalry officer scratched his head in dismay when he saw the lone policeman, for he knew the fierce reputation of the Sioux fighters. He looked at the police constable. He said, "Only one man? Surely you didn't come out here with these people all by yourself."

The constable smiled and said, "Oh no. This is a pretty important detail. They wouldn't send me out alone. The other guy is over on the other side of the hill cooking breakfast."

That's the difference between the Royal Canadian Mounted Police and any other police force. Two men could escort the whole Sioux nation because they were willing to talk.

ROYAL CANADIAN MOUNTED POLICE

Inspector James Walsh of the North-West Mounted Police

Marie Anne McLean of Edmonton, Alberta, is an elementary-school teacher and a librarian. She is a member of the Alberta League Encouraging Storytelling (TALES). She tells "prairie tales," original stories of the small prairie towns that are disappearing because of agricultural change. Through her stories she tries to help the little places live on. She has told stories at festivals and conferences, on radio and TV, and in schools, nursing homes, clubs, and churches.

Aunt Clara Brown

Kay Negash

This story chronicles the life of a woman born into slavery in Virginia around 1800. Sold at age 3 along with her mother, she was taken to the Kentucky wilderness. There she grew up, married, and had four children, only to see them and her husband sold away from her. In her early fifties she was freed and began a lengthy search for her one surviving daughter. Her journey took her through St. Louis; Leavenworth, Kansas; and the Pikes Peak region during the gold rush. All of the events described here are true. Some names and conversations have been invented.

AUNT CLARA BROWN WAS BORN INTO SLAVERY SOMETIME AROUND 1800. SHE never knew the exact date because people didn't write down slaves' birthdays. The first thing she did remember was that when she was only 3 years old, she and her mother were sold away from the rest of the family. Slave owners disapproved of selling children away from their mothers before they reached age 10.

She and her mother were bought by a Mr. Ambrose Smith, a tobacco farmer in Virginia. When Clara was 8 or 9 years old, Mr. Smith's family and five other white families decided to go pioneering and moved to the wilds of Kentucky.

They traveled in covered wagons, and the trip was terrible and grueling. When they finally arrived, Clara and Mr. Smith's two sons, who were about her age, helped clear off the land so the big house could be built, with the slave quarters out back.

There wasn't much social activity in the Kentucky wilderness, but every once in a while a traveling preacher would come through and hold a revival meeting. Mr. and Mrs. Smith were very religious and went to every one. Once they invited Clara and her mother to go along. That was when Clara first heard the story of how Jesus had suffered and died for her sins. When she heard that, she knew the Lord would never ask anything more of her than he had of his only son.

In time, when Mr. Smith's two sons went off to college, he needed more help on the farm. That's when he bought Richard, the handsomest man Clara had ever laid eyes on. It was love at first sight. Soon they got married and started having children. First came young Richard, then Margaret, and then the twins, Liza Jane and Paulina Ann. Mr. Smith promised Richard and Clara that as long as he was alive, he would never sell any of them away.

One day when the twins were about 9 years old, Clara was in the big house ironing, when suddenly Liza Jane came running in, shouting.

"Mama! You gotta come quick—Paulina Ann went swimmin' in the creek! I told her not to, but she did anyway! You gotta hurry, Mama!"

Clara grabbed the dinner bell, rang it as hard as she could, and then went running with Liza Jane down to the water. When they got there, Liza Jane pointed to a place where the water was very still and the willows were hanging low. She said, "That's where she went down, Mama. I'm so sorry! I hope I didn't wait too long."

About that time Clara's husband, Richard, and Mr. Smith came running. Richard jumped in the water with all his clothes on and dived under again and again. Finally, after what seemed like much too long, he came up, carrying Paulina Ann's cold, still little body. There were weeds all tangled around her ankles and feet.

They buried Paulina Ann on Mr. Smith's farm, but the family's pain over the loss of that little girl didn't go away for a long, long time. It was worst for little Liza Jane because she thought she'd killed her own sister. She began to have hysterical trembling fits and terrible nightmares. The doctor had to give her medicine so she could sleep at night.

Eventually the pain went so deep inside that somehow life went on as before. Then one day about a year later another terrible thing happened. This time it was Mr. Smith who died. Clara and her family truly mourned his death, but they also wondered and worried about what would happen to them now.

Their worst fears came true. They found out that they would all be sold away on the next auction day in front of the courthouse in Russelville. It was up to Clara and Richard to tell their children that their life as a family was ending forever.

Auction day came, and there they were, standing by the auction block in front of the courthouse along with Mr. Smith's other possessions—his farm equipment, his furniture, his livestock. Then it came time to sell Mr. Smith's estate. First they called up Margaret. She just stood there with her head hanging low, and she was sold for $250.

Next it was Richard Senior's turn. When he got up, a man from the crowd shouted, "I'd like to examine the merchandise before the bidding begins." He came and felt Richard's muscles to see how strong he was. He opened Richard's mouth to look at his teeth. And he ripped Richard's

They buried Paulina Ann on Mr. Smith's farm, but the family's pain over the loss of that little girl didn't go away for a long, long time. It was worst for little Liza Jane because she thought she'd killed her own sister.

shirt off his back to see if there were any whip marks on him. The bidding started and went higher and higher until Richard was sold for $1,000. A man with a mean, pinched-looking face led him off.

That same man bought young Richard and took them both right past the spot where Clara was standing. But they couldn't even look at one another—they knew that if their eyes met, they would all have broken down and cried.

Now it was Liza Jane's turn. Clara was worried about all her family but most concerned about her little Liza Jane. She was so small and frail and just 11 years old. Clara had dressed her up in her prettiest pink pinafore, hoping she'd go to a kind master. But when Liza Jane got up on the block, something terrible began to happen. She started having one of her shaking and trembling hysteric fits. Then she threw up all down the front of her pretty pink pinafore. The auctioneer finally let Clara come and clean her up with her hankie. Clara did her best and then took her youngest by the shoulders and said, "Now, Liza Jane, you got to be strong today. You just straighten up."

Clara was sent back to her place, and all she could do was close her eyes and ears because she didn't want to see or hear what was going to happen next. She kept them closed for a long, long time, and when she finally opened them and looked around, her little Liza Jane was gone.

At last it was Clara's turn. She was bought by a Mr. George Brown that day. He was a friend of the Smiths so she knew she'd be treated kindly. She stayed with the Browns for the next 20 years.

During that time they tried to help her find out what had become of her family. She learned that Margaret had died of a respiratory disease two years after the sale. Her two Richards had been sent downriver to the huge cotton fields in the Mississippi Delta and to certain death. Liza Jane had been bought by a Mr. James Covington over in Morgan County, which was too far away to permit any communication.

When Mr. Brown died, Clara was in her early fifties. His oldest married daughter, Mary Prue, saw to it that Clara got her freedom papers. But she had to leave Kentucky, the only home she'd ever known, before the end of one year or she'd have to go back to being a slave again. Mary Prue had some friends in St. Louis, a Mr. and Mrs. Jacob Brunner, so she wrote Clara a letter of introduction to them. The letter said, "This is to introduce Aunt Clara Brown. She is a good cook, a fine domestic servant, and a woman of sterling character. Anything you can do to help her find gainful employment would be most appreciated."

Mary Prue also gave her the money to travel to St. Louis, and when Clara finally found her way to the city and the Brunners' front door, the family hired her as their cook right then and there.

At the Brunners she was free for the first time in her life. She earned her own money and could come and go as she pleased. She even joined a church. Samantha, the Brunners' other employee, warned her about slave hunters in St. Louis. They could snatch her off the street and sell her into slavery again if she couldn't prove she was free. Samantha took Clara to the courthouse so she could get her freedom papers registered.

After Clara had been in St. Louis just a short while, the Brunners decided to move to Leavenworth, Kansas, and they asked her if she would like to go with them. She said yes. She'd often wondered if Liza Jane, a grown woman by this time, might have gone west too. Clara hoped she would find her daughter out West—maybe even in Leavenworth. She kept her eyes open and asked everyone she met if they knew her Liza Jane.

When Clara got to Leavenworth, she was surprised to find a Negro Baptist Church there. She joined it, and it was at that church that she met the best friend she would ever have, another former slave and a woman about her own age. Becky Johnson was a laundress in business for herself. The two women had many good times together, laughing and gossiping and doing church work.

Aunt Clara Brown

Then one day the Brunners told Clara they were moving again, this time all the way to California. Once more they invited her to come along. But this time Clara wasn't sure she wanted to go. She was afraid that California was too far west and that she might never find her Liza Jane if she traveled that far. Still, Clara had never lived on her own before, and she wasn't sure she could do it. She went to Becky for advice.

Becky told her, "Shoot, girl, you can do just fine on your own. You could be a laundress like me. I got more customers than I know what to do with. I'll help you get started. And I'll bet the Brunners won't want to be carrying their boiler and tubs all the way to California. You can probably buy them from them cheap."

So that's what Clara did. She bought the Brunners' boiler and tubs and had her laundry business going before the Brunners left for California.

Now, Clara noticed lots of black people passing through Leavenworth and heading for the Pikes Peak region in Colorado, and she wondered if her Liza Jane might be out there. The more she thought about it, the more she wanted to go find out.

One day she heard some white men on the street talking about taking a wagon train across the great desert (now western Kansas and eastern Colorado) to prospect for gold. She asked if she could go too and work out her fare by doing laundry and cooking. The man in charge said, "Ma'am, I have to ask you this question. Why would a woman of your advanced age want to take such a grueling trip?"

Clara got a little huffy about that. She was still in her fifties. She told him flat out that before he was even a twinkle in his mama's eye, she was pioneering from Virginia to Kentucky. He and the other men started discussing the fact that among the travelers there would be 30 to 35 single men on that wagon train with no wives to cook for them or do their laundry. Eventually they decided they'd be fools to turn her down. They even agreed to let her take her boiler and tubs so she could make a living once she got there.

Clara hurried to go tell Becky. Her friend helped her sell her things and buy what she needed for the trip: heavy, warm winter clothes and light, airy summer clothes. The wagon train would be crossing the desert in April 1859, and in April it could be blistering hot one day and freezing cold the next. She also needed heavy thick-soled leather shoes because they wouldn't be riding across the prairie: they'd be walking. The oxen would need all their strength just to get the mining gear across.

They started out on a cold, blustery morning in April. They followed the Republican River for a while, but then they came to a 100-mile stretch where there was no water. People got so thirsty, they started sucking bullets because they thought it made their throats feel cooler. Some people's tongues swelled up so big that they couldn't shut their mouths. And some just fainted dead away. Clara and some of the other strong women on that wagon train nursed those sick folks all the way to Denver City. Many told Clara later they would never have survived without her.

Two months later, when they finally arrived in Denver City, Clara didn't think it was much of a city—just a scattering of cabins, some half built, some abandoned by disappointed gold seekers. She bought a cabin for $25 and started her laundry business up right away. She also delivered babies as a midwife. Again she looked for and asked about her daughter, Liza Jane. But no one had heard of her.

In Denver City she helped poor miners and their families whenever she could, giving them food, clothing, and money. Later she traveled up to Mountain City (Central City today) because she heard that there were enough Negroes up there to warrant a whole Negro cemetery. She thought maybe she'd find Liza Jane there. But still she had no luck.

After the slaves were freed in 1865, Clara was free to travel anywhere she wanted. She decided to go back to Kentucky and find out what had happened to her youngest daughter. With Mary Prue's help, she searched the courthouse records and discovered that Liza Jane had left the area five years before she had, but there was no record of why she'd gone or where. She was more discouraged than she had ever been. She prayed and prayed, and when her answer came, she knew what to do. She would bring 15 poor but deserving former slaves back to Colorado with her and support them until they found jobs and became self-sufficient.

Once again—in the 1870s—she went in search of Liza Jane, this time to Kansas. She had heard that a runaway slave named Benjamin Singleton had gone to Kansas after escaping to Canada. He'd bought some good farmland for the purpose of giving destitute ex-slaves a start in farming. Singleton had made up some handbills that said COME TO KANSAS, LAND OF OPPORTUNITY, AND GET A LITTLE PIECE OF LAND FOR $5. Then he passed them out to former slaves all over the South.

Clara heard that thousands of people were pouring into Kansas to get their little piece of land. In her seventies and in failing health now, Clara still had not given up on finding her daughter. She hoped she would find Liza Jane in Kansas. She went there and stayed a year, searching and asking and also feeding, clothing, nursing, and burying the desperate and destitute who had come to Kansas, literally dying for a little piece of land all their own. But once again, she did not find Liza Jane.

Clara by this time had lived in Colorado nearly 20 years, and though she was poor herself, she always helped those less fortunate than herself. She had also contributed to the building of all denominations of churches and synagogues because she believed God was in all of them.

As her health continued to deteriorate and she became less and less able to work, a campaign was begun, unbeknownst to her, by some influential people who appreciated her caring generosity. They said, "She's been helping people all these years. Now she needs our help. What are we going to do for her?" They decided to try to get her designated as an official Colorado Pioneer. This meant she would get a pension for the rest of her life. Until that time, only white men had been eligible. There was a lot of wrangling and arguing over the issue, but when the final vote was counted, Clara became the first black and the first woman to become an official Colorado Pioneer.

Through the years she had continued to correspond with her old friend, Becky Johnson. Around 1880 Becky moved from Leavenworth to Council Bluffs, Iowa, to be with her widowed daughter and grandchildren. Once she got settled and joined a church, she wrote Clara, telling her of her new life and mentioning a Mrs. Brewer she had met. She said, "She kind of reminds me of you, Clary, a hard-working churchwoman."

She prayed and prayed, and when her answer came, she knew what to do. She would bring 15 poor but deserving former slaves back to Colorado with her and support them until they found jobs and became self-sufficient.

By this time Clara had pretty much given up on ever finding Liza Jane. She was about 80, ill, and unable to get out of her bed much—until she got Becky's second letter from Council Bluffs.

Becky wrote,

I was talking with this Mrs. Brewer today, and I told her about my old friend, Clary, who'd searched the West, looking for her daughter, Liza Jane. Well, that woman got a funny look on her face and said, "My name's Liza Jane." Well, I started questioning her, asked her where she came from. She said from Kentucky . . . that she had been a twin and that her sister had drowned . . . and then she was sold away from the rest of her family. Now, I don't know just how sick you are or even if this is your Liza Jane. But if I were you, I'd get up out of that bed and get myself to Council Bluffs and find out.

After Clara got that letter, she started to feel a little better. She did get out of bed, and she started telling people about this Liza Jane in Iowa. Soon some generous friends gave her a train ticket. In March 1882 she was on a train headed for Council Bluffs. She had just received a letter from this Liza Jane telling her what to do when she got there. She was to catch the trolley at the train station and take it to Second Street, get off and wait, and Liza Jane would meet her there.

When Clara got off the train, it was snowing and blowing. She was glad the trolley was waiting. She got on, sat right behind the driver, and said, "Please, sir, tell me when we get to Second Street." He said he would. But it didn't matter. Every stop, she'd ask him, "Is this Second Street?" and he'd say, "No, ma'am, but I'll tell you when we get there." Pretty soon everyone in the whole trolley knew she was waiting and watching for Second Street. When the trolley finally did get there, everyone in the whole trolley shouted, "Ma'am, this is Second Street!"

Clara climbed down into the sleet and rain, looked up and down the street, and didn't see anyone. She wondered if maybe she'd gotten the directions wrong or if something had happened to this Liza Jane. Then she saw a tall, strong-looking woman walking in her direction, and when that woman saw her, she started to run. In a moment they were hugging and crying out there in the wet, stormy weather.

Clara finally stepped back and gave her a good look. Then she said, "I know for sure you're my Liza Jane because you favor your father, who was the handsomest man that ever walked this earth."

Mother and daughter had lots of catching up to do. Clara found out that Liza Jane was a widow—her husband, Jeb, had fought in the War

Between the States and had never come home. Clara discovered she had three grandchildren. The youngest, Cindy, in her early twenties, lived with Liza Jane. Clara stayed a month and tried to get Liza Jane to come back to Colorado with her. But Liza said she couldn't. She had her work there, people depending on her. But Cindy could come. So Clara returned to Colorado with her granddaughter but without her Liza Jane.

For the next three years Clara hung on but got sicker and sicker. It was good that Cindy was there to care for her. In the summer of 1885 Clara and Liza Jane both got letters from the Society for Colorado Pioneers saying a banquet would be held in Clara's honor. Liza Jane was sent a train ticket to come. By this time Clara couldn't walk, dress, or feed herself. The night of the banquet, she had to be dressed, carried out to the wagon, carried into the hall, and fed once she got there.

But it was a beautiful evening for Clara, with her daughter on one side and her granddaughter on the other. Many wonderful things were said about her that night. But people were saying things about her behind her back too—things like, "Poor old Aunt Clara. She's probably not going to make it through another winter." And they were right.

Clara lived until October of that year. She had been sleeping almost around the clock. But on one flaming autumn evening just at sunset, she opened her eyes wide and looked toward the window as if she saw something. She called out, "Mama, Mama . . ." and then she closed her eyes and died.

After her death a church in Central City to which she had generously contributed included her name on the plaque on its cornerstone. In the Central City Opera House the names of many famous Coloradans are carved on the chairs in the orchestra section. Clara's name is on one of them. In the Colorado State Capitol Building in Denver her portrait appears in a stained-glass window. All these visible tributes speak of Coloradans' appreciation for her kindness and generosity and ensure that they will never forget Aunt Clara Brown.

Kay Negash of Boulder, Colorado, has been a professional storyteller since 1983. A co-founder of the Rocky Mountain Storytellers Guild and a Colorado Artist-in-Residence, Negash leads workshops for participants from kindergarten age through adulthood. She has received grants for storytelling projects with seniors, low-income groups, and at-risk teenagers. Negash regularly tells star stories at the Colorado University Planetarium. In 1994 she performed at the Derry Storytelling Festival in Ireland.

Launching a Scientist: Robert Goddard's First Attempt at Rocketry

Kendall Haven

The world of science is filled with gripping stories. Some of the most fascinating ones are those that give us a glimpse of future scientists long before they conducted the experiments for which they became famous. This story is about Robert Goddard, the scientist and engineer who developed the first liquid-fueled rocket, which ultimately allowed man to escape Earth's gravity. Even as a 6-year-old boy Goddard was an eager and thoughtful experimenter. The dates, locations, characters, personalities, and events of this story are historically accurate. Only the dialogue has been fictionalized, and even it is true to the documented interactions of the characters.

ON A BRISK SATURDAY AFTERNOON IN SEPTEMBER 1887, WITH THE LEAVES JUST beginning to turn, two 6-year-old boys played in front of a modest two-story house in Boston.

"It won't work," repeated freckle-faced Percy Long.

"It will too!" insisted the dark-haired shorter boy.

"You can't fly, Bobby. Only birds fly," yelled Percy.

But young Bobby Goddard was not going to back down. "This is called science. You just start counting once I take off from the front-porch railing."

Bobby fished a 10-inch-long zinc rod out of his pocket. It was as thick around as his wrist.

"What's that?" asked Percy suspiciously.

"It'll help me fly. Now, you just remember to count. Get ready!"

Bobby banged the front door open and dashed into the living room. Then he slid his shoes along the thick woolen carpet, shuffling back and forth across the room.

"Hurry up!" called Percy from outside. "I can't wait around all day."

"Just a second!" Bobby shuffled two more laps across the living-room carpet. "Here I come!"

He sprinted out the open front door, stepped once on the low bench he had positioned next to the railing, once on the railing itself—and with a mighty leap, he launched himself into space, holding the zinc rod high over his head with both hands. "Count!" he yelled.

"One . . . two . . ."

Thud! Bobby slammed into the soft dirt of his mother's flower bed just below the railing.

Percy Long laughed so hard he almost fell over. Bobby had crumpled two blooming chrysanthemums and left deep holes where his elbow and knees had hit. "I told you you couldn't fly."

Bobby sat up thoughtfully and rubbed his sore knees. "Maybe I didn't get enough of an electrical charge." He climbed out of the flowers and back onto the front porch.

"Where are you going?" demanded Percy. "Giving up?"

"No. I'm going to try it again. This time I'll get a better static-electricity charge. So you be ready to count!"

Bobby stepped into the house and began to shuffle across the living-room carpet—back and forth, scraping his shoes across the carpet, time and time again.

"Here I come!" Being careful not to touch anything and lose his electrical charge in a harmless spark, Bobby raced back onto the front porch. One foot on the bench. One foot on the railing. And 6-year-old Bobby Goddard launched into the clear blue sky again. Again he lifted the zinc rod high overhead.

Percy stared and counted. "One . . . two . . . three . . . four . . ."

Smash! Bobby wiped out two hydrangea bushes as he crashed down and rolled out onto the grass.

Again Percy laughed. But Bobby leapt to his feet. "Don't laugh. I flew longer than last time. It worked better."

Percy squeaked to a stop in the middle of a laugh. It was true. Bobby had stayed up almost twice as long that time.

"Bobby Goddard!" his mother called from the porch. "I've told you a thousand times not to leave this door open." She reached the porch railing, looked over, and gasped, "My land! What have you done to my flowers?"

"He was crashing, Mrs. Goddard," said Percy with a shrug.

"I was flying, Mom," corrected Bobby, and he glared at Percy.

"Flying?" exclaimed Mrs. Goddard. "Where on earth do you think you're going to fly to?"

"Not on Earth, Mom. I'm going to fly to the Moon."

"Well, so far it looks like you've only managed to get as far as my flower bed. And right now, young man, you will put my flower bed back in order."

Bobby lowered his eyes and softly sighed, "Yes, ma'am."

Bobby's father marched out onto the porch, still carrying the newspaper he had been reading. "What's all the commotion out here?" he asked.

"Bobby's been wrecking my flower bed. That's what!" snapped Mrs. Goddard.

"I was flying, Dad," corrected Bobby.

"Mostly he was crashing," corrected Percy.

Mr. Goddard squatted down on the porch and looked at his son standing before him. "How were you trying to fly, Bobby?"

"Electricity, Dad. If I could only get a big enough electrical charge."

Mr. Goddard nodded. "So that's what all that shuffling across the living room was about. You were building up a static-electricity charge. And here I thought you were just wearing out the rug." Mr. Goddard thought for a moment. "What I don't understand, son, is the zinc rod. What was it supposed to do?"

Bobby shrugged and answered, "You told me yesterday that when I shuffle my feet on a rug, electricity rises up from the carpet to my feet. I knew zinc was a good conductor, so I figured if I held a zinc rod up real high when I jumped, maybe the electricity would rise up through me to the zinc. And maybe it would carry me up with it as it went."

Mr. Goddard clamped both hands over his mouth to cover up the laugh that threatened to jump out of his throat.

Shooting for the Moon

THE FIRST SUCCESSFUL FLIGHT OF A LIQUID-FUELED rocket took place March 16, 1926, in Auburn, Massachusetts. The rocket, powered by gasoline and liquid oxygen, reached a height of 41 feet; its flight lasted two and a half seconds. Its inventor was Dr. Robert Goddard, a professor of physics at Clark University in nearby Worcester.

A conservative, private man, Goddard proposed and patented many inventions and improvements—from a solar sail for interplanetary travel to a device for removing impaled leaves from rakes. He is best known for his steadfast, quietly stated insistence that it was possible for a multistage rocket to reach the Moon.

His inventions changed the face of warfare before they altered our view of the universe, as his patents were used by the Luftwaffe to build the V-1 and V-2 rockets used against Great Britain in World War II.

A rocket launched by Goddard and his crew on March 26, 1937, rose between 8,000 and 9,000 feet. This rocket, also fueled by liquid oxygen and gasoline, was equipped with a gimbaled gyroscopic stabilizer. A spinning gyroscope resists changes in motion and, attached to steering fins, would straighten the flight of an errant rocket. The use of this type of stabilizer was another of Goddard's innovations.

—David Rhoden

Bobby looked glum and dejected. "Well, it sort of worked. I flew longer the second time." Then little Bobby sighed. "Maybe I just jumped harder."

Mr. Goddard rose and turned to his wife. "*Now* what do you think of this boy, Fannie? I tell him one thing about electricity, and he puts it together with two or three other ideas and comes up with a science experiment."

"What he came up with was the destruction of my flower bed," said his mother.

"What he came up with was a crash," Percy reminded everyone.

Mr. Goddard nodded and looked back at his son. "So your experiment was a failure?"

Sadly Bobby nodded. "I guess so . . ."

"Good," exclaimed Mr. Goddard.

"What?" Bobby was startled.

"Failure is how a scientist learns," his father explained. "You try something. It flops. That leads you to a better idea for the next try. The important thing is never to stop trying. Now, before your next try, you might spend some time thinking about what kind of force could be strong enough to overcome gravity and drive something up into the air. I think it's time I told you about Sir Isaac Newton's laws of motion."

Percy fidgeted back and forth from foot to foot. "I, uh, think I have to go home now." He leaned close to Bobby and whispered, "Yuck! That sounds boring."

On a cloudy afternoon three days later Mrs. Goddard climbed the basement stairs with a load of wash and glanced out the kitchen window. Then she dropped the laundry basket and screamed. Her son was balanced on top of the back-yard fence. In his hands Bobby held two enormous balloons. "He must be six feet off the ground!" she gasped. Then she sucked in a great breath and yelled, "Bobby Goddard, you get down from there this instant! But be careful!"

She raced out the back door just as Percy Long's countdown reached "three . . . two . . . one . . . go!"

Mrs. Goddard screamed again as Bobby leapt from his precarious perch high into the air. Bobby yelled, "Count!"

As he jumped, Bobby relaxed his tight grip on the necks of the two bulging 24-inch balloons. With a piercing high-pitched screech, air rushed out the bottom of each balloon.

Percy counted. "One . . . two . . . three . . . four . . . fi-" Thud!

Bobby crashed to the soft grass. The whine of his two balloons slowly died away to a faint hiss as they deflated. Bobby sat up and shook his head to clear away the stars before his eyes as his mother rushed over.

"What on earth do you think you were doing?" she demanded.

"I was flying, Mom," he answered.

"You mean crashing," corrected Percy.

At dinner that night Mr. Goddard asked, "What's this I hear about you trying to fly again?"

"He just about broke his neck is what he did," said his mother.

"I was using balloons for thrust, Dad, like what you told me Mr. Newton said. When the air rushes out the bottom of the balloons, it pushes the balloons up. I figured they'd take me up with them."

Mr. Goddard smiled. "Did you hear that, Fannie? What do you think of our boy now?"

Softly Bobby asked, "Is this another failure, Dad?"

"You just need more lift, son, more power. A lot more power. Oh, and maybe it's time to stop sending yourself up with your rockets. Safer for you to watch from the ground. Yup. A few more experiments and a little more power. I think you'll get it."

Nearly 40 years later, on March 16, 1926, Robert Goddard launched the world's first liquid-fueled rocket. It rose 50 feet from the ground. By 1937 one of his rockets thundered 9,000 feet into the air, and the space age was launched for mankind. In another 25 years rockets would regularly blast free of Earth's gravity to place satellites and manned capsules into orbit. But that's another story.

Robert Goddard in 1935, working on a rocket in his shop at Roswell, New Mexico

The only West Point graduate to turn professional storyteller, Kendall Haven has performed for two million listeners in 36 states and conducted workshops on the teaching power of storytelling for more than 10,000 teachers. Haven has published four audiotapes and three books of original stories and won five national awards for his radio drama on the effects of television. He has written 50 stories (Marvels of Science: 50 Fascinating Five-Minute Reads, Libraries Unlimited, 1994) to help make the process of science fascinating and compelling to youngsters. He lives with his wife and nephew in the rolling vineyards of rural Northern California.

This story is one of 50 historical science stories in Kendall Haven's book *Marvels of Science: 50 Fascinating Five-Minute Reads*, published by Libraries Unlimited, P.O. Box 6633, Englewood, Colo. 80155, 800-237-6124. Reprinted by permission.

The Year of the Turnip in Oklahoma

Fran Stallings _____

In 1889, back in the cities, if you had the money you could buy fine ready-made clothes, eat in fancy restaurants, and read your newspaper by gas or electric light. But on the frontier, poor settlers had only what they could bring, make, or grow. This story was inspired by the experiences of my husband's granduncle Charlie and grandaunt Clara Macmillan, who homesteaded west of Oklahoma City. Since the Macmillans died before my husband was born, we have few details directly from them. However, whenever I tell the story in the presence of other descendants of early Oklahoma families, those folks eagerly share bits from their own ancestors' experiences. Those details, plus my historical research, have helped me develop this story.

WHEN CHARLIE AND CLARA MACMILLAN HEARD ABOUT THE OKLAHOMA LAND run, they realized it was their chance. "All we have to do is stake a claim, live on the land, and improve it. It'll be ours—almost for free!"

They had tenant-farmed in Illinois, Missouri, and Kansas, and most of each year's crop went to pay the landlord. They were tired of seeing all their hard work slip away. They were tired of moving from place to place. Although the children hated to move again, they agreed that it was worth a try.

In May 1889 they packed their belongings in their wagon. It wasn't much bigger than a pickup truck, but Charlie built tall hoops over it, and Clara covered it with canvas so they could pile things high inside. Still, they had to sell or give away everything they wouldn't absolutely need. Clara carefully packed a box of books for the children, though: there was no telling how long it would be before a school opened in the new territory.

They said goodbye to their friends, hitched their horses Brownie and Jed to the wagon, and tied their three cows on behind. The chickens rode in a crate tied to the back of the wagon. It was a slow trip—cows walk slowly. There was no room to camp inside the wagon, so each night the family curled up in their blankets underneath it.

At last the Macmillans arrived in "Ark City" (Arkansas City), Kansas. Up until three days before the land run, it was still against the law for non-Indians to live in Oklahoma Territory.[1]

"Clara," said Charlie, "I'm afraid this wagon isn't strong enough to make the run. What if we hit a rock and a wheel flies off? The whole thing would crash apart. No sense risking life and limb, and our claim too. Why don't I just take Brownie and go by myself? She's faster than old Jed."

It sounded like a good plan to Clara. "The children and I can bring the wagon along later if you send us a map," she said. "We'll be just fine in Ark City until we hear from you." So Charlie went on alone into Oklahoma Territory, to the border of the Unassigned Lands.

The weekend just before the land run was a long and fretful time for Clara and the children. The run would start at noon on Monday, April 22. April 21 was Easter Sunday. That night Clara could hardly sleep for worry. What if Brownie broke a leg in a rabbit hole? What if she stumbled and Charlie fell under the hooves of the other animals? People were going to make the run on racehorses, farm horses, mules, and donkeys, driving wagons and buggies and racing surreys. There were even a few folks on newfangled bicycles. Clara was so worried for Charlie's safety that she could hardly think about the land he hoped to claim.

That Monday morning, April 22, people gathered in Arkansas City to watch the town clock's hands inch around to noon. At that moment, they knew, the cavalry soldiers would fire into the air to signal to the waiting homesteaders. But that was more than 50 miles away: the folks in Ark City wouldn't hear it. All they could do was cheer as the clock struck.

It was almost a week before Clara got the letter from Charlie: "My dear ones," he wrote, "our prayers have been answered. I met a fellow who suggested circling around to the west border of the Unassigned Lands instead of waiting with the crowd on the north. It was good advice. I found us a fine claim west of Oklahoma Station,[2] where the land is flat and green. It will make fine winter-wheat fields. But there's also a hill for our dugout house and a little spring with a pond for our animals. It even has three trees! It will be paradise for us."

---

1. By 1889 there was a sizable population of white and black folks in Oklahoma (Oklahoma Territory and Indian Territory) who had married or been adopted into Indian families or were legally working for them. All other non-Indians attempting to settle there were considered "Boomers" and were ejected by the cavalry. "Sooners" were those who trespassed into the settlement area immediately before the run. If caught, they lost any right to file a claim. Only the Unassigned Lands, a patch in the center of Oklahoma that did not belong to any of the Indian nations at the time, was settled by the land run of 1889. Later other areas were opened by runs and lotteries.

2. Oklahoma Station, just a stop on the Santa Fe Railroad's north–south line from Kansas to Texas, later became Oklahoma City.

Clara and the children took another week to bring the wagon across the Cherokee Outlet and down into the Unassigned Lands. It was May before they started to get settled. First they tended to the animals, building fences and pens. The weather was mild; there was no hurry about building their dugout house. But they put in a garden so that they could have some fresh vegetables soon.

Clara found a rotted haystack that must have been made by Boomers who had tried settling a few years before, and she planted cucumbers in that rich compost. They grew as fast as Jack's beanstalk! When the children got fed up with cucumber salads, she made pickles: not just jars of pickles but barrelfuls. "What do you want with all those pickles?" asked Charlie.

"It's food; we mustn't waste it," she replied. And it turned out that they were lucky to have those pickles.

You see, they couldn't plant field crops that first summer. It was too late to start most crops. Besides, the prairie grass had never been plowed, and it took most of the summer to prepare the first few fields for September planting with winter wheat.

All fall and winter the wheat would put down roots and gather strength so that in spring it could start growing strong and fast. By April 1890, it would be almost knee-high. By late May it would be golden, heavy with ripening grain. In June 1890 they would have their first harvest: wheat to sell so they could pay off their debts and buy badly needed supplies, wheat to grind into flour for their own bread, seed for next September's planting. But first they had to get through the winter of 1889–90. Aside from what they'd gotten from the garden, they had been unable to grow any food to live on.

The three cows grazed on prairie grass and gave milk. Clara and the girls set the milk cans in the cool spring water until the cream rose to the top, then they churned it into butter. They sold the butter in town and bought wheat flour from Kansas. With the flour, they made biscuits.

So the family ate biscuits, skim milk (which was left after the cream was removed), and pickles for lunch. Biscuits, skim milk, and pickles for supper. Biscuits, skim milk, and pickles for breakfast . . . all that winter.

It wasn't so bad. The biscuits gave them lots of energy. They got protein, calcium, and minerals from the skim milk. And the pickles had vitamin C. Many of the families who had no pickles or sauerkraut got scurvy that winter: their skin got patchy, their gums bled, and their teeth fell out. But the Macmillans stayed healthy, thanks to Clara's pickles— thanks to those Boomers' haystack.

By spring they were eager for that wheat harvest! But something happened in 1890 that happens every now and then in Oklahoma. There was a drought.

The year started well, with ample moisture, and the winter wheat came up green and strong. But then March passed without any rain. When April continued dry, people really worried. The wheat, which should have been knee-high, was only a few inches tall and shriveled. Charlie and the boys had plowed up more fields during the winter for spring plantings of corn and beans. But the seeds couldn't sprout in the dry dusty dirt.

May went by without rain, and the creeks were drying up. June came, and a few lucky farmers were able to harvest a bushel or two of wheat per acre—but that's barely enough to save for replanting, not enough to sell or grind into flour.

Neighbors came by the Macmillans' place. "Your spring hasn't run dry yet? You want some extra livestock? We can't keep 'em." The pond couldn't spare water for a garden that summer.

By July and August the wagons were rolling again—but this time they were heading out of the territory and back to Texas, Kansas, Missouri. Folks said, "You can't make a living farming if you can't count on the rain." As the wagons passed, Clara saw barefoot children walking alongside, searching the roadsides for green leaves they might eat, they were so hungry.

In September the rains came at last—a three-day deluge. When the land drained enough to be worked, it was time to plant winter wheat again. The Macmillans and the few other families who had hung on through the drought borrowed money from the Santa Fe Railroad to buy seed. The fields turned green with promise. But now they had to get through the winter of 1890–91 without a harvest behind them. And this time Clara had no pickles.

Luckily there is one vegetable you can plant in September in Oklahoma that will grow big enough to eat before frost comes: turnips.

They planted turnips. Not just garden rows but whole fields of turnips. And those turnips grew so well that they proved the richness of Oklahoma soil, if you could just get some rain on it! Folks say those turnips grew as big as a child's head. They even say some grew as big as a dishpan—but maybe dishpans were smaller in those days. So the settlers had plenty of turnips to eat.

They had crispy raw turnip salads. They had boiled, mashed, broiled, and fried turnips. They had stewed turnip greens. They tried every recipe they could think of for eating turnips.

They fed turnips to their animals too. The trouble is, when cows eat

Luckily there is one vegetable you can plant in September in Oklahoma that will grow big enough to eat before frost comes: turnips.

turnips, their milk comes out tasting like turnips. So the butter and cheese . . . *tasted like turnips.* [Note: Pause in your reading aloud, and listeners will readily join in this refrain.]

They fed turnips to the chickens, and the eggs came out . . . *tasting like turnips.*

They fed turnips to the hogs, and when it got cold enough for butchering, the hams and bacon and pork roast all . . . *tasted like turnips.*

So the flavor of turnips was everywhere! They could get a little variety by putting melted butter or cheese on their turnips, but the butter and cheese . . . *tasted like turnips.* They could season their turnip greens with some ham or bacon, but the ham and bacon . . . *tasted like turnips.* They could even have a dish of turnip pie or turnip cobbler with a nice cold glass of milk, but the milk . . . *tasted like turnips!*

That's how they got through the winter of 1890–91. In fact, they called 1890 the Year of the Turnip. People even decorated their Christmas trees with 'em!

The spring of 1891 was worth waiting for. The rains were steady and good. The wheat grew strong and tall. The harvest in June 1891 let the Macmillans and their neighbors pay off debts, buy plenty of long-needed tools and supplies, and eat bread made from their very own flour. Oklahoma looked like paradise after all! The Macmillans prospered and raised their children and sent word to their relatives back in Illinois to come live in the Promised Land.

But the descendants of those settlers remember the hard early years. At Thanksgiving you will often find a big bowl of turnips on the table. Some folks really like turnips, and they're thankful to have some. The rest of us are thankful that now—unlike those months in 1890, the Year of the Turnip—we can have something else.

Fran Stallings grew up in a storytelling family. Trained as a biologist (that's another story), she tells nationwide at festivals and teaches workshops, including courses at the 1988 NAPPS Summer Institute and the 1991 Congress on Storytelling in Education. Since 1985 she has conducted school residencies for the State Arts Council of Oklahoma. Her publications include fiction, songs, and many professional articles. She lives in Bartlesville, Oklahoma, where she directs the Sunfest Storytelling Festival and edits The Territorial Tattler.

Zayde's Trunk

Karen Golden _____

This is the story of my grandfather's journey to and across the United States, beginning in 1888, as he might have told it as a teenager. I gathered the story from my mother, who always regretted not asking him more questions. I filled in some of the missing details by adding my own time line, dialogue, and descriptions of the way things must have looked and felt to a teenager, but the people and events are all real. I put myself into his shoes to try to understand the social and historical issues and themes this story addresses: anti-Semitism in Eastern Europe, the journey to America, sweatshop conditions, the transcontinental railroad, western migration, and finally the Wild West. The trunk still sits at the foot of my aunt's bed as a reminder that we would not be here if it weren't for Zayde's spirit and tenacity.

EVERY TIME I VISIT MY AUNT LILIAN, I OPEN THE LITTLE BLACK TRUNK THAT SITS at the foot of her bed. She keeps extra blankets inside for those chilly Wisconsin nights. Sometimes when I open the trunk I smell herring or even the salty ocean—but once I heard the voice of a 16-year-old boy telling the story of how he brought that trunk to Milwaukee more than 100 years ago. That boy was my "Zayde," my grandfather, Itzchock Henoch Peretsky . . .

IT HASN'T ALWAYS BEEN AS CLEAN AS IT IS NOW. SEE THAT LITTLE DENT BY THE latch? That happened in February 1888 when I was unloading it from Mama and Papa's wagon. It was covered with snow and ice, and it slipped from my hands and crashed to the ground. It seemed heavier then because I was a lot smaller. I was only 12. Mama and Papa took me to the meeting spot outside our village in Lithuania.

It was dark, and Papa said we had to be very quiet so the Cossack soldiers wouldn't hear us and take me away to the army. They took lots of boys away for 20 years or more. Papa was so nervous, he kept pulling pieces of straw from his long white beard, and poor Mama was crying. I gave her my handkerchief to wipe her tears. I'll never forget the way they looked—Papa in his long black coat with the fur collar and Mama in her heavy gray wool shawl. That was the last time I ever saw them.

Then Mama said, "Remember, Itzi, in 32 days it will be your bar mitzvah. Then you will be a man. And remember always to live by what you feel in your heart." I understood about the bar mitzvah, but I didn't really understand what it meant to live by what I felt in my heart.

"Don't worry, Mama. I'll act like a man even though I haven't had my bar mitzvah yet." I climbed out of the wagon with my wooden trunk and jumped into the neighbors' wagon. The horses pulled forward, *clippity clop, clippity clop*, and we were off. I watched Mama and Papa wave, but then it got so dark that all I could see was the stars.

I had never been away from home in my whole life, and I felt a mix of adventure and sadness. I hid the trunk under the straw and remembered all the wonderful things Mama had packed inside. A *pereneh* (feather quilt) and pillow, a prayer book, a tallis (prayer shawl), two pairs of pants and three shirts that Papa had sewed himself, eight loaves of bread, and a wooden box filled with salt herring. There were lots of other people in the cart, and we all lay quietly. Every once in a while a baby would cry, "Waaaaa," piercing the stillness, and we would jump. And then it would be quiet again, *clippity clop, clippity clop*.

I wasn't sorry to be leaving. I was only sorry that I had to leave Mama and Papa behind. I wouldn't miss those mean Cossack soldiers who came storming into our house in the middle of the night to search us, and I wouldn't miss hearing the gunshots. The soldiers killed people for no reason at all! Our little village, called a *shtetl* in Yiddish, had become a place filled with terrible things. We weren't safe even when we went to the outhouse.

As I lay in that cart, my mind filled with the many thoughts I hadn't had time to think about over the past few weeks. I remembered how Mama had first told me I was going to America. We were in the kitchen, and she was stirring a pot of soup on the stove. Then she started to tell me about the time my older brother Pincus drank some starch water she was boiling to use on the laundry. He thought it was soup! She made the same funny face that Pincus made when he put the spoon to his lips. We both laughed.

Then she stopped laughing and got very serious and said, "Itzi, you will be seeing your brother soon." I didn't know what to say, so I just sat there silently. I wanted to see Pincus, but I would have to leave home, never to return. "Pincus sent the money for your boat ticket. You will leave next week with the Kleinmans. Papa is too old to make the journey. We will stay behind."

"Can't I wait until after my bar mitzvah?" I begged Mama, but she shook her head. "The Kleinmans are good people. They've been our neighbors for many years, and they will watch after you."

"But I will be a man after my bar mitzvah—I will look after myself."

Mama smiled and said, "Yes, Itzi, you will be a man, but you will always be my baby."

And now I was in the wagon, listening to the horses' *clippity clop, clippity clop*, over the crunchy snow. The ride seemed to last forever! We had to travel at night because we weren't really supposed to leave.

Suddenly the horses stopped short, and I covered my head with straw. I heard Mr. Kleinman talking in Russian, which sounded funny since I didn't understand a word. I only knew Yiddish. I peeked out of the straw and saw a shiny gold coin drop from Mr. Kleinman's hand into the hand of the guard at the Prussian border. Then the guard opened the gate, and our wagon rolled through. Not long after that I smelled the salty sea air, heard the waves crashing against the dock, and saw the big boat.

Hundreds of people were waiting, and everyone was carrying either a trunk or a bundle wrapped in cloth. We steerage-class passengers were told to wait in line. We were packed so tightly together that I couldn't even move my arms from side to side.

The boat sounded a low whistle, and we were off . . . to freedom! Ah, freedom. It seemed so simple, but on the boat I learned what steerage class meant, and freedom felt very far away. We had to sit and sleep on the floor, and the only food we had was a thin potato soup and what we had brought. I almost forgot—we didn't have showers or baths. We washed ourselves with wet *shmattes*, rags.

The first few days were exciting. I made four new friends: Moishe, Yankel, Dovid, and Mendel. We sang songs and told jokes to the other steerage-class passengers. We called ourselves the *Shpielers*, or players. We weren't allowed to go upstairs where the rich people sat. We heard that they had beds and washbasins!

Soon the days grew long and boring. Our jokes became old, and there was nothing to do and no place to go. And then people started getting sick. Moishe got a bad case of the measles, and we weren't allowed to play with him anymore. He got so sick that he died. The captain of the boat said his body would have to be thrown overboard. I didn't watch them do this. I was too sad.

And then I remembered the words of Mama, not to forget about my bar mitzvah. I had never met anyone who had a bar mitzvah on a boat, and I was afraid I would forget the days of the week because they all seemed the same. So I made myself a bar mitzvah reminder stick. Every day I carved a notch in the stick. And when I had carved 28 notches, I began telling everyone in the lower deck of the boat, "I'm having a bar

I peeked out of the straw and saw a shiny gold coin drop from Mr. Kleinman's hand into the hand of the guard at the Prussian border. Then the guard opened the gate, and our wagon rolled through.

mitzvah in four days." After I carved each notch, I practiced the special bar mitzvah prayers. I wouldn't be reading from the Torah scroll because there wasn't one on the boat.

Thirty notches . . . "My bar mitzvah is in two days!"

Thirty-one notches . . . "Tomorrow is my special day!"

When I woke up on day 32, I felt the notches in the stick and shouted, "Today is the day!"

Mr. Kleinman picked me up, put me on his shoulders, and carried me around the boat until we came to a group of men gathered at the far end of the deck. They recited a few prayers and invited me to join them. This was the first time I was ever invited to pray. I sang the Hebrew songs loudly, wrapped in my blue-and-white-striped tallis with the long fringe. That was it! Now I was a man!

But I didn't feel any different. I didn't feel any braver or stronger or anything. I just felt like the same skinny black-haired Itzchock from Volkameer, Lithuania, on my way to America. Then Mrs. Kleinman pulled out a little tin box of sugar cookies from my mama. I missed her so much that I didn't share them with anyone.

The last few weeks on the boat went by slowly. It was cold and windy, and we wanted to be in America already. And then it happened: another big day—even bigger than my bar mitzvah day!

I was lying under my *pereneh* when I heard a lot of screaming, and I saw everyone running toward the upper lookout deck and shouting. Dovid and I pushed through the crowd and climbed up the railing instead of on the stairs. When we got there, we saw Lady Liberty holding her big torch. Everyone was yelling "*Freiheit*," which means freedom. We finally made it!

I couldn't take my eyes off her. She was the most beautiful woman I had ever seen. The boat sounded one final whistle, and we all packed up our things and ran to the exit. We came to Castle Gardens, which was the immigrant station in New York. I held onto my stick and felt the 32 notches, and I remembered the second part of Mama's wish—that I should live by what I feel in my heart. I still didn't know what this meant, but I was sure I would figure it out in America.

I wished we could just jump off the boat, but we had to wait in line. Waiting, waiting, waiting . . . We waited to get off the boat, we waited to pass inspection, we waited to receive the right papers. In one of the lines I got a new name: "Isador Henry Cohen." They said, "Isador Henry sounds more American, and Cohen is easier to say." I didn't ask questions because I didn't speak or understand English. When I was finally through waiting, I saw . . . could it be Pincus waving from the dock? Yes!

It was Pincus, with a small beard and a tall brown felt hat. I shouted, "Pincus, Pincus!" I sure was glad to see him.

I had made it to America! But that is only half the story of how the trunk got to Wisconsin. Pincus and I walked around New York with my trunk on his back. There were tall buildings everywhere and crowds of people walking and riding on bicycles and in wagons. There were clothes hanging above the street on clotheslines and garbage cans overflowing with papers. Everywhere I looked, I saw things I had never seen before. I saw black people for the first time and even Chinese men and women. Finally we came to the Lower East Side, where Pincus had rented a little room. I felt like I was home because all the signs were in Yiddish and everyone was Jewish.

I knew I would have to work in America, but I never imagined that the next day Pincus would take me with him to his work to find me a job. We walked to a dirty old warehouse with crumbling bricks. Inside was a sweatshop that was a sewing factory. The noise was so loud that I could hear it from a block away, *rat-a-tat-tat-tat-tat-tat-tat-tat*.

Rows upon rows of people were sitting at sewing machines, frantically stitching together underwear. Many of them were little children even smaller than me, and I was a very short 13-year-old. The whole room *rat-a-tat-tatted* with the nonstop noise of the sewing machines. The foreman came over to my brother and shook his head: "No work today."

I was very happy! I didn't want to work in that horrible place. That afternoon I was on my own again. Pincus had to work every day, and he even brought work home with him. He looked funny carrying a mountain of underwear on his back.

I had walked back to the water to think about my old life in Lithuania when I heard someone shouting, "Hey!" I turned around and saw a man with a thick black mustache. I just nodded because I still couldn't say anything in English. The man motioned for me to follow him. The next thing I knew, I was learning how to tie packages for the steamship line. With a roll of twine at my side and a knife, I found my first job in America. And the best thing of all was that I could sleep on the empty shelves when they weren't full of packages. Soon I brought my trunk from Pincus's room, and that place became my home. I made $2 a week! I even learned a little English because no one spoke Yiddish there.

I soon became the best package-wrapper in New York. I could tell just from looking at a package how much twine I needed to tie it up. I wrapped packages nine hours a day, and sometimes my boss, Mr. Johnson, gave me an extra penny for my hard work. The steamship company was alongside the water and on a railroad track. Every day I watched the trains pick up the packages, and I followed them a little ways down the track—a little farther each day until one day I followed them all the way to the train station. There I saw a sign that read TRAINS TO THE WEST $1! ONE WAY ONLY! FREE LAND! YOU NEED A FARM! HERE IS ONE YOU CAN GET SIMPLY BY OCCUPYING IT. ALL ABOARD!

I was only 15, and I didn't really want a farm, but I did want an adventure. So I picked up my trunk from the steamship company and my bar mitzvah stick, I said goodbye to Pincus, and I bought my ticket and headed west.

Every few hours the train stopped—sometimes in a small town and sometimes in a big city. I got off the train and walked around, and I noticed that some towns were so small, they didn't even have stores. I decided I would become a traveling store, a peddler.

With my savings I bought a small cart and knives, forks, and spoons; needles and thread; mirrors; and even religious pictures. I figured the farther the train was from a big city, the more the people would miss going to church, so they would want to buy religious pictures. I was right! My religious-picture business was a big success, and when I finally reached Oregon a few weeks later, I had more money than I had started with.

The streets of Portland looked much different from those of New York. I saw a lot of Indians with their long black braids and colorful beaded shirts and dresses. I also saw cowboys and bandits.

ARCHIVE PHOTOS

Almost there: A boat-side view of Bedloe, or Liberty, Island and the Statue of Liberty

I met a 15-year-old boy named Jack at the synagogue. He was very lucky because he didn't have to work. He got to go to school because he lived with his parents. Oh, how I wanted to go to school and learn. I knew that I needed to find a job if I wanted to stay. So I got a job in a store that sold cloth, buttons, thread, and sewing machines. I decided that someday I would open my own store in Portland, and this would be the end of my journey. I wanted to live in a land of adventure with cowboys and bandits and Indians!

Well, that's what I thought until I was shot. I had just bought myself a tall, rounded brown felt hat. It was my first American hat. Until then I had worn a flat black hat with a little rim like people wore in the old country. Now I walked proudly down the street with my new American hat. I even took out my bar mitzvah stick and held it like a cane. I felt like I had finally become an American, and I was only 16 years old.

I was feeling so proud that I wasn't watching where I was walking. I was looking up in the air, and suddenly I walked between two big men wearing black cowboy hats and pistols at their sides. They were shooting at each other! No wonder there was nobody else walking down the street.

A bullet flew through the air and went right through the middle of my hat. I got shot in the hat!

I could hardly believe how lucky I was to be alive. My whole life had flashed before my eyes. I'd seen Mama and Papa standing next to their cart, sending me to America, and I recalled the second part of Mama's final words: "Remember always to live by what you feel in your heart."

I now knew what this meant. My heart said, "Get on the next train going east." That's exactly what I did! I picked up my trunk and my bar mitzvah stick, and with my holey hat on my head as a reminder I got on that train. I had had enough adventure to last me for a long time. And that's how the trunk ended up in Milwaukee. I got off the train there because I spotted a pretty redheaded girl outside the window. Oh, I almost forgot to tell you . . .

SUDDENLY I HEARD MY AUNT CALLING ME. "ARE YOU OK IN THERE? YOU'VE BEEN gone a long time."

"Yes, I'm fine; I'll be out in just a minute," I yelled back. I looked into the trunk and said, "What did you forget?" The 16-year-old voice of my grandpa returned: "I forgot to tell you that I lost my bar mitzvah stick and my hat on the train on my way here. But now you have the story, and that's much more important. Don't forget to tell it."

"I won't," I said. As I slowly closed that little black trunk, I heard the familiar squeak of the hinge. But I also heard the voice of my great-grandmother say, "Always live by what you feel in your heart," and I heard a soft but unmistakable *clippity clop, clippity clop, clippity clop* . . .

Karen Golden began telling stories at the dinner table at age 3, and today her table is the size of North America. A Los Angeles–based storyteller, musician, writer, and workshop leader, Golden specializes in Jewish, multicultural, personal, and historical stories. In 1993 she was featured in the Los Angeles Times *and on National Public Radio and published an audiotape,* Tales and Scales: Stories of Jewish Wisdom. *In 1994 five of Golden's original stories were published.*

Scott Joplin: Master of Ragtime

Bobby Norfolk

Scott Joplin can easily be considered the American counterpart to the Euro-pean composers of classical music. He was the prime motivating force behind the development of the various genres of American music as we know it today. Born in the postbellum South, Joplin very early showed a gift for music and was particularly drawn to the piano. No other human being on the planet had the impact Joplin did in creating a new style of music based on African polyrhythms and a European beat—a style that defined early 20th-century culture. Jazz, rock 'n' roll, punk, pop, country, rock (both hard and acid), rockabilly, and rap all followed the masterly foundation laid by Mr. Scott Joplin.

IF YOU EVER HEAR A TUNE PLAYING CALLED "THE ENTERTAINER," THAT'S MY song. I wrote that fine song when I lived in the city of St. Louis in 1901. Even my business card reads just that way: Scott Joplin, "The Entertainer."

In 1973 a movie came out called *The Sting*, starring Robert Redford and Paul Newman. That movie's success—millions of records and tapes were sold, and two Academy Awards were won—brought my music back into style after many years of neglect.

In 1902 an impressed newspaper critic writing about my song "The Entertainer" for the now-defunct *St. Louis Globe Democrat* said: "'The Entertainer' is a jingling work of a very original character, embracing various strains of a retentive character which set the foot in spontaneous action, and [it] leaves an indelible imprint on the tympanum."

This classic form of American music is known as ragtime. Now, that's a compound word, but let's take that word and break it into its two components—and let's take the second word, *time*, first. In true ragtime the time part is kept by the piano player's left hand and has an even and steady beat like the ticking of a clock. The rag part is kept by the right hand, and it has a rhythm that is uneven, choppy, and "ragged." That's called a syncopated rhythm. Syncopation is what you hear when you listen to the likes of jazz, rock, reggae, punk, pop, and rap. The important thing to remember is that before there were jazz, rock, reggae, punk, pop, and rap, there was rag and there was time. Put them together, and you have classic ragtime!

Now, there were other types of music being played in these United States before the advent of ragtime. For example, people used to listen to waltz music and marches.

But they really weren't the kind of music I had inside me. Where I came from, in East Texas, we didn't know about waltzes and marches. I was influenced by other kinds of music. Both of my parents loved music: my father played the violin, and my mother played the banjo.

I remember my mother well, and her music had a strong influence on me. She would play while she sang old work songs and church hymns. The banjo was a popular instrument throughout the South. People fashioned the banjo from an earlier African instrument. An animal skin was stretched across a box to make the sound box, and strings were stretched across to create the different pitches. I always loved that sound, and the banjo became an important part of my music.

But another big influence on me—probably the biggest one—was the music of the church. Our church was a wooden building with tall twin towers. Inside were rows and rows of wooden benches, and on Sunday morning, how that room would come alive. People would rock and shout and sing and clap their hands. They would stamp their feet and sway in the rows like great waves upon the sea. That was where I first saw how the piano could make people feel joy. I loved to see people so happy, and I couldn't wait to play that instrument.

I finally got my chance to play the upright piano when my parents let me take lessons. In those days my mother was working for the Cook family over on Hazel Street in Texarkana. While she dusted and mopped, I'd go into the parlor and play the piano that was there. First I'd practice a scale or two.

Then I'd play a few arpeggios to warm up my fingers. The Cooks had a wonderful collection of sheet music, so one by one I learned the popular songs of the time. I even learned to play the music of such great masters as Beethoven and Mozart. And sometimes I just sat and improvised my own tunes.

By the time I got to high school I had gotten pretty good as a pianist. People started to call me "the musician in residence," and I played for school assemblies, parents' programs, award days, and graduation.

I worked on my music all the time. My family finally bought an old secondhand piano, and then I got to practice every free minute I had. My practicing was really starting to pay off!

Now, let's figure the place of the piano in my day. Around the 1890s traveling musicians would play throughout the South and Midwest, and I was one of them. Those itinerant musicians were in great demand, and their arrival in any town was a big event. Some were teenagers, and some were old-timers. They sang, they danced, and they played on pianos, on banjos, even on spoons!

In those days I was always looking for inspiration for songs. I found it in an amazing event staged in 1896. On September 15 of that year nearly 40,000 people came to rural Texas from hundreds of miles around to see two locomotives ram into each other at 60 miles per hour. I called my song about the event "The Crush Collision" because in it you can actually hear the two trains building up speed and then colliding.

Scott Joplin, the King of Ragtime

And the man who devised this little scheme was named William Crush. What a play on words that was!

As time went by, I started getting a little antsy in Texarkana and had the urge to see what was happening in the big city. I heard that things were really hoppin' in St. Louis—the "Gateway to the West," they called it. St. Louis was the center of activity in the Midwest.

Trains, riverboats, streetcars—people going east, people going west. What a city! What excitement! The center of the action in town was near Union Station in an area called "the sporting district." There were restaurants, saloons, and music halls all along Market Street. The most elegant men and women would stroll down the street, arm in arm, dressed in silks, jewelry, big bonnets, and derby hats.

I got a job playing at the Silver Dollar Cafe owned by Charles and Tom Turpin. It was one of the most popular clubs around. A lot of pianists were working in the sporting district, and there was a lot of competition to get recognition. You really had to be good to gain the respect of your peers, but once you did, you earned the title "Professor."

Everything seemed to be going my way. I had gained a good reputation among the musicians and the public, and life was exciting. But I knew something was still missing. You see, I would make up tunes and play them, but I wanted to know more about music so I could share my compositions with the world.

When you really want to know about something, there's only one way to find out more about it—and that's to study. You read, you practice, you take lessons, and you learn from others. That's why I decided I should continue my education.

I heard that in Sedalia, Missouri, there was a college where I could learn more about music. It was called the George R. Smith College. So I went to Sedalia and became a student again. Every day I went to classes, and I learned about music theory and composition. I learned how to write down melodies, harmonies, and rhythms. Finally I had learned how to make my music available for others to play.

While I was living in Sedalia, I had to earn enough to cover my living expenses, so I did what I knew how to do best: I started playing in the clubs. I found a job at the Maple Leaf Club, and I played there in the evenings after spending the whole day in class. It was about that time that a new kind of music was becoming the rage in the dance halls.

It was ragtime! I loved that new music, and with it I had finally found a way to express everything that was inside me. When I played that music, I felt my soul come alive. I was so inspired by school and my life in Sedalia that I wrote a ragtime tune and dedicated it to the Maple Leaf Club. I called it the "Maple Leaf Rag," and it was a rag in the classic sense.

I knew my next step was to get a publisher for my music. In those days there were no records, no radio, no MTV, no VH-1, no Friday-night or Saturday-night videos, and certainly no Nintendo games! The only way for a popular musician to gain recognition and to earn a living was to have his music published by a sheet-music distributor. The public would buy sheet music, and the family would sit in the parlor in the evenings and make music together.

In Sedalia there was a man who had established a sheet-music publishing business. His name was John Stark, and he was one of the most important people I ever met. I got him interested in my "Maple Leaf Rag," and he agreed to publish it for me. It was 1899. A new century was about to begin, and a whole new life was about to happen for me. Sales of my first ragtime tune started out slow, but by the fall of 1900 orders for it were flooding John Stark's office. All I had learned at school about writing music was paying off.

I wrote ragtime tunes just as fast as they came to me. Sometimes a piece would come to me but I couldn't think of a name for it. One day I went to John's office with a new piece I'd written with Arthur Marshall. I played it for him, and he really liked it, but neither one of us could think of a name for this tune. All of a sudden we heard a loud commotion outside the door of the office. We ran to open the door, and there we found two boys in tattered knee-pants fighting each other with all their might.

They were kicking and scratching and biting and tearing like we had never seen. We pulled them apart and sent one of the boys on his way. The other one came into the office and told us what had happened. It seems the two were newspaper boys, and this one said, "That other boy was selling papers in my territory." That's against newsboy ethics, you know, and he was fightin' mad about it. But he was embarrassed that he had been caught fighting, and he had a guilty look on his face—like he had just swiped cookies from Grandma's oven. That word struck us both, and we decided to call my unnamed piece of music "Swipsey"! John had a camera in the room, so he took a picture of the boy, and we used that picture on the cover of my new rag.

The ragtime craze brought some new dances with it. During the 1890s the most popular dance was called the two-step. So when ragtime became popular, it was natural that the new dances would be variations of the two-step. One of them was called the Cakewalk Dance. It was a high-stepping dance, with steps like you'd use if you were walking across the icing of a cake.

In dance halls everywhere there were cakewalk contests, and the winning couple of the night would receive a big cake with creamy icing for the prize. From those days on, when something was the best in its class, people would say, "That takes the cake!"

As soon as I finished my studies in Sedalia, I decided to follow John Stark back to St. Louis. He had moved his publishing firm there because business was really hopping. The sheet-music business was doing quite well. I was ready to write music full time and dedicate myself completely to my music.

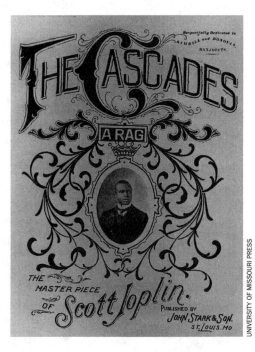

The sheet-music cover for "The Cascades," a piece Scott Joplin wrote especially for the 1904 World's Fair in St. Louis

The next few years were the best years of my life. I married a girl named Belle Hayden, the sister of my good friend Scott Hayden. He was also a ragtime composer, and we played together often at a club owned by Tom Turpin. I bought a house on Delmar Boulevard and settled into the feeling of success. Everything seemed to be going well, like I just couldn't lose, so I wrote another ragtime piece called "Easy Winners."

Of all the tunes I ever wrote, I think that one's my favorite—written at the best time of my life. For the next few years my compositions sold all over the country—in fact, all over the world. Ragtime was being heard in the ballrooms and the saloons of Paris, London, and Vienna. The tunes that started out as background music in little music halls and saloons became the rage on dance floors everywhere.

In 1904 St. Louis hosted the World's Fair. People were coming from far and wide to see the Louisiana Purchase Exposition. My career was at its height, and I had become known as the King of Ragtime. I had achieved what I set out to do in my early days: to express everything I had inside me through my music. I wrote a rag especially for the World's Fair and dedicated it to that great event in the history of St. Louis. The song was called "The Cascades," inspired by a great waterfall in Forest Park that was lit up at night.

This is the essence of my story, and although there was more music and more traveling, you're getting the general sense of my life and of ragtime. The 20th century marched on, and ragtime music faded for a while. Times were changing. People changed, and so did music.

America moved through the Roaring Twenties and the jazz age and into swing, bebop, and rock 'n' roll. We passed through the Great Depression, when the whole country went broke, and were nearly ripped apart at the seams during the two world wars. Then came the civil-rights movement and the emergence of equal rights for women. Through it all, there was music—different kinds of music for Americans in this changing century.

Hollywood rediscovered ragtime when all of that great music was added to the soundtrack of the movie *The Sting*. Ragtime music is a testimony to turn-of-the-century America, and we're safe in assuming that it is here to stay . . . which is more than you can say for me.

I'll be on my way now, but when you hear ragtime music, remember me—Scott Joplin, the Entertainer, the King of Ragtime.

Bobby Norfolk of St. Louis began his career as a National Park Service Ranger, developing and presenting first-person historical narratives for tours at the Gateway Arch in St. Louis. He has won three Emmy Awards for his work on the TV program Gator Tales *and produced three award-winning audiotapes. An accomplished writer and director, Norfolk blends new stories with old favorites as he travels around the world, performing in concerts and giving workshops.*

The Courage of Ed Pulaski

Jim Cogan

This story examines the real, though seemingly incredible, events surrounding forest ranger Ed Pulaski in the summer of 1910. The backdrop of the story, set in the rugged mountains and forests near Wallace, Idaho, is the Great Idaho Fire. Historically accurate, the story reveals the essence of this calamity by focusing on the actions of one man. The addition of fictional dialogue helps illuminate the experience of people in crisis and puts a human face on the qualities of knowledge, duty, cooperation, love, trust, and courage. Though this fictional addition moves the story into the category of American folklore, it preserves the truth of the episode while personalizing actions that have been remembered in near-legendary tones by the people of Idaho and the northern Rockies.

SATURDAY, AUGUST 20, 1910, WAS A DAY EDWARD C. PULASKI WOULD REMEMber for the rest of his life.

Ed worked as a ranger with the Coeur d'Alene National Forest in the rugged mountains of northern Idaho. Each summer he trained firefighters near Wallace, a small town of 3,500 that lay nestled in the deep canyon of the Coeur d'Alene River 15 miles west of the Bitterroot crest. The wild, remote geography surrounding the Coeur d'Alene and St. Joe rivers was covered with an ocean of forest: thick stands of white pine, blue spruce, silver fir, Douglas fir, and tamarack. Big trees, they all but hid the scattered logging and mining camps, the hamlets and railroad towns—Cataldo, Kellogg, Wallace, Mullan, Burke, and Avery. The woods provided the region's 7,000 residents with a respectable livelihood supplying a growing nation with natural materials for homes and businesses.

Every summer, though, thunderstorms would build over the Bitterroot Mountains and throw down bolts of lightning, igniting countless fires that needed to be put out, lest the winds rise to fan them into a conflagration that could wipe out the whole region.

It had been one of the hottest summers on record in the northern Rockies. No rain had fallen since April. The dry lightning storms of June and July sparked more than 2,500 fires across this forest; thousands more burned in central Idaho and Montana. The smoke was so thick, people couldn't see the sun. The mines closed. The economy stopped. Every able-bodied person hustled into the mountains to fight the fires.

And Ed was training them. Tall, handsome, and intelligent, Ed finished his forestry training at Yale, traveled west, found Idaho, and fell in love with the region's beauty. Joining a handful of dedicated professionals in the recently created U.S. Forest Service, he learned to recognize every flower, tree, creek, lake, meadow, ridge, mountain, mine tunnel, timber camp, fishing hole, watering hole, squirrel hole, shack, barn, and pretty girl in the mountains.

He married a beauty too, and when Emma Pulaski had given birth to their first child, Elsie, he had had lakes named for both of them.

Today, standing amid the smoke atop the St. Joe Divide, the usually calm and confident Pulaski fretted. The air was hot . . . too hot. In front of him were 40 men. Like hundreds of others lured to Wallace recently by the promise of work, they had little in common except for the fact that, as far as firefighting went, all of them were green. Most had never seen these tools or steep mountains, let alone forest fires. As soon as they stepped off the Northern Pacific train, Supervisor William Weigle sent them right up to the St. Joe Divide, then told Pulaski to start training them.

The day before, Ed had said goodbye to Emma and Elsie at the Placer Creek trailhead, pulled his two packhorses up the ridge, and met the men. Despite having worked 10 days straight, he approached them with his usual calm, confident, and meticulous manner.

He taught them how to properly use an ax to cut trees and a mattock and shovel to scrape a fire line clear of anything that would burn. He also taught them to communicate and work together. "Be a team. Look to your partner. Help each other out," he preached. "Your lives depend on it."

By midafternoon on the 20th, the men had a line started. Ed's friend Frank Foltz had come up to cook and just about had a meal prepared. One of the men, George Howard, started asking the questions Ed had been expecting.

"What happens if everything around us starts to burn, boss?"

Ed saw the immediate rustle of nervousness run through the men. Putting his thumbs through his suspenders, he smiled and spoke softly. "Down below you to the south, there's a tongue of fire coming toward us now, off Striped Peak. That's where all this smoke is coming from. Behind you, to the north, there's a fire burning at the head of Placer Creek, just south of Wallace, where you came in on the train. If the wind stays down and we can get a wide line cut, there won't be any fuel on the ridge left to burn. We'll be fine."

He paused before giving voice to his next thought. He didn't want to scare the men, but George had asked a good question. "If that wind does blow up, this ridge will become a living hell in minutes. We'll need to get out of here—fast! If you hear me call you, bury your tools in the cache, grab a blanket, line up, and follow me . . . if you want to live."

Looking at the fear and panic coloring each man's face, Ed added a small prayer, then calmed the men with the words, "But everything is as still as a reflection in a lake right now, so don't worry. Take a break. Get some grub."

Ed never had any grub that day. The only thing he would eat were those last words.

A few minutes later, about 4 p.m., a pressure-driven wind roared east off the Palouse plains and funneled into the west-sloping canyons of the Bitterroots. Small fires raced across the forest floor, igniting brush, spewing embers into the trees, climbing up tree trunks. Pushed by a Pacific storm, this hot, dry mass of air became a gale that fanned the larger fires into maelstroms.

Entire ridges burst into flame. The superheated air ignited anything combustible and instantly turned the sap of the conifers into steam. Swaths of trees literally exploded sky-ward, sending limbs thousands of feet into the air. Red-orange arcs of flame leaped from ridge to ridge, propelled by a wind that topped 70 miles per hour. Smoke billowed up 70,000 feet. People on ships in the Pacific could see the clouds. Burning brands dropped out of the skies over eastern Montana.

Ed Pulaski near the mouth of the tunnel that saved his men's lives

Even the worst-case scenario for Coeur d'Alene did not conjure up this reality. The end of the world had come to northern Idaho.

Far up the ridge to the east, the men were grabbing food in the smoky stillness. Only Ed picked out the distant cannonades of the blowup. He stood silent for a moment . . . listening . . . looking. The treetops slowly began to sway toward the east. Then the smoke began to move. The heat increased. The men looked up, saw Ed, and stopped talking. Now everyone could hear the distant roar.

"Stash those tools, grab your grub, take some blankets, and line up," yelled the suddenly animated Pulaski. "Put the blanket under one arm, and place your other arm on the man in front of you. Let's move! Frank, bring the horses up behind."

They ran to the north, down a steep ridge, toward Wallace. Ed hoped he could pick up the Placer Creek trail and get off the mountain and into Wallace before the fire hit.

He had experienced one firestorm years earlier, and that was enough. By the time this one made it to the Wallace area, it would be a tower of flames, sucking up air, feeding itself, creating its own weather, reaching miles ahead with flaming debris and incinerating everything in its path.

It had already gotten that bad. One engineer coming out of Kellogg saw a whole section of the St. Joe turn into a mountain of flame. "The flames went straight up . . . 200, 300 feet," the engineer said later. "Then I felt this rush of air through the cab toward the fire. The flames began to twist higher. It looked just like a tornado. I saw trees coming out of the top . . . flaming arrows they were. I opened the throttle and ran at top speed toward Wallace, sounding the horn all the way."

Wallace was a beehive of activity. Seeing the smoke and feeling the first winds, the town had mobilized. Hospitals were readied. Telegraph operators alerted crews and remote camps. Wooden buildings were torn down lest they add fuel to the fire. Trains started hauling people east as the sky grew dark and the devil winds roared in.

Emma wrapped little Elsie in a blanket and fled from the Pulaski home, a few miles up Burke Canyon just northeast of Wallace. An old slag pond up canyon offered an open, treeless, moist flat for local residents. Looking back, Emma felt the full force of the wind, then saw the entire wall of the canyon above the south side of Wallace burst into flames.

"Ed!" she screamed. Nearly collapsing, she stared at the conflagration, watched it leap across the canyon toward them, took one look at little Elsie, and ran with her neighbors to the relative safety of the pond.

Up on Franklin Ridge the wind now bent trees to the point of snapping. The smoke poured past them, parting now and then to give Ed a glimpse of Wallace. The east end of town was in flames! The Placer Creek fire was blowing up . . . coming right up the mountain for them.

"We're not going to make Wallace in that direction, boys!" he yelled.

Suddenly the St. Joe Divide crackled behind them. They all stopped and turned. A huge wall of flame reached up from the north side and consumed the entire ridge line where everyone had been standing just a few minutes earlier. The heat was so intense that hair singed, clothing started to smoke, exposed skin blistered. Men screamed. Some fell to their knees. They knew they were trapped. Everyone thought he was going to die.

Everyone except Ed Pulaski. Despite the terrifying thoughts created by the vision of Wallace burning—*Did the fire hit Burke Canyon yet? Where are Emma and Elsie? Did they make it to the slag pond?*—Ed kept cool. There was one hope. He knew of an old mine tunnel in the upper reaches of the West Fork of Placer Creek. It was about 100 feet long. A small creek trickled across its floor. Maybe they could get there before the fires met.

"Come on, men," he said. "I know a place we can hide. Keep an eye on the man in front of you, and let's head straight down this slope until we hit the creek bottom."

The men plummeted down the loose slope—running, stumbling, sliding, but somehow staying together. Visibility was almost zero. Reaching the canyon floor more than a thousand feet below, Ed herded them down the now-dry creek bed until he saw a trickle of water coming in on the left.

"The War Eagle Mine!" he yelled. "Here it is. Get in there. Drop down to the ground. Splash water over your clothes. Cover yourselves with blankets. Keep your lips close to the water; the air's better there. Let's move!"

George Howard stopped at the timbered entrance dug into the hillside, turned to Ed, and hollered, "We'll all cook in there. I'm not goin' in!"

Ed would have to do a little persuading. He always carried a .45 strapped to his belt for just such occasions. Pulling it out, he leveled it at George and said, "You might die in there, or you can die out here. Take your pick!"

George dived through the tunnel, and the rest of the men followed. The horses were already too burned to be saved. Ed shot them. With Frank's help, he set a few timbers across the entrance and stretched the remaining blankets across them.

"That's to keep the air in and the fire out. Now, everybody drop, and stay calm. Things are going to get pretty nasty any minute now."

They could all hear the roar. It sounded like a hundred freight trains coming around the bend all at once. Ed could see the blankets being sucked outward by the approaching storm. Some burst into flames. He beat them out.

"I can't breathe," cried someone at the back. Suffocation was the biggest killer in all fires. Ed stayed at the entrance, patching holes and dousing flames, getting scorched and choked in the process.

The world outside exploded. The fires met right near the mine and leapt skyward. The 2,000-degree heat consumed everything right down to the mineral soil. A few burning trees fell across the outside of the tunnel. The wail of the firestorm drowned out the cries of the men, their gasps, coughs, moans, thoughts all swallowed by the scream of the fire.

Then all grew still inside the tunnel. The fire raced east, toward Montana, lighting up the approaching night and leaving behind a scene of utter devastation.

The people of Wallace made a heroic stand and saved half the town. A freak wind shift helped blow the fire to the north, around Burke Canyon instead of through it. Emma, Elsie, and all the residents were safe.

After spending the night watching the terrible beauty of wildfire dancing along the St. Joe Divide, Emma and her neighbors walked out of the pond to find that the fire had missed their homes. Looking up at the St. Joe Divide, all they could see was black earth, rock, and smoke. Few trees were left standing. The entire divide was destroyed.

The neighbors stayed close. Emma broke into tears. Many of her neighbors had friends and relatives in the forest, but right now they turned to Emma. Things didn't look good for Ed.

The silence of the War Eagle Mine seemed eternal until George Howard coughed. Other coughs followed. Smoke-filtered light poured in through the charred tunnel entrance. Men began to move and slowly realized they weren't dreaming. They had survived.

The man who had saved them lay in a crumpled heap at the entrance. George Howard struggled to his feet and saw Ed Pulaski's body.

"The boss is dead," he said. "Let's get out of here." And he stepped over the body.

"Like hell I'm dead," came a gasping reply from below him. Then George heard the click of metal and looked down the business end of Ed's .45.

"Help me up. I can't see. Did everyone make it? Don't go out there yet. Too dangerous."

With that, Ed collapsed. He was burned and blind and could barely talk. Reviving him with sips of water, George propped him up. Ed spoke again.

"We are going . . . to walk . . . out of here," he said haltingly. "But single file. It's going to be damned hot out there. Lots of fire still in the trees, in the holes on the ground, falling snags everywhere. George, how are your eyes?"

"Great, boss. Why?"

"I need you to walk with me at the front," Ed whispered hoarsely. "You're going to see for two. With your sight and my memory, I think we can get out of here OK. It's three miles to Wallace, so let's get moving."

Led by this unusual man, 33 survivors walked out of the War Eagle Mine and through the charred wreckage of Placer Creek. Seven lay behind in the back of the tunnel. Their lives had run out with their air. Many of the survivors were horribly burned. Some walked nearly naked.

Boots smoldered and disintegrated in the hot ashes. As they staggered into Wallace, shouts of alarm and cries of disbelief echoed through the streets. Townspeople came running. One by one the men were led away to Hope and Providence hospitals.

After the last man was cared for, Ed asked George to lead him up to Burke Canyon. Making his way through the narrows, Ed could hear the voices, feel the life there.

"What do you see, George?" asked Ed.

"Houses. People . . . and a woman running toward us," he replied.

"Ed! Ed! Is that you?" Emma ran toward the men as fast as her legs could carry her. She saw them coming and recognized her husband in a second.

"Emma? Emma!"

Ed could feel her hands in his again. Emma looked at the charred figure of the man she loved—wounded badly but alive and kicking—the most wonderful sight she ever did see.

George Howard sat down on the roadside and cried like a baby.

A smokechaser, left, speaks with Ed Pulaski in 1924. The firefighter carries a Pulaski tool on his shoulder.

Two days later that Pacific storm arrived and drenched the region with rain. The Great Idaho Fire of 1910 was history. It killed 85 people, burned dozens of towns, mines, and camps. More than six million acres of virgin forest went up in flame and smoke. The ash traveled halfway around the world, blotting out summer in most of the Northeastern United States, changing the climate even in Europe.

The people of northern Idaho, long accustomed to cooperation in the face of adversity, put their lives back together. They rebuilt their towns, established new logging camps, reopened the mines. Train whistles soon came calling over Lookout Pass at the Bitterroot crest. Placer Creek played its sweet music all of the following summer, even if the sounds turned bittersweet at the War Eagle Mine.

The 33 men saved by the courage of Ed Pulaski told this story again and again. And although Ed Pulaski became something of a legend, the story is true.

Ed survived. His eyesight returned. Though he was plagued with lung problems the rest of his life, his keen mind and kind heart remained steadfast.

A few years later he developed a firefighting tool that would save many more lives. Mounted on the end of a wooden handle, it had an ax on one side that tapered to a heavy adzlike hoe on the other. Today it's the standard firefighting tool for urban, industrial, and forest firefighters all over the world. There's a story in it too because to this day it's still officially called . . . a Pulaski.

Thirty years in the mountain West as a student, a naturalist, a historian, a journalist, a teacher, a father, and a performer shaped Jim Cogan's vivid, animated style of telling. Now touring from Ojai, California, Cogan weaves history, legend, folklore, and myth into his retellings and original pieces. Cogan has performed at festivals, fairs, conventions, colleges, and schools. He teaches at educational conferences and workshops and specializes in children's programming (Storytime, KCET-TV, Los Angeles), literacy programs, and library concerts.

The Laundry Man Who Overthrew the Qing Dynasty

Charlie Chin

Like many legends, this one is based on historical fact. At the turn of the century Chinese immigrants living in Canada and the United States donated immense amounts of money to the revolution led by Dr. Sun Yat-sen against the Manchu Qing Dynasty. Dr. Sun, who was known as the Father of the Chinese Republic, is the main character in countless Chinese-American folk tales that describe events said to have taken place during his tours of the United States. As a teenager I spent my summer months with my immigrant father, working in a Chinese hand laundry as a shirt presser. To help pass the time during their 12-hour shifts at the ironing tables, my father and the other Chinese men told stories. I first heard this one in the summer of 1958.

NOW, EVERYONE KNOWS THAT DR. SUN YAT-SEN LED THE REVOLUTION OF 1911 and became the first president of the Republic of China, but few know the story of the man who was really responsible for bringing down the Qing Dynasty.

The last ruler of the Qing Dynasty was a Manchu empress, of a people from beyond the north of China, and she didn't care what happened to her Chinese subjects. She was old, weak, and easily frightened. That's why by the year 1900 a number of foreign nations had boldly cut up China like a ripe melon and ruled whole provinces as they pleased. The people suffered, and everywhere in China there was talk of revolution.

During that time Dr. Sun Yat-sen, an educated man and a great leader, founded the Young China party. Its purpose was to replace the Qing Dynasty with a democratic republic. For this the Manchu government labeled Dr. Sun a traitor and put a price on his head. He was forced to flee overseas and hide with friends in Europe and America. When he traveled through the United States, Dr. Sun used every occasion to spread his message of ending Qing Dynasty rule and forming a republic to the Chinatown family and benevolent associations.

Many of those who listened agreed with him. He stirred the hearts of the overseas Chinese so deeply that thousands reached into their pockets and gave freely to finance the coming revolution. One day in 1910, just after he had finished a passionate speech in the city of Chicago, Dr. Sun was approached by a humble Chinese laundry man who offered him a cloth sack.

Dr. Sun asked what was in the bag, and the little man said, "Dr. Sun, I have worked as a laundry man for more than 30 years in America. When I was a boy, China's poverty forced me to leave my family and look for work in another land. I had hoped to return home to China someday as a rich man. But after listening to your speech, I see that China's fight for freedom is more important than my personal happiness. I give you my life savings."

Dr. Sun was very impressed. The money was every cent that the laundry man had in the world. Dr. Sun took the bag respectfully with both hands and said, "On behalf of China, I thank you." Dr. Sun passed the bag to his assistant and turned to go, but the man held his arm and made a request.

"Dr. Sun, I give this money for the cause, but there is something special I want you to use it for."

Dr. Sun stopped and asked, "Loyal son of China, what are your instructions?"

The laundry man explained, "I have heard of a new thing. It is called an airplane. It is a machine that can carry a man inside and fly. I would like this money used to buy one of these airplanes for the army of the revolution."

Dr. Sun nodded and asked, "And what will be the purpose of this machine?"

The laundry man described his plan: "With it someone could fly over the Forbidden City and drop a bomb on the empress's head."

Dr. Sun was an honorable man, and he would never betray a supporter's trust, so he turned to his assistant and said, "Please write this down. This money is to be used only for purchasing an airplane that will fly over the Forbidden City and drop a bomb on the empress's head." He thanked the laundry man again and went to his next appointment.

Dr. Sun Yat-sen's people carried out his orders and went about trying to buy an airplane, but in 1910 there weren't very many airplanes in existence. It took several months before an airplane for sale was found in California, and the laundry man's money was used to buy it.

But none of Dr. Sun's people knew how to fly an airplane. In any event, it was useless sitting in California, so they decided to send the plane by ship across the sea to China.

When the freight ship carrying the airplane arrived in Canton, China, the local people saw the strange device being loaded onto the dock and asked what it was. Such large crowds were gathering to see this novelty that the Chinese newspapers sent reporters to the docks to find out what was going on.

When the reporters asked the ship's captain what the large thing was and why it had been sent to China, he really couldn't say. He had no idea how it worked, and until the machine had been brought aboard his vessel, he had never seen anything like it. All he could do was read the instructions that had been sent along with the airplane. He announced to the reporters and the waiting crowd, "This is an airplane—a machine that can carry a person and fly in the air. The airplane is being sent to the patriotic revolutionaries of China for the purpose of flying over the Forbidden City and dropping a bomb on the head of the empress."

The reporters asked, "When will the pilot come to fly the airplane?"

The captain guessed out loud, "I suppose he will be on the next ship." But of course there really wasn't anybody who knew how to fly it. The people on the dock who heard the captain's words cheered, and the next morning the story was in every newspaper in the country.

As it happened, the empress was having breakfast when she read the newspaper story of the airplane's arrival. In a panic she called all of her ministers and advisers and said to them, "The newspapers say that Dr. Sun's revolutionaries have an airplane. Is that true?"

Next she said, "And the newspapers say they are going to fly it over the Forbidden City and drop a bomb on my head. Can they do this?"

The ministers threw themselves to the floor, banged their heads against the tiles, and howled in sorrow. "Your Highness, against such an attack, the palace guards are helpless. There is nothing we can do to protect your imperial person."

Realizing that there was no way to stop the revolutionaries from attacking her, even in her own bed, she told her ministers to contact the rebels and tell them that she would surrender.

So the Qing Dynasty fell, the Manchu people left, and Dr. Sun Yat-sen became the first president of the Republic of China in 1912. If you read the history books, Dr. Sun is the one who gets all the credit, but the old-timers in Chinatown know that it was really a laundry man from Chicago who overthrew the Qing Dynasty.

W. D. "Charlie" Chin has performed, composed, written, and taught for more than 30 years. In honor of his lifelong interest in collecting and performing Chinese and Chinese-American folk tales, the Smithsonian Institution awarded him a Community Folklore Scholar Certificate in 1989. His book, China's Bravest Girl, *was published by Children's Book Press in 1993. Born and raised in New York City, Chin now lives in San Mateo, California.*

Stagecoach Mary

Sharon Y. Holley

Mary Fields, known as Stagecoach Mary or Black Mary, was a real pioneer of the West. Her story takes place in the late 1800s and early 1900s in Cascade, Montana. Her early life is sketchy and may have included her bondage in slavery since slavery was not abolished in the state of Tennessee until 1865. Her reported connection to the Dunn family is significant in that Mother Amadeus's name before she took her vows was Sarah Therese Dunn. The late actor Gary Cooper, a native of Helena, Montana, heard the stories of Mary Fields as a young boy while visiting relatives in Cascade. He related these memories in an October 1959 Ebony *article that depicts photos of Mary Fields at home in Cascade. This story addresses the migration of African-Americans from Southern slaveholding states to new territories in the West after the Civil War.*

A SMALL WOODEN CROSS IN HILLSIDE CEMETERY OUTSIDE CASCADE, MONTANA, marks the gravesite of Mary Fields. There is no indication on the marker that the grave holds the Western frontier spirit of a six-foot-tall, 200-pound, cigar-smoking, gun-toting, strong, and independent black woman known to many as Black Mary or Stagecoach Mary.

Mary Fields was born in 1832 in Hickman County, Tennessee. The exact date of her birth and the details of her early life are sketchy. Some reports say, however, that she grew up a slave in Tennessee and worked for the Dunn family. After the Civil War she moved with the family to Ohio, where she worked at the convent run by the Ursuline Sisters. Other reports have her on the Mississippi River as a chambermaid on the riverboat *Robert E. Lee* when it raced Steamboat Bill's *Natchez* on June 30, 1870.

Wherever the stories meet, it is Mary Fields's friendship with Mother Amadeus, a nun from the Ursuline convent in Toledo, Ohio, that places her in Western history.

In 1884 Mother Amadeus responded to a plea from Bishop Brondell, the first bishop of Helena, Montana, to go to Montana to minister to the Blackfeet Indians and to establish a school for girls. Unaccustomed to the harsh winters, Mother Amadeus became very ill. When Mary heard of her plight, she hurried to Montana to nurse her back to health and stayed on to help at the mission.

Montana was just a territory in 1884, and there were few black settlers in the area. Mary was a commanding figure whose image stayed in the minds of all she met. She was six feet tall and weighed more than 200 pounds, smoked black cigars, dressed in men's clothing, and wore a .38 strapped to her waist and covered by an apron skirt. Living at St. Peter's Mission, she ran errands for the nuns and began to haul supplies to the mission from Cascade, Montana. As she was coming from town one night with supplies, her wagon overturned, and she was surrounded by wolves. Brandishing her .38, she kept the wolves at bay until morning.

Mary was known to have quite a temper, and she feared neither man nor beast. While she worked at the mission one day, a hired hand refused to take orders from Black Mary and hit her. She challenged him to a gun battle, and when the smoke had cleared, Mary was still standing. Her reputation traveled all the way to Bishop Brondell in Helena, who told Mother Amadeus to let Mary go. It was not the kind of publicity the mission needed.

Mother Amadeus had to do as the bishop ordered—and after 10 years of working with little or no pay, Mary was asked to leave. Mother Amadeus helped Mary open a restaurant close by. But Mary's kind nature to the cowboys and hired hands caused her business to fail, as she gave away more meals than she sold.

Then the U.S. government talked about opening a mail route between St. Peter's Mission and Cascade. With Mother Amadeus's help, Mary got the job, and history records that she was the first African-American woman and the second woman ever to become a stagecoach driver for the U.S. Post Office. Stagecoach Mary was the epitome of the motto "Neither snow nor rain nor heat nor gloom of night stays these couriers from the swift completion of their appointed rounds." For eight years she commanded the two-horse team while driving the stagecoach between St. Peter's Mission and Cascade, always delivering the mail on time. She met every train, and when the winter blizzards came—as they often did in the mountains of Montana—and her trail was impassable by coach, she picked up the mail and hauled it on her back.

In 1903, at the age of 70, Mary gave up the mail route and moved into Cascade, becoming the town's only black resident. In 1910 Mother Amadeus was sent off to open new missions in Alaska. Still feeling the entrepreneurial spirit, Mary began to take in washing and later turned her entire home into a laundry. Mary was still armed, but she had tamed her temper, and she was popular with the residents, enjoying special privileges as the only woman in town allowed to drink and smoke cigars in saloons with men. Legends say that as a man passed the door of the saloon one day, Mary recognized him as someone who owed $2 on his laundry bill. She left her seat, confronted the man, knocked him out with a punch, took the money he owed, and returned to the saloon, proclaiming, "His bill is paid in full."

After her laundry business closed, Mary took to babysitting for some of the townspeople, charging $1.50 a day. She was fond of the Cascade baseball team and was its biggest fan, often honoring home-run hitters with large bouquets of flowers from her garden. The town of Cascade celebrated the birthday of Mary Fields—sometimes twice a year or whenever she'd declare it. Schools and businesses would close for the occasion.

When Stagecoach Mary died in 1914 at age 81, she was mourned by the entire town. They buried her body at the foot of the mountain, by the road that leads to St. Peter's Mission. The late cowboy artist Charlie Russell preserved her image in a pen-and-ink drawing, *A Quiet Day in Cascade*, that hangs in the Cascade Bank.

Sharon Y. Holley is a storyteller and a librarian for the Buffalo and Erie County Public Library in Buffalo, New York. She is a member of Spin-a-Story Tellers of Western New York and a board member of the National Association of Black Storytellers. She performs with Karima Amin as "We All Storytellers." Holley, who incorporates songs, chants, and rap in her performances, is the author of "African-American History Rap," which appears in Talk That Talk: An Anthology of African-American Storytelling, *edited by Linda Goss and Marian Barnes (Simon & Schuster, 1989).*

An ancient motto

THE WORDS "NEITHER SNOW NOR RAIN NOR heat nor gloom of night stays these couriers from the swift completion of their appointed rounds" are not the official motto of the U.S. Postal Service, as its representatives are careful to point out when any of these conditions cause a notable interruption in service. The phrase comes from Herodotus (c. 485–425 B.C.), who used the phrase to describe Persian messengers in his *Histories* (book VIII, chapter 98). It became associated with the U.S. Post Office when it was called into use as an inscription over the front façade of the General Post Office in New York City. The post office, built in 1913, was designed by William Mitchell Kendall of the well-known firm McKim, Mead & White. Kendall himself apparently selected the text for the inscription, which may have garnered so much attention because of its length. At 280 feet, the inscription is probably the world's longest. Each letter is about six feet high.　　　　　　　　　—David Rhoden

The Horse That Went to War

Sheila Dailey

This story describes an experience my mother-in-law, Evelyn Gunn Carroll, had as an 8-year-old girl growing up in Ontario in the years immediately before World War I. The story is special to me because it underscores the emotional toll that war can take as well as the unexpected heroism and personal growth that often occur during war.

IN 1914 CANADA WAS GEARING UP TO SEND MEN AND SUPPLIES TO JOIN THE war at the Western Front in Europe. My mother-in-law, Evelyn Gunn Carroll, was only a young girl of 8 at the time, but she showed the same courage and capacity for sacrifice as did the soldiers who went to war. It all had to do with a horse, and it happened this way:

Evelyn's mother died shortly after giving birth to Evelyn's younger sister, Gertrude. Evelyn was only 2 years old at the time, and her father, a logger, was ill-prepared to raise two young girls alone. It was determined that the maternal grandparents would take Gertrude and the paternal grandparents would take Evelyn.

So Evelyn went to live in southern Ontario with Mary and John Gunn, her dour Scottish grandparents, who ran a hotel in Glamis. Glamis, now a ghost town, was on the Bruce Peninsula, a finger of land jutting out into Lake Huron, and the town was a carriage stop for tourists and other travelers. The land around Glamis is hilly and rock-strewn, and the winters can be fiercely cold. Evelyn remembers seeing horse-drawn sleighs pulling up to the front entrance and visitors tumbling out from under their buffalo robes into the warmth of the hotel.

Evelyn grew up surrounded by the bustle and noise of hotel life. The hotel regulars—besides herself and her grandparents—were an array of hired help for cooking, cleaning, and taking care of the horses. It was a lonely life for a child since there were few children about. Feeling like a loner in the midst of all this activity, Evelyn tended to drift to the horse barn, where the guests' horses were stabled. In the same barn were several carriage horses owned by the hotel.

All the horses were looked after by Dirty Billy. The poor fellow was given that name by the household help because his work in the stalls

135

made him smelly and dirty, and he seldom cleaned himself up. Dirty Billy was Evelyn's friend, and he often talked to her as he worked about the stalls.

One day when Evelyn was 6, Grandmother and Grandfather Gunn bought a new workhorse for the hotel.

Big Jim, Grandmother Gunn, and Evelyn Gunn in 1914

When Evelyn saw Big Jim, it was love at first sight. Her grandparents decided to give her the horse for her own, though he would still be used to haul heavy loads and plow fields around the hotel. After Big Jim's arrival, Evelyn hung around the barn more than ever to offer him a carrot or an apple or just to talk to him. Occasionally she rode him bareback. Big Jim and Evelyn were seldom far from each other. They became best friends.

A year and a half later, in the winter of 1913, rumors of war reached Glamis. By the following spring Canada was preparing to enter the war, and young men from British Columbia to Nova Scotia joined up as patriotism swept the country. People throughout Canada were being asked to donate funds, goods, and time to the war effort.

In late May 1914 all the snows were gone in Glamis, and the apple tree in the yard was in full blossom. One day a man from the government pulled up in a wagon and asked to see Grandmother and Grandfather Gunn. The adults talked for a time, and then Grandmother Gunn went looking for Evelyn.

Finding her with Big Jim, Grandmother began to explain that a man from the army was going around Bruce County to draft strong horses for the war. He had asked if the army could take Big Jim into service. In those early days of the war, horses were still used to haul munitions and even to carry soldiers into battle. Big Jim would be used to pull heavy loads in France. But Big Jim was Evelyn's horse, so she must be the one to decide if he should go. Then Grandmother paused and said quietly, "It would be a way for the Gunns to do their part for the war."

Evelyn's heart sank. Give up Big Jim? Still, everyone she knew was doing something for the war. Even the children at school were rolling bandages and knitting socks for the soldiers. Evelyn struggled with her feelings. The man was waiting for her decision. She wanted to do her part for her country, yet Big Jim was her friend. Finally, reluctantly, she said yes, her horse could go to war.

Grandmother Gunn led Big Jim from the stall, and Grandfather ran for his box camera to capture the moment. Evelyn could only manage a frown for the camera. But as sad as she was to see her friend go, she had a deep sense of satisfaction, knowing she had made a difference in the war effort.

After Big Jim was gone, Evelyn often thought of him, working in the battlefields of France. She realized that since he was doing something for his country, she must too, and she began to roll bandages and learned to knit socks for the soldiers. She and her grade-school friends also made box lunches to sell and donated the proceeds to the war effort.

Evelyn never heard anything more about Big Jim, but of course, she never forgot him. She told me this story as a woman in her eighties, yet her memory of that day is as sharp as the black-and-white photo that Grandfather Gunn took.

Sheila Dailey of Mount Pleasant, Michigan, has been telling stories for 13 years. Two of her special interests are family stories and Great Lakes history. She researches and tells tales from her Irish ancestry and her childhood, and she has produced a tape and curriculum guide, Land of the Sky Blue Waters: Stories and Legends of the Great Lakes *(Storytime Productions, 1986), on early Great Lakes history. Her most recent book,* Putting the World in a Nutshell: The Art of the Formula Tale *(H.W. Wilson, 1994), is a collection of stories for beginning tellers.*

Say Goodbye to Papa: The Regina Sinreich Barton Story

Annette Harrison

This is the story of Regina Sinreich Barton, my husband's mother, now 94 years old and living in Selma, Alabama. In the early 1970s her daughter, Evelyn Weisfeld, asked Regina to write down her immigrant experience to share with Evelyn's eighth-grade class. I based this story on her wonderful account, although I have created dialogue and highlighted the father–daughter relationship. Regina's story is typical of those of European immigrants of the early 1900s. Many came to America from cities, but others, like the Sinreichs, had a more difficult transition because they came from the farm to live in the big city. The story addresses people's burdensome work situations, and listeners begin to understand why workers needed to organize and why child labor was outlawed. By living the experience with Regina, we learn firsthand how hard it could be to assimilate into the American culture.

MAMA WOKE US UP EARLY THAT MORNING: "REGINA! . . . LEON! . . . MARY! . . . Time to get up!"

"So early, Mama?"

"Children, come say goodbye to Papa."

I wondered where Papa was going, and then I remembered. I said with a sinking feeling, "Papa's leaving for America."

"The land of milk and honey," said Leon.

"And the streets are full of gold," I said.

"Yes," said Mama, "where the streets are paved with gold. Hurry, Papa is waiting."

"Mama, why can't I go too? I love milk and honey, and I'm 8 years old, almost all grown up."

"Regina, we lost our money from the drought. We have only enough for Papa and Willy to go. They will find work and send back money, and then we will *all* go to America. Come now; Papa is all packed and ready."

Papa and Willy had eaten a hearty breakfast and were standing beside two large cardboard boxes wrapped up with heavy string. Papa held out his arms, and the three of us ran into them. He gave us one big hug. I loved the way Papa looked . . . big, strong, with his curly red hair and rosy cheeks . . . and he always smelled of the outdoors.

Papa was the youngest of 12 children. He had chosen to stay on the farm and work with Grandpa. But now he was leaving the farm to find work in America.

I looked up into Papa's face, and I saw tears.

"Papa, don't worry," I said. "We'll write you long letters; we'll tell you *everything*. Will you write us back?"

"Tell us about the gold," said Leon, "and the milk and honey."

"I will, and you write too, little Miss Mary," Papa said to his youngest child.

"Goodbye, Papa . . . see you soon . . . don't forget to write!"

That same week we moved away from our farm to my other Grandma and Grandpa's house. It was all right living there, but I thought about the farm a lot. I missed the way the wheat looked when it waved in the wind. I especially missed the harvest celebration. When all the work was done and the wheat had been gathered and was ready to be shipped, Grandpa would give a huge party for all his workers. When the sun went down, they would come in their colorful best clothes, laughing and talking. First there would be a feast, and then the dancing would begin. It was a sight to behold! They danced all night.

Regina Sinreich Barton in 1918, outside Montgomery, Alabama

My life on the farm was relaxed. For fun we would walk and talk and visit friends and relatives. In my family we would sit and talk for hours. In the summer Willy, Leon, and I would go into the forest and pick berries and mushrooms. We could always tell the difference between the poisonous and the edible ones. We would eat as many warm berries as we gathered, and Mama would yell at us. My mama made the best fresh mushroom soup in Austria!

But we weren't always playing. Even when we sat around and talked, we crocheted, sewed, and embroidered. Mama believed that children should never be idle. Even though a woman from the village helped Mama with the household chores, we still had specific duties to perform. All I wanted to do was go outside and play, but instead I was learning how to hold a broom a certain way. If you didn't turn it from side to side, it would get a tail.

Life on the farm was good until the drought came. Then the wheat didn't grow, and the horses, cows, and sheep died of the disease called cholera. Papa said we were penniless, and that was why he and Willy had to go to America.

Papa wrote us from America, but he didn't write about the golden streets or the milk and honey. He told us about his job. Willy, who was 14, went to live in the Midwest, but Papa worked in the garment district in New York City. He made it sound like a good job. He sent money back home so we could save enough to buy tickets to come to America. It took four long years, but finally it happened.

We packed all of our things into boxes so we could go and join Papa in America. We crossed the ocean in a big ship in steerage class. We were in the hold of the ship with 500 people for 12 days. It was a stormy, bumpy trip, and many people got sick. It was smelly, crowded, and unbearably hot. Mama brought some food along, but none of us were hungry. When we finally landed at Ellis Island, everyone cheered.

Papa was waiting for us. But he didn't look like Papa at all. Could four years in America change my handsome, strong father into an old man? Mama cried when she saw him. He looked pale, thin, and sick. His red curly hair looked dull and gray, and his rosy cheeks were gone.

"I'm fine," said Papa. "Don't worry. Now that my family is together, I will be just fine."

But Papa was not fine, he was very ill . . . he had tuberculosis. He coughed all the time and slept when he was not working. For most of his four years in America Papa had bent over his sewing machine, sewing together shirts and pants for 12 hours a day in what was called a sweat-shop. It was very hot, and there was no ventilation.

Papa said that the bosses treated them like slaves. He had slept on the floor of the sweatshop at night and eaten only one meal a day so he could send more money back to Austria. It made me sad and angry that my sweet, kind, gentle papa had to be treated this way.

When he knew we were coming, he rented a three-room apartment in an old tenement building on Delancey Street. The rent was $10 a month. The first time we opened the heavy door, we smelled the awful smell of cooked cabbage, rancid oil, and dirt. We saw peeling wallpaper and worn linoleum and a light bulb hanging from the ceiling.

At first it was hard to sleep because the elevated trains were so noisy at night. But the worst part was the uninvited guests . . . the mice, roaches, and *bedbugs*! We could cope with the mice and the roaches but not the bedbugs. Every Friday morning we would wage war against them. All the tenants would work together, spraying down the walls and the halls of the building with kerosene. Then the bugs would creep out of the walls, mattress springs, furniture . . . from *everywhere*. It was disgusting to watch them crawling all over our things.

We were very poor, but we were never hungry. Somehow we always had food in the house. Mama was a magician in the kitchen. A five-cent soup bone made a huge pot of delicious barley soup that would serve the whole family for a week.

In my school in Austria we spoke German, but in America we could speak only English. Most of the Jewish students could speak Yiddish, but Leon and I had never learned it. It was very hard and frustrating for us. All the foreign students in my grade were put into one class. An Italian girl and I were the only clean heads in the class—the rest had to wash their hair every night with kerosene because they had lice.

I loved my teacher. She was a saint! She insisted on speaking English in class, but outside of school she spoke German with me and became my friend. She would come to our apartment on Sundays with a picnic basket and take me on little trips around New York. We'd go to the park, to the zoo, and to see plays. One day she took me to the Bronx Opera House to see *Pollyanna*.

But Papa grew sicker and couldn't work any longer. So I had to quit school and find a job.

"Mama, it isn't fair! I love school! What about my friends? Why is Papa sick anyway? I hate America!"

But there was no choice. I was the eldest child living with my family, so I had to go to work to help support the family. I understood this, but still I cried and cried.

So there I was, Regina Sinreich, a 14-year-old Austrian immigrant living in America, the land of opportunity, and I had to go to work! I envied my school friends when I saw them rushing off to school each day.

Papa went into a TB hospital, and I went to work. I was an errand girl on 42nd Street for Mr. Schwartz's upholstery shop. Mr. Schwartz was an immigrant too, and his English wasn't any better than mine. I reminded him of his daughter, so he hired me. The company made draperies and upholstered furniture for very rich families in New York.

"Regina, take these trimmings to the Steinway home"—where the famous piano people lived.

"Regina, go to Riverside Drive, and take this package to . . ."

I was what was called a runner. When the men needed extra material or trimmings, I would deliver them. I got to go inside many mansions, and to me they looked like castles. One day I was sent with a package to Carnegie Hall. I heard violins and beautiful music, and I was enchanted! I forgot all about delivering the package and sat down in the corner of the hall, enjoying the music and eating my lunch. I stayed all day. Mr. Schwartz sent the police to find me. There I sat—it was five o'clock in the evening, and I was still listening to the beautiful music!

So there I was, Regina Sinreich, a 14-year-old Austrian immigrant living in America, the land of opportunity, and I had to go to work! I envied my school friends when I saw them rushing off to school each day.

I was able to go to night school for a while, but then Mama needed me to work at night too. Mama was pregnant again, and she was sick all the time, so I had to help her. We worked together, making silk bows for the inside of men's hats. We got 10 cents a gross: a gross was 144 bows.

Poor Leon. He was always tired because he had to walk 25 blocks to pick up the material and 25 blocks to take back the bows. Who had five cents for carfare? He also helped out by delivering newspapers before and after school. We all had to help support the family.

I never had any money of my own, but my friends and I still found ways to have fun. Every Saturday we'd walk to Wanamaker's Department Store and spend hours going up and down the escalators. Fun for free!

I was 15 when Papa died. Our relatives in Montgomery, Alabama, sent us money to come and live with them. We buried Papa in New York City. All of us huddled around his gravestone.

"Goodbye, my beloved papa. Rest peacefully."

We headed south.

"Mama," asked Leon, "what is it like in Montgomery, Alabama?"

"I don't know, my son, but I do know it will be better than our life on Delancey Street in New York."

When we arrived, our relatives gave us a warm welcome. The weather was sunny, and when I looked around, I saw trees, flowers, and beautiful scenery again. I said to myself, "Heaven couldn't have been prettier!"

I knew I had finally come home.

Annette Harrison of St. Louis has been a storyteller and an educator for 17 years. She is the co-author of Storytelling Activities Kit *(Prentice Hall, 1992) and the author of the award-winning* Easy-to-Tell Stories for Young Children *(National Storytelling Press, 1992). She is co-host of* Gator Tales, *a weekly children's television program. Harrison performs and teaches in schools and at conferences across the country and is writing a book on conflict resolution and storytelling.*

Rider on an Orphan Train

David Massengill

For 75 years, from just before the Civil War to the eve of the Great Depression, the orphan train ran west, carrying thousands of unwanted, often abandoned children from the slums of Northeastern cities. The train's purpose was to give these children a better chance in life by placing them with adopting families in the Western states. The families agreed to educate them until they were 16 and to raise them as their own. In the main, the children were wanted for their labor, but at least they were wanted.

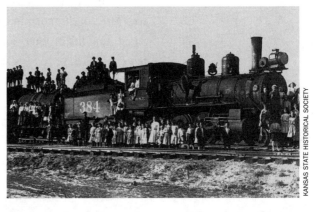

In the mid-1850s the Reverend C. L. Brace had founded a Children's Aid Society in New York City to provide food and shelter for abandoned children. There were so many orphans that only a small portion could be placed in foster homes. In order to survive, the rest often had to shift for themselves. Some sold newspapers or shined shoes, others ran with gangs, some begged, and many resorted to crime. Laws were harsh. Children as young as 12 could be hanged for stealing food. The Reverend Brace felt there had to be a better way.

Farmers out West were always in need of extra laborers, so Brace conceived of an orphan train to help place these children where they might be wanted. Ideally it was to be a mutual medicine; the reality was sometimes cold.

Typically the orphans were put on a train and sent across the country from Maine to Texas. Along the way the children could be adopted by any willing farmer or family. Often the orphans were lined up, and people would pick and choose which child they liked. Imagine the feelings of the children who were not picked, town after town.

Those orphaned children were accompanied on the train by an agent from the Children's Aid Society to see that they were protected and well-placed. The agent's intent was to make sure that the children weren't used just for labor. Sometimes investigations were called for and children relocated. The agent also tried to keep brothers and sisters together—or at least in the same community—but sometimes they were separated, never to see or hear from each other again.

Nearly 150,000 children rode the orphan train during its 75-year history.

The orphan trains helped populate states along the way: New York, Ohio, Indiana, Michigan, Illinois, and Wisconsin. A greater number of the children were delivered to settle Iowa, Missouri, Minnesota, Nebraska, and Kansas. In later years they were also sent to Texas, Colorado, and California. Over the years nearly 150,000 children were given a new start with new families in the mostly rural settings of the Midwest and the West.

By the 1920s the conditions that had supported the orphan train were changing. The demand for farm labor waned as infant survival rates in the Midwest rose. Most states began taking over their own foster care. The last orphan train traveled to Missouri in 1929, capping a 75-year run.

My own interest in the subject and the consequent song were sparked when I was contacted by one Don McClanahan, an orphan whose birth name was Massengill, born in the era of the last orphan train. He had been separated from his brother James as a child, and he thought I might be James. I felt compelled to tell his story in song, set in 1929.

Each lost child had a story. Here is one.

ONCE I RODE AN ORPHAN TRAIN,
And my brother did the same.
They split us up in Missouri;
James was 5 and I was 3.

He got taken by some pair,
But for me they did not care.
We were brave and did not cry
When they made us say goodbye.

That was the last I saw of him
Before some family took me in.
But I swore I'd run away
And find my brother James someday.

I went back when I was grown
To see how old the Children's Home.
And I asked for to see my file
Of when I was an orphan child.

"It's sad," they say, "there's been a flood—
File washed away in Missouri mud."
Sometimes life is a stone wall;
You either climb or else you fall.

In every town on every street,
All the faces that I meet—
And I wonder, could one be
My brother James come back to me?

Though I don't know where he's gone,
I have searched my whole life long.
Now I roam from town to town,
But there's no orphan Lost and Found.

Sometimes I dream a pleasant sight:
My brother James and I unite.
Remembering our last goodbye,
No longer brave, we start to cry.

I hope he lives a life of ease,
All his days a soft warm breeze.
May he sit upon a throne,
And may he never sleep alone.

Once I rode an orphan train,
And my brother did the same.
They split us up in Missouri;
James was 5 and I was 3.

Moderate; ♩ = approx. 92

1. Once I rode____ an or-phan train and my broth - er did the same. They split us up____ in Mis-sour - i. James was five ____ and I was three. —bye. That was the last____ I saw of him be-fore _ a fam - ily took me in. But I swore I'd run a - way____ and find ___ my broth - er James _ one _ day. —lone.

David Massengill is a native son of Bristol, Tennessee, where he once chased a bobcat and vice versa. He now lives in New York City, where he chases dreams and catches a few. The Roches, Joan Baez, and Nancy Griffith have recorded his songs. He accompanies his ballads on mountain dulcimer and guitar and tells stories about family, mountain folk, and the times. His recording Coming Up for Air *(Flying Fish, 1992) won a New York Music Award for best independent album.*

145

The Herring Shed

Jay O'Callahan

This story of World War II is seen through the eyes of 14-year-old Maggie Thomas. Maggie works in a herring shed and becomes aware that her nation, Canada, is helping to feed England during the war. The story is partly about her coming of age but also about the importance of community. It is also a story about the blindness of war. Maggie's mother is blind but sees more clearly than those who would make war. I met Maggie Thomas and Charlie Robertson, and we talked over a period of a month. By then Maggie was in her sixties and blind. I based the story on my conversations with Maggie and Charlie. The story is also an attempt to capture the beauty of the land and the hardness of rural life.

NOVA SCOTIA. WORLD WAR II. THIS IS CAPE TORMENTINE. THAT'S THE NORTHumberland Strait down there, and way beyond it is Prince Edward Island. It's six in the morning, spring here. All these people in the farmhouses around are up, and tonight they'll be turning on their radios to listen to the news about the war. We've all got people over there.

That's Maggie Thomas who just came out on the porch. She's 15 now. She worked in the herring shed last year, and the season's beginning again this morning—one hour from now, seven o'clock. She's the one to tell you about the herring shed.

I'm Maggie Thomas. I couldn't sleep last night. I was thinking about last season at the herring shed. I'll tell you, and you'll know why I couldn't sleep. I got to be down there in one hour. Oh, before I tell you, that's Papa's boat. See? Out in the strait with the brown-and-white sail. The best thing about the war is there's no gasoline, so you make your own sail. I helped Papa.

Well, let me tell you about last season. As a girl of 14, I was very, very keen to take on the work in the herring shed. In years before, my brother, Harry, had worked there, but he was fighting in the war so I got the job in the herring shed. At seven in the morning I stepped into the shed—Peg to my right, Mrs. Fraser across. Peg is 15, and she has long black braids and merry eyes, and Mrs. Fraser has the longest nose I ever saw and the nicest smile. She's my boss, a widow Mama's age.

"Maggie?"

"Yes, Mrs. Fraser."

"Now, Maggie, I know your brother, Harry, worked here, but just let me explain everything. The great big barrel outside—that's the pickle barrel, and the herring come right down on the slides. See? They're coming down now right onto the zinc table. You get on the rubber apron. That's it. You don't want to be wet because then you'll be cold. All right. Now, what you want to do is put 18 of the herring on the rod—it's called stringing it—and you put the rod on the rack there, and Corner Murdock will come and bring it to the drying shed. You know Corner?"

"Yes. He has a hole in his fence, so his cows are always on the corner."

"That's right. All day he's sipping at a vanilla bottle. Gets kind of silly. Pay no attention."

"I won't."

"Fine. Now, you pick up the rod like this, put your thumb in the gill, open it up, and slip the herring right onto the rod. Wait a minute. There's a rhythm: Thumb in the gill, open the mouth, slip it on the rod in the herring shed. Thumb in the gill, open the mouth, slip it on the rod in the herring shed. All right?"

"Yes. I can do it." I gave Peg and Mrs. Fraser a nod, and I picked up a rod and began the work in the herring shed. "Thumb in the gill, open the mouth, slip it on the floor . . . I'm sorry."

"Slow, Maggie. Slow. Slow."

"Yes, I will. Thumb in the gill, open the mouth. There, I got it on. Don't look at me. Thumb in the gill, open the mouth, slip it on. I've got it. I'm all right, Peg." Thumb in the gill, open the mouth, slip it on the rod in the herring shed. Thumb in the gill, open the mouth, I was doing the work in the herring shed. Eighteen on a rod, put the rod on the rack, pick up a rod without any slack, and go on with the work in the herring shed. Thumb in the gill, open the mouth, the hours passed by in the herring shed.

"Peg, I know we've got to do a lot for 45 cents, but how much?"

"What you do, Maggie, is a hundred rods. That's called a bundle, and that's about 45 cents."

"A hundred rods? That's 1,800 fish. It'll take me all summer."

"No, it won't. You'll do a bundle in a week or so. You're fast."

"I better get a lot faster." Thumb in the gill, open the mouth, slip it on the rod in the herring shed. Thumb in the gill, open the mouth, it was getting so cold in the herring shed. The floor was dirt, the sea to our backs, and the door was open so Corner Murdock could pick up the racks and bring them across to the drying shed.

"Peg, I don't want to complain, but I can't feel my feet. Honest!"

"Well, it's almost lunch. Just dance or something. Go ahead."

"Well, I will." Thumb in the gill, open the mouth—I can't get it on the rod this way. Slip it on the rod in the herring shed. Thumb in the gill, open the mouth . . . oh, at last it was noon in the herring shed.

We stepped outside, and the sun was warm. Our lunch was a potato and a herring without its head. We talked of the war and the farms around and then went back to the cold, cold ground of the herring shed. Thumb in the gill, open the mouth, slip it on the rod in the herring shed. I finished the day, my very first day in the herring shed.

"Thank you, Peg. Thanks, Mrs. Fraser. A quarter. Oh, thank you. I'm faster than Harry."

I ran on home, straight by the sea, glad to be free of the cold of the herring shed. Charlie Robertson's wheat was tiny and green in the evening light, a sight to be seen.

"Hello, Charlie."

Charlie Robertson is the most wonderful farmer. He's the kindest man. You've got to say his name right—Charlie Robertson. He's a Scotsman and proud of it.

"Charlie, you didn't have to come over."

"Well, of course I did. You finished the day. You did a bundle."

"Oh, I didn't do a bundle, Charlie, but I did more than half a bundle. I'm faster than Harry."

"Oh, of course you're faster than Harry. No question about that."

"I was looking at your wheat. It looks good."

"Well, you know, I told you. There are wet seasons and dry seasons and good seasons. It's going to be a good season."

"I think it will. I'm going to show my mother the quarter. I'll see you later."

"I hope so, Maggie."

I ran home, up the porch steps, but I didn't go in. I turned around, and I looked at the herring shed. It was my herring shed now. Not just Harry's and Mama's and everybody's. It was mine.

I was going to run in and say, "Look, Mama." It's silly, but we all do it. Mama's gone blind, the way her mama did and her mama before her. They say someday I might go blind. Anyway, I knew just where Mama would be. She'd be sitting on the couch, right by the fire, kneading the bread. I opened the door quietly. I don't know what it was. Maybe it was making the quarter. Mama's pretty and young, but she looks so frail.

"Mama! Open your hand."

"Maggie! You finished the day, dear. Come over. I'm so proud of you,

Maggie. I know it's cold. And aren't they wonderful, Mrs. Fraser and Peg? I suppose Corner Murdock's still got his vanilla bottle. Don't tell your father. He doesn't think that's funny. All right? You can have my hand. A quarter! You're faster than Harry. You take it. You're wonderful. Oh, I hear your father, Maggie. You show it to him."

Well, Papa came in, and he was stringing the herring net across the room. It divided the room. He did it to mend the net. Papa doesn't frown, and he doesn't smile, but I knew he was proud of me.

"Look, Papa, a quarter. I'm faster than Harry; I'm faster. No, I want you to take it, Papa. I want you to take it. I'm helping like everybody."

Well, Papa took it, and that night for a change I did all the talking at supper. I told them about everything—about Mrs. Fraser and Peg and Corner Murdock and his vanilla bottle. Papa didn't think that was so funny. I was eating my chicken to the rhythm. Thumb in the gill, open the mouth, slip it on the rod in the herring shed. I must have sung it 50 times for Papa. Thumb in the gill, open the mouth, slip it on the rod in the herring shed.

"Thanks, Maggie, very much. I've got hold of it now."

"You're welcome, Papa."

After supper we did the dishes, and Papa went over and snapped the radio on. They were talking about Dunkirk, and so many people were killed there. Papa went over and snapped the radio right off because that's where we thought Harry was.

I've never gone to sleep so fast in my life. I dreamed of Harry, and he was far from dead. I could see him with that wild red hair, laughing at the cold in the herring shed.

At seven in the morning I was back in the shed—Peg to my right, Mrs. Fraser across. I gave them a nod, and I picked up a rod and went on with the work in the herring shed. Eighteen on a rod, put the rod on a rack, pick up a rod without any slack, and a week went by in the herring shed.

I was going fast one day, and Peg shouted, "You can do a bundle today, Maggie! Keep it up!"

"I will! I will!"

Thumb in the gill, open the mouth, slip it on the rod in the herring shed. Thumb in the gill, open the mouth . . . I did it! I did a bundle in the herring shed!

"Thank you, Mrs. Fraser. Forty-five cents. Thanks, Peg. See you later."

I was so happy and proud. And I'm glad it happened, because the next day was terrible in the herring shed.

We were working away. Thumb in the gill, open the mouth, and the rector came into the herring shed in his odd, shy way. The rector's got the worst job. He's 26 and has never been a rector before. Whenever anyone dies in the war, the station agent gives the telegram to the rector, and it's got so no one wants to see the rector coming up the path. Well, he's sandy-haired, and he leaned forward. "Maggie, could you come outside?"

I knew my brother, Harry, was dead. For a moment I couldn't move. I saw the telegram outside the shed. It was at Dunkirk.

"Thank you, Rector."

"I'm sorry, Maggie. I'm going to take you home."

"No . . . please. I don't want to go home. I'm sorry, Rector. I won't be any good to Mama like this. Let me get my feet on the ground. I would be very glad if you'd come tonight, Rector, with everybody."

And I went on with the work in the herring shed. Thumb in the gill, open the mouth, I went on with the work in the herring shed.

That night at home the neighbors came around. Mrs. Fraser brought pie; Peg brought bread. "Thanks, Mrs. Fraser. Come on, everybody. Sit down."

We must have had 30 people sitting in the kitchen. We just had the one kerosene lantern. People were telling funny stories and sad ones about Harry, and we were laughing and crying. All of a sudden the door opened, just about six inches.

"Mama! It's all right, Mama. It's Harry! It's Harry!"

I threw the door open and threw my arms around him. "Harry!"

"It's me, Corner Murdock, Maggie! It's Corner Murdock!"

"Oh, I'm sorry, Corner. I'm so sorry. Come on in."

Oh, I was so embarrassed. I wanted to run out into the night. Well, Mrs. Fraser took care of me, and Papa took care of Corner. Papa even gave Corner a whole bottle of vanilla. He never did that before.

I couldn't tell anyone why I did it. Well, I did it because of the way Corner opened the door. Ever since my brother, Harry, was about 8, he'd open the door six inches until everybody looked, and then he'd throw the door open and come in. That's what Corner had done.

I was so glad to be alone when everybody left. I went up to my room and looked out at the stars. "Why did you take him, God? Do you need him up there?"

And for hours I looked out into the blackness. I was looking at the strait, and I was trying to find the burning ship. For a hundred years, they say, there has been a burning ship out there. They say the people won't give up until they find a port.

Charlie Robertson saw it. Mama saw it before she went blind. And Harry saw it on his birthday. Well, it wasn't there.

At seven in the morning I was back in the shed—Peg to my right, Mrs. Fraser across. Peg held my hand, and Mrs. Fraser gave me a big hug. The strange thing was that I felt so numb, I just wanted to eat and sleep and work. So I went on with the work. Thumb in the gill, open the mouth, slip it on the rod in the herring shed. He lay in the ground, in the cold, cold ground, the ground that was cold as the herring shed. Thumb in the gill, open the mouth, slip it on the rod in the herring shed. Thumb in the gill, open the mouth, the weeks went by in the herring shed. Thumb in the gill, open the mouth . . . I didn't realize it, but I was so fast one day, Peg shouted, "You can do two bundles, Maggie!"

"I will! I will!"

Thumb in the gill, open the mouth, slip it on the rod in the herring shed. Eighteen on a rod, a hundred to a bundle, 45 cents. I did it. I did two bundles in the herring shed.

"Oh, thank you so much. Ninety cents, Mrs. Fraser. We'll buy a whole herd of cows. I'll see you later."

I ran on home, straight by the sea, glad to be free of the cold of the herring shed. Charlie Robertson's wheat was tall and green in the evening light, a sight to be seen.

"Hello, Charlie."

"Hello, Maggie. You were looking pretty far down there for a while. Good to see you."

"Oh, we're better. We're much better. Honest. We still wake up crying, and Mama says we'll do that for a year. Oh, Charlie, thank you for everything you and Margaret sent—all the meat and vegetables."

"Oh, listen, would've gone to rot at my place."

"They wouldn't have gone to rot, Charlie. You're wonderful. We talk about you all the time. Charlie, can I ask you something?"

"Well, I hope so, Maggie. What is it?"

"Were you ever lonely when you were my age?"

"Oh, I was lonely all right. I don't remember so much about being 14 and 15, but I was lonely. When I was 9, 10, 11, I had nobody to play with. I used to go outside. Who was I going to play with? Jimmy Davis's boy? Little brat. I wouldn't play with him. I made up an imaginary friend. Nobody could see him but me. Jimmy Scotsman. He was enormous, had big shoulders. I'd come out, and I'd say, 'Jimmy Scotsman, take my hand.' As soon as he took my hand, I was 19, enormous."

"I want to meet someone like that but someone real."

"Oh, you will, Maggie."

"I don't think so. Papa doesn't approve of dances. He says I can never go to a dance."

Thumb in the gill, open the mouth, slip it on the rod in the herring shed. Eighteen on a rod, a hundred to a bundle, 45 cents. I did it. I did two bundles in the herring shed.

"There are other ways of meeting someone."

"Do you think I'm pretty?"

"I think you're pretty, Maggie. I think you're pretty wonderful."

"Thank you. I'll see you later."

"Well, I hope so, Maggie."

Thumb in the gill, open the mouth, slip it on the rod in the herring shed. The weeks passed by in the herring shed. Thumb in the gill, open the mouth, slip it on the rod in the herring shed.

One day I must have had a good sleep or something because I was flyin'. By ten-thirty I had done a bundle, and Peg shouted at me, "Maggie, you can do three bundles today! You might never do it again, but you can do three today!"

"I will! I will!"

Thumb in the gill, open the mouth, slip it on the rod in the herring shed.

"Peg, I'm not going to have lunch. Get a potato, and stick it in my mouth."

Thumb in the gill, open the mouth, slip it on the rod in the herring shed. By two o'clock I could barely move, but I was going to do three bundles that day. I kept at it. Thumb in the gill, open the mouth, slip it on the rod in the herring shed. Thumb in the gill, open the mouth . . . I did it! I did three bundles in the herring shed.

"Oh, I'm so proud, Mrs. Fraser. I never thought I'd do it. A dollar thirty-five. We can buy a new farmhouse. Oh, thank you. I'll see you later."

Well, it was a wonderful day. I felt so good. But the next morning when I got there, I was so stiff I could barely pick the rod up. I picked it up, and I felt awful giddy, so I started laughing and pretending I couldn't even get the fish on. I pretended to groan. Thumb in the gill, open the mouth . . . Well, Peg started laughing, and the two of us were laughing, pretending we couldn't get the fish on. Thumb in the gill, open the mouth . . . We looked at Mrs. Fraser, and we were trying to make her laugh, but nothing breaks her concentration. Her hands are like fairies gone mad. Thumb in the gill, open the mouth, slip it on the rod in the herring shed. Thumb in the gill, open the mouth, slip it on the rod in the herring shed.

The two of us bent over, calling, "Mrs. Fraser." We said it slow as molasses. Thumb in the gill, open the mouth . . . We saw the littlest bit of a smile, and we knew we had her. Peg picked up her black braids and pretended she was an opera star. Thumb in the gill, open the mouth . . . And I bent over with my rod. "Mrs. Fraser." Thumb in the gill, open the mouth . . . She couldn't resist us. She dropped the rod, and she bent back and started laughing and clapping. And we danced around. Thumb in the gill, open the mouth, slip it on the rod in the herring shed.

We were dancing around, and Corner Murdock came in. He looked like an elephant's trunk, and he bent over and picked up the drying rack, and all of a sudden Peg got one arm, and I got the other. Thumb in the gill, open the mouth, and we danced around with him. I was dancing with a man, even if it was Corner. Thumb in the gill, open the mouth, slip it on the rod in the herring shed.

"All right now," Corner said wildly. "Thank you very much. That's enough."

We wouldn't let him go, and he stared at Mrs. Fraser. She picked up a rod and pretended she was conducting. Thumb in the gill, open the mouth . . . Well, poor Corner Murdock dropped the rack and ran outside, and with all of us watching, he opened his vanilla bottle and drank it down. Oh, we laughed and danced and sang, and Mrs. Fraser told stories about her grandmother. And we worked too. I made 6 cents that day. It was the most wonderful day of the whole summer, and it was good that it was, because the next two days were the worst.

We were back to normal the next day. We were working away at 10 o'clock. Thumb in the gill, open the mouth, and the rector came into the herring shed. He leaned forward in that shy way. "Mrs. Fraser, will you come outside?" She came right around the table. She wasn't going out.

"It's one of my sons, isn't it? Dead?"

"I'm sorry. It's Jack."

"Oh, God!"

She wept right in front of us, and then she straightened up, and she cried, "Well, please God, if it has to be one, it should be Jack! Gannett's got a wife and a son. You know that."

"I've got the car outside. I'll take you home."

"I'm not going home, Rector. Thank you. There's no one at home. I'll finish the way Maggie did. But I'll be very glad if you come tonight with everybody."

And she went on with the work in the herring shed. Thumb in the gill, open the mouth, the war came home to the herring shed.

I ran on home, straight by the sea, glad to be free of the cold of the herring shed.

"Hello, Charlie."

"I'm sorry, Maggie. Sad day. Is she all right?"

"She's a strong woman, Charlie. She kept working to the end. We'll see you there tonight. We'll bring the chicken."

"We'll bring the scalloped potatoes."

"See you later, Charlie."

"Well, I hope so, Maggie."

At seven in the morning we were back in the shed—Peg to my right, Mrs. Fraser across. She came to work despite her loss, and we went on with the work in the herring shed. Thumb in the gill, open the mouth . . . The rector came in at 10 o'clock, and Mrs. Fraser came right around.

"Rector, very kind of you, but I'll be all right now. I've got Peg and Maggie here, and at least Gannett's alive."

And the rector was still.

"Gannett's alive, isn't he?" she cried out. "Gannett's alive?"

"No, he's dead."

"God! Oh, God!"

And she fell to the floor in the herring shed. She was taken on home and put to bed, and we went on with the work. Thumb in the gill, open the mouth, slip it on the rod in the herring shed. We went on with the work in the herring shed. I ran on home, straight by the sea, glad to be free of the cold of the herring shed, and I swore I'd never go back there. It was too cold, and it was too sad. I'd make money some other way.

"Hello, Charlie. Don't want to talk, Charlie. I'll see you there tonight."

We paid Mrs. Fraser another evening call and brought food. Then we went home, and Papa turned on the radio. Mr. Churchill was speaking, and he sounded so strong. His words were old and simple and bold: "We shall not flag or fail. We shall go on to the end. . . . We shall fight on the beaches, we shall fight on the landing grounds, we shall fight in the fields and in the streets, we shall fight in the hills. We shall never surrender." We sat at the table, and our eyes were wet, and I looked at Papa, and his fists were set. Papa stood up, and then he smashed the table with his fist and cried, "Damn it, Maggie! We'll go on to the end!"

At seven in the morning I was back in the shed—Peg to my right, and Mrs. Fraser came in. She looked so old and so thin. But she gave us a nod and went on with the work. Thumb in the gill, open the mouth, slip it on the rod in the herring shed. The herring that are dried are put on the ships and sent to England for hungry lips. We went on with the work in the herring shed. Oh, we went on, yes, we went on; dear God, we went on with the work in the herring shed.

Well, the season finally ended, and I was so glad. I stood outside until Corner Murdock snapped the lock, and it was done.

It was harvest season. Everyone had to help, even Mrs. Fraser. You couldn't be too sad. And finally winter came, and I'll never forget. It snowed all day and all night, and Mama said we'd find the laughter underneath the snow. She was right. Sometimes there would be six or seven people sitting around the kitchen at night, telling stories. It was fun outside too. I built a snowman one day.

"Charlie! Charlie! Who do you think the snowman is?"

"I don't know, Maggie."

"It's you."

"Well, I thought so."

"You did not."

"Well, listen. Your father doing the cutting?"

"He's cutting, all right. Four cords of wood for you on Friday."

"What about the grain?"

"He's going to bring the grain over as soon as the ice is hard. Let's have a snowball fight."

"I think I'll pass it up, Maggie."

"I'll see you later."

"Well, I hope so, Maggie."

I wanted the winter to go on forever. But it's over. You can smell the air this morning. It's spring. Oh—it must be seven o'clock. I'm going to have to hurry! That's Peg going into the herring shed. Mrs. Fraser's already there. Well, now you know why I couldn't sleep. But before I go, that's Papa's boat you see down there. I told you the best thing about the war is there's no gasoline. You make your own sails. I helped Papa make those. Well, I've got to go. I'll see you later.

Thumb in the gill, open the mouth, slip it on the rod in the herring shed. Eighteen in a row, a hundred in a bundle, 45 cents. We'll go on with the work in the herring shed.

"Hello, Mrs. Fraser. Nice to see you. Hello, Peg. Your braids look so nice. Mrs. Fraser, you'll have to tell stories again this year. Oh, I'll never be as fast as you."

The herring that are dried are put on the ships and sent to England for hungry lips. We'll go on with the work in the herring shed. Thumb in the gill, open the mouth, slip it on the rod in the herring shed. Thumb in the gill, open the mouth, that is my tale of the herring shed.

Jay O'Callahan of Marshfield, Massachusetts, has performed from Lincoln Center to the Abbey Theatre in Dublin. In 1991 he was awarded a National Endowment for the Arts grant. He performed at the Winter Olympics in 1980 and was commissioned by the Boston Symphony Orchestra in 1983. O'Callahan has written three children's books: Tulips *(Picture Book Studios, 1992),* Orange Cheeks *(Peachtree, 1993), and* Herman and Marguerite *(Peachtree, 1995).*

Rosie the Riveter

Judith Black

Between 1941 and 1945, five million women poured into the U.S. work force. These women, who worked an average of 56 hours a week while maintaining their homes and families in wartime conditions, did not consider themselves heroines. I do. Rosie the Riveter was the media's prototype for the woman who donned overalls and a visor snood and punched in each day. This tale, researched primarily at Radcliffe College's Schlesinger Library, is written as a piece of folklore. The issues it deals with, however—sexism, denial of the Holocaust, and the racism that workers faced daily on the job—were all part of the very fabric of Rosie's America.

> Morning, noon, or night,
> Rain or shine,
> Rosie's always on
> The assembly line.
> Let them hoot and jeer,
> Her name malign,
> She'll still make her quota
> On the assembly line.

JUNE 4, 1942, THE BATTLE OF MIDWAY; 6:52 A.M.

ROSIE MCRIVET PASSED UNDER THE GREAT WROUGHT-IRON GATE, HER TIMECARD in one hand, her work orders and lunchbox in the other. A dozen pairs of eyes and a few wise mouths followed her overall-clad, only slightly discernible female form as she marched down that long shop floor.

"Hey, baby, don't get your skirt caught!"

"Hey, honey, what're ya doin' after ya shift?"

But Rosie kept both her flaming Irish temper and her red hair snugly secured beneath the visor snood atop her five-foot-three-inch frame. Her clear green eyes focused straight ahead, toward the riveting shop. She emerged from the deluge of comments, whistles, and slights and handed her work orders to the burly foreman.

"Well, little lady, it says here you did just fine in the night-school riveting course."

"Sure," shot one of the guys from the floor. "She was probably flirting with the teacher."

Rosie, who could barely contain herself another second, shot a look at that man that was like fire cutting into ice. He was silenced.

Rosie listened as the foreman explained that she was the first woman ever to work in the riveting shop and that it might take the boys a while to grow used to her. He then called Big Lenny, the set-up man, to give her an assignment. Lenny, whose belly preceded him in all things, let it oft be known that in his view, women were useful only in the kitchen and the bedroom. The entire shop leaned in to catch this first meeting. Big Lenny approached Rosie. She didn't step back an inch but remained silent.

"OK, girlie," he said in a loud, laughing sneer. "Do you know what this is?"

"Main girder," Rosie answered in a quick, efficient way.

"OK! Good start, honey. Do you know what to do with it?"

Quietly she asked, "Should I put on me arm and leg guards now?"

Laughing so loudly that he could be heard down in the barrel shop, Big Lenny spit out, "Only if ya want to keep your arms and legs!"

As a matter of fact, he was laughing so loud and long, he didn't really notice Rosie slip on her arm and leg guards. He didn't notice her survey the job and determine that additional rivet holes were needed. He didn't see her take an air drill with a flexible shaft, with which she could traverse the corner. He didn't see her drill a neat series of holes that, though unmeasured, were an exact equal distance from one to the other. He didn't see her leave the metal clean and free of any nicks or scrapes. As a matter of fact, he didn't notice anything until she was by his side again seconds later, stating simply, "I'll need a bucker now."

Big Lenny's jaw dropped when he saw the girder, and he pointed to a lanky straw-haired man. Rosie addressed him in a quiet, precise manner: "You'll need a diamond-studded bucking bar for this job. Please display your equipment."

The bucker, who stands opposite the riveter, makes sure that once the rivet is sunk through the hole, it's secured on the opposite side. This bucker silently pulled out his bucking bar. For the first time some color rose to Rosie's cheek.

"Look at that bucking bar! A nick or scrape in your bucking bar could cause an inconsistency in the equipment we are working on, which could result in deaths on the front! Do you want to be responsible for that? Get yourself a disk sander and some coarse emery, and clean that bar up."

Rosie then walked in small clipped steps over to the tool cage, where she chose a corner gun and flat-head, tubular-head, and brazier-head rivets. She adjusted the rpm on the gun, placed the manufactured head of the rivet into its proper position, and pressed it into one of the holes she'd so neatly drilled.

"Excuse me, ma'am," drawled the bucker, "don't you think these rivets you chose are a little small?"

Rosie took a quick breath and without losing her momentum replied, "These rivets are exactly 1.4 times the square root of the thickness of the plate we're working on. Go ahead; check it if you like." She tossed an extra rivet over the girder. It bounced from the bucker's head into his hand. He shot a look at Big Lenny, who with a nod had to confirm that Rosie was right.

Rosie pushed the rivet in again. The bucker pressed back, signifying that he was ready. Rosie exerted a slight amount of pressure on the gun trigger, and two taps came from the other side of the girder. One or three taps from a bucker indicated that the rivet had been incorrectly sunk. Rosie always got two taps . . . correct. She knew her bucker. She knew the job.

Within seconds a sound like a hundred woodpeckers hard at work filled that area, and a little cloud of dust rose around them for a full six minutes. When the noise stopped and the cloud settled, there sat a perfectly completed main girder that a whole team of men had hoped to complete by the shift's end.

Rosie, cool and calm, said to Big Lenny, "You'll have to excuse me. I'm way over my usual time. That bucker you gave me . . . slow as molasses."

Crawling on his hands and knees from behind the main girder, gasping for breath, the tall, lanky straw-haired man inched his way over to Big Lenny. The entire shop leaned closer to hear him choke out, "Lenny, you might have to get a younger guy to work with her."

And Lenny, whose jaw was still slack from watching her drilling, whispered back, "Yeah, but, Tom—you're only 19!"

In the end Rosie McRivet had three buckers assigned to her. All three were women, as it was determined that their stamina was far greater than that of their male counterparts.

Morning, noon, or night,
Rain or shine,
Rosie's always on
The assembly line.
Some want a rest,

Say the enemy's benign;
Rose doubles her quota
On the assembly line.

JULY 10, 1943, MONTGOMERY AND PATTON INVADE SICILY; 2:55 P.M.

Rose Rivitchsky lumbered beneath the great wrought-iron gate, her timecard in one hand, her brown-and-white checked thermos in the other. As she plowed slowly, determinedly toward the riveting shop, her ever-present worries went with her.

"Good afternoon, Rose."

"Good afternoon, Mrs. Rivitchsky."

In her middle-European accent she replied to no one in particular, "Would be better afternoon if people, they stopped killing each other." Once she arrived at the riveting shop, the brown-and-white thermos went into the locker,

A real-life Rosie the Riveter, left, and her bucker assemble an aircraft engine mount.

her arm and leg guards were secured, and Rose, with dogged determination, went to work.

As the war stretched on, so did the work required to support it. Initially the women, who also maintained their homes and took care of their children, were asked to put in a 40-hour week. But that soon turned into 45, 50, and often 55 hours a week. The two 10-minute breaks the workers got during each shift were desperately needed, and when they came, Rose Rivitchsky would lumber to her locker, pull out her brown-and-white checked thermos, and call, "Come on, everyone. Chicken soup!"

As she poured steaming cupfuls for everyone in the shop, she said, "Herman, look at you; you're disappearing! You'll need double soup today."

Herman, a small man with thin, angular features, had a nervy edge to him that afternoon. "I tell you, Rose, if they ask me to work one more minute this week, my back's gonna break."

A short breath like a train whistle escaped her lips. "Trust me, Herman, working so hard as the boys on the front, you're not. They carry those guns 24 hours a day against the Nazis."

Herman stood, and though he was a good 70 pounds smaller than Rose, he was peeved with patriotism and let it be known. "Nazis, shmatzis. You know, I need a break too."

This time Rose took a long, deep breath, riveted Herman with a stern look, and spoke in slow, measured tones.

"Nazis, shmatzis, Herman. Herman, it's the Nazis burning the books. It's the Nazis killing the Jews . . . Gypsies . . . and intellectuals. Herman, it's the Nazis taking little blond-haired children into rooms and teaching them to hate. Think about that, Herman, and see if it doesn't give you the strength you need to keep working."

Not a soul spoke. Herman tried to shrug it off.

"Come on, Rose, no one really believes all that stuff. It's just propaganda. They tell you horrible things about your enemy in every war so you'll work harder. For God's sake, this is 1943. No one really believes that the Germans . . ."

Rose corrected him. "The Nazis, Herman . . ."

". . . that the Nazis are really killing Jews and Gypsies and, and . . ."

She helped him finish. "Intellectuals, Herman."

"Yeah, no one believes that. Even President Roosevelt doesn't believe all that stuff. If it was true, he'd have been takin' in all those Jewish immigrants instead of makin' them go back to Europe. So are you tellin' us that President Roosevelt is lettin' all those people get killed? Come on, Rose, let's be realistic! Who here on the shop floor believes what Rose is sayin'?"

A big debate ensued. Some agreed with Rose that a Holocaust was being perpetrated in Europe, but many agreed with Herman that this was merely propaganda to inspire American workers. Rose, who had not heard from her mother or sister in Germany since the day the Reichstag building was burned by the newly victorious Nazi party, listened for a minute, raised her thick arms in the air, and in a voice that commanded attention, announced, "What I believe, I'll show you."

She lumbered over to the tool cage, took three different kinds of riveting guns and six types of rivets, and motioned for her three buckers. Within seconds it sounded like a dozen machine guns opening up on the front. The entire floor trembled with the intensity of their work, a dust cloud surrounded them, and the heat they emitted caused the other workers to back away.

After five minutes a hand motioned from the cloud for a fourth bucker. They worked like this for 35 minutes until the dust settled on a perfectly completed fighter-bomber. Then the four buckers sat against the cinder-block wall, sweat pouring off their trembling, heaving bodies, and Rose Rivitchsky, looking 10 years older than she had only 35 minutes ago, pulled herself out from under the belly of that plane.

She lumbered over to the tool cage again, silently picked up a hand-riveting gun and hand rivets, lumbered back to the bomber, and pressed herself down to the just-completed bomb-release hatch. Her shocked co-workers remained silent as they heard her drilling a neat series of hand rivets. She dragged herself back out, looked around, and simply said, "Come, everyone, we have a lot of work to do."

It wasn't until mealtime, when Rose was pouring soup from that brown-and-white checked thermos (it never did seem to empty), that a girl from the shop crawled under that fighter-bomber. There on the bomb-release hatch, written in neat hand rivets, were the words A HALARI-AH ON YOUR SOUL.

For those of you who don't know Yiddish, Rose had placed a curse on the souls of those who killed six million.

Morning, noon, or night,
Rain or shine,
Rosie's always on
The assembly line.
That set-up man
May be a swine;
Rose triples her quota
On the assembly line.

FEBRUARY 21, 1944, SAIPAN ATTACKED BY AMERICAN FORCES; 10:55 P.M. Rosella Riveton eased on through the great wrought-iron gate, her time-card in one hand, a brown lunch bag in the other. There was a war on, and this deep-brown-skinned daughter of a Southern preacher-man knew what she was fighting for.

"Hey, Susie girl. I been meanin' to ask," she said, smiling from ear to ear because it was the same question she asked every night, "Is that college education helping you out on the assembly line?"

"Hi, Rosella." Flaxen-haired Susie had initially been self-conscious about coming in after her college classes. Not anymore. She shot Rosella the ritual answer: "It's helping me figure out when they've miscalculated my paycheck."

"OK, girl, I'm gonna have to have you check mine too. Bosses can't cheat us with a college girl on board." Susie smiled and headed toward the shop as Rosella spotted another co-worker. "Hey, my man Manuel, another sucker for the old midnight shift."

The tall, thin Mexican immigrant grinned. "Hey, Rosalita, you know I like an active nightlife."

"Well, my man, we'll see how active you can get. You try to make one-third my production level," Rosella challenged.

Manuel graciously tried to slip out of the challenge. "Rosella, I be too busy lookin' at you, woman. You turnin' heads tonight."

She smiled. "Yes, brother Manuel, you best be sure I am: round heads, brazier heads, and tubular heads!"

Then she spotted Ho Trung. He was a slight Tonkinese man. He was alone, without his family, and Rosella took care to greet him each night.

"Hey, my man Ho Trung, how's it goin'?"

His eyes never met hers, but a shy smile bespoke his enjoyment at having her notice him. "It go good, Rosella."

"You catch the newsreels last night?" She knew he fought off loneliness by going to the movies each day. "What they talkin' 'bout now?"

Ho Trung blushed slightly. "They talk about too many girls in factory. Find girls in back room, kissing with foreman."

Rosella's voice grew loud enough for the whole shop to hear. "Best not get my brown self back there with our night set-up man. We'd make sparks."

Everyone understood her irony, but it was Ho Trung who made his first public joke: "Not make too many hot stuff, Rosella. Casings for fighter-bomber explode!"

They all laughed and reported to their stations by the 11 p.m. starting bell. Their conscientiousness never stopped that night shift's set-up man.

He was a tall, nervous man in his late twenties with thin, oily hair and a world-view that had never grown beyond his small south-side neighborhood. Whenever it was allowed, a cigarette that he tapped incessantly hung from his pendulous lips. His high-pitched voice seemed to scrape the air: "Red and black and yellow and brown—let's get my dull little rainbow to work."

Rosella would walk in front of him and calmly remind everyone, "Let's remember the big enemy and get to work."

The World War II era was the first time in this nation's history that women, immigrants, and African-Americans could get the kind of skilled training necessary to hold responsible, well-paying industrial jobs. The bosses were willing to trust them to perform a single function, but the role of supervisor was still ritually reserved for white men. Too often the men they found did not deserve to be called *boss*.

That night set-up man paced the shop floor like a cold wind at everyone's back. "Hey, Susie girl, why don't you stay after your shift? I'll teach you something they don't learn you about in college . . . Hey, Manuel, spic! You know, if you washed a little more often, things wouldn't slip through your fingers, and you'd get more work done." He continued down the line. "Hey, Rosella, yeah, nig . . ." But he thought twice before finishing that bit of invective. Besides, his eyes latched onto a more vulnerable victim.

"Hey, Ho Trung, you know, I think I'm gonna have to report you to the boss for stealin' secrets. See, you look like a Jap to me. All them Japs are in camps now so they won't steal things. Best you be with them, little man."

Ho Trung, who had never spoken to the set-up man, stopped his work and turned. Though his eyes looked down, his voice reached toward the taller man.

"I not Japanese. I Tonkinese. Not same."

The set-up man lit a cigarette as a thin line of amusement spread from one side of his mouth.

"You look Jap to me. That's good enough. Think I'll go tell the boss right now. Gotta keep our factories safe from the enemy."

Ho Trung's small voice pleaded over the factory noise. "Please no. I need job. Bring wife, bring children here, please." He took a small step toward the set-up man.

"Please."

With a single movement the set-up man brought a strong arm down to stop the gently approaching Ho Trung. The worker was set off-balance and fell backward, his head missing a moving lathe by half an inch. The set-up man loomed above him.

"Were you talking back to me, boy?" It was then that the night set-up man felt a warm vibration at the nape of his neck. As he turned toward it, it intensified, and he somehow knew Rosella had her riveting gun pointed at the base of his brain. As she gently increased the gun's speed, he could imagine a neat hole running from the nape of his neck straight through his forehead.

That woman, who'd seen the Klan burn crosses on her daddy's lawn and knew Jim Crow better than she wanted to, understood the enemy. She gave the set-up man time to think, then calmly suggested, "If I were you, mister mister, I'd help that man up." Additional pressure on the trigger convinced him she was right, and without grace he helped Ho Trung up.

She continued in a deadly calm voice, "Now dust him off." The set-up man began to complain, and Rosella repeated herself, just a little louder. "I said dust him off."

And once it was done, the set-up man began to turn. But she stopped him cold.

"Now *apologize*. Apologize to that human being right now."

With a single movement the set-up man brought a strong arm down to stop the gently approaching Ho Trung. The worker was set off-balance and fell backward, his head missing a moving lathe by half an inch.

The intensity of her voice and the sensation of the rotating bit at his neck were reasons enough. He bit his thick lips and forced out the words "I'm sorry, Ho Trung. That was an accident. And as for you, girl, we are going down to see the night foreman. We are going right now. Right this instant . . ."

He was trembling, and his cigarette fell from his lips to the cement floor. Rosella extinguished it with her toe. "I'm right behind you," she said.

They walked down the long shop floor, her riveting gun never leaving the nape of his neck, until the door to the foreman's office opened.

A few moments passed. No one worked. No one spoke. Ho Trung drew himself up to his full height and said, "I go talk for Rosie."

Flaxen-haired Susie chirped, "Not without me. I'll speak up for Rosie."

And Manuel smiled. "Hey, I'm talkin' for my Rosalita too."

One by one, all 22 people from that shop joined the line behind Ho Trung Nguyen and marched down to the boss's office. They heard angry voices, but none of them was Rosella's.

The night set-up man: "This here girl is dangerous. She wants to run the dang shop."

The foreman: "We've never had a complaint about Rosella before. She's always had an incredible level of production."

The set-up man: "At what cost? You let her stay on the floor, soon they ain't gonna listen to you or me or no one in power . . ."

For the first time in his life Ho Trung Nguyen opened a door without knocking. The night foreman looked out and saw 22 pairs of angry eyes all riveted to his set-up man. The air was thick with their feelings.

Silence.

Then the foreman spoke. "Rosella, I want you to accept my apologies for whatever happened tonight. Your production level and your attitude have never been in question with me. Would you do me a big favor and please, please, go back to work?"

Rosella stood slowly, dusted herself off in the direction of the set-up man, took one step down from the foreman's office, and looking at her co-workers, simply said, "One enemy down. Come on, you all, we got a lot of time to make up for."

Rumor has it that the night set-up man was made one of Rosella's buckers. And in his honor she worked even faster!

Morning, noon, or night,
Rain or shine,

Rosie's always on
The assembly line.
No matter what the problem,
The girl's got spine,
Quadrupling her quota
On the assembly line.

Judith Black of Marblehead, Massachusetts, creates and tells stories from American history, her unique observations of human behavior, and world folklore. A frequent keynoter on this topic, she has been commissioned to create historic tales for such auspicious organizations as the U.S. Department of the Interior, the U.S. Constitution Museum, and National Public Radio. She has performed throughout the continent, from the Montreal Comedy Festival to the National Storytelling Festival in Jonesborough, Tennessee.

Such Things to Write About

Paul Q. Lipman, edited by Doug Lipman

This story consists of actual letters written from Europe by my father, Sergeant Paul Q. Lipman, U.S. Army Corps of Engineers, during the final months of World War II. I read about 50 of the letters that Paul wrote to my mother. In the story I have generally included complete letters—with small deletions and word substitutions. I consolidated two of Paul's fellow soldiers into one character, Lieutenant Spero. I have also added several sentences to clarify Paul's conflict with his father. The story touches on many themes: relationships between husbands and wives and between fathers and sons, prejudice on the basis of religious background and nationality, Jewish identity in the United States and its relationship to intermarriage between Christians and Jews, the Nazi Holocaust, the experience of European immigrants and the relationship of U.S. culture to Europe, the experience of war by nonprofessional soldiers, and personal letters as historical documents.

JULY 27, 1944

My BELOVED VIRGINIA,

It's so strange to sit here in the supply tent and look out upon the English landscape. It's so strange because things appear to be normal . . . yet they cannot be normal because you are not here.

The English scene is pretty and very, very green. It lacks the rugged wildness, the majesty and profusion of our terrain back home, yet its greatest attraction is the subdued and quaint quality of its fields and woods.

Its towns too (or at least the ones I've seen) are a thing of constant interest to my confused mind. It seems that when living in the country, the British have all the space they can possibly use, yet when they group together in a borough, they try to crowd as many humans as they can into the smallest possible area.

It's almost bewildering to ride through wide expanses of farmland for miles and then suddenly come upon a hamlet about the size of a city block . . . and as crowded.

We know as little about what's actually happening as you do—all our information comes from the BBC on the radio.

During news broadcasts everyone gathers around just like people do in the States—except the progress of the war means so much more to us in this country.

No wonder wars start in Europe—this rainy climate alone is enough to make anyone fight.

Virginia—remember what our friend said when we were married . . . our marriage is itself a step toward peace . . . love and beauty and peace don't have any religion or race. They're just as abundant as this English countryside . . . and they're there for the taking.

It must be about 10 o'clock now, and the dusk is just beginning to make its presence known. I sit here on a case of ammunition, looking at the fading day, and I find it quite difficult to keep from blubbering all over the typewriter.

Evening has always meant Ginny-time, and now the evenings come and go and there is no Ginny. No nothing, really.

Tomorrow may bring a letter from you (I feel better just planning on that!) and the next day or the next or the next may bring the end of this war, and then I'll really be able to plan.

Love me, my sweet, and believe in me. I'll come back to you safe and sound and make you forget these past months.

Your devoted, loving, faithful, adoring, heartsick own husband, Paul

AUGUST 19, 1944

I'm in the command car, and we're moving up front. We are in a long convoy, and the head of it—tanks—is meeting resistance as we move along. So we sit and wait much more of the time than we actually move.

I started to write to you Sunday, but by the time my duties were completed and I was getting comfortable, a call came through for a reconnaissance party. So off I went in a convoy of three jeeps loaded down with machine guns, grenades, and so on.

We barreled through France for hours—found ourselves in enemy territory, got the information we were sent for, and got back just at dusk. It's dangerous getting back after dark because our own troops shoot at just about anything that moves at night.

Yesterday we moved all day, and I decided that if I didn't write you while on the move, it might be weeks.

The towns we pass through now are not so badly shot up. Once in a while we still find one leveled to the ground, but I guess the Germans are more interested in getting away now than in fighting.

On the reconnaissance Sunday we passed through Chartres. It's filled with American troops who are rebuilding it rapidly. They are using the parks to bury the civilians killed by shells.

The townspeople keep giving us flowers, apples, and tomatoes as we go through. They offer wine too, but riding in the command car means *no wine*. So I sit back here and drool, but it's still *no wine*.

It's been three weeks since we've had any mail, and God knows when we will. We are moving too fast for almost any sort of supplies to get to us.

Now we're in a fairly large town. In England it was "Gum-chum, gum-chum, any gum, chum?" In France it's "Cigarette? Cigarette?" I sometimes wonder if they're as happy to see us as they pretend or if it's just the stuff the Americans throw at them.

There are ambulances rolling back, so I guess the fighting up ahead is fierce.

Your husband is dirty. I bathed in a stream some time ago but have not had my clothes off since.

Don't know just what lies directly ahead of me—but I do know what lies far ahead of me—when I can go home to you.

Be there, waiting for me, honey. Be there, loving me. I'll be back. To stay. To stay with you. Forever.

AUGUST 25, 1944

Today is a red-letter day for us. A little mail finally caught up with us, and I got two letters from you!

I feel so different now that I have received something from you. The day seems warmer and the sun brighter. I love you.

We had another skirmish two days ago. We helped in crossing a river. Lieutenant Spero and I led the way. I won't go into the details, but there was hell to pay. We had one man killed and three wounded.

I get quite depressed sending personal belongings back home from men killed in action. That's why your two letters today mean so much.

The trucks are warming up, so I'll bid you adieu now, my beloved. I hope more mail comes to us soon. Keep your chin up, and wait for me.

P.S. The imprints of your lips look just like 'em.

NOVEMBER 24, 1944

Got a nice letter today from my brother. It was very nice of him to clean up all the business mess I left when I was drafted. I guess that even though he wouldn't stand up as our best man in that Christian church, he really is on our side.

It was brave of him too to store my things in Pa's basement. If Pa were to find out about it, he'd be angry. . . .

I must tell you about today. The town we came to had been mostly evacuated, but the civilians, it seems, came back before we got here, and living space is quite scarce. So I, with a German-speaking helper, tried to find a decent place for a command post. We found it. We found a woman, about 50 or so, and she was very happy to give us rooms in her house. She had been waiting for the Americans to get here for three years—or so she said. She told us how she'd had to send her children somewhere or other because there was no food in this town. She told of her two sons who had been taken by the Germans and are now in German uniform somewhere. She could not do enough to please us. She gave us three rooms in her house and scrubbed every one of them before we moved in. She put clean sheets on beds and had fires going in the stoves. She gave us a miniature-sized bathtub to bathe in and is now heating water for us. She will wash our clothes tomorrow. Just like home, no?

This woman is hard to form an opinion about. Is she French and sincere toward us, or is she German and pretending happiness on our arrival? There's a "diploma" on the wall showing that her aged husband has performed 15 years of faithful service for the Republic of France as a fireman. When she utters the name of Hitler, she spits. I guess the thing about her that got my sympathy was the way her face screwed up and tears came to her eyes as she told of how the Germans came and took her sons. It was just the same way my mother would cry when she spoke of tragedy.

When she utters the name of Hitler, she spits. I guess the thing about her that got my sympathy was the way her face screwed up and tears came to her eyes as she told of how the Germans came and took her sons.

Tonight I'll be sleeping in a bed. I know I'll dream of you. I always do. And that way, even if the days drag on, the nights go swiftly.

SEPTEMBER 13, 1944

I hope, at this writing, that you have an apartment. An "apartment" sounds so secure—so safe—so comfortable. I don't think I will ever again gripe about minor (or even major) inconveniences. I really believe that every night I shall pray and thank God for a home—a clean bed—a bath. Things that were so taken for granted. The hell with everything else— you and a home are all I ask.

I love you with all the calm and peace these woods suggest—I love you with all the fury and violence the shells around us insist upon.

FEBRUARY 16, 1945

Today has been mail-less. No sweet words from you today—no words to help the day go faster—to make it easier. But those words are somewhere on their way to me, and they will have their effect when they get here.

There are many of those words being flown in planes, rushed by truck, by rail, from you to me, each bearing its message of love, of hope, of cheer. They'll get here.

I feel like talking to you, and the only way I can is on paper.

Pa hasn't sent me even a postcard. He doesn't know—or seem to care—about any of the things I've been through. I can't understand why a man who left so much of his Judaism back in Europe would be so upset because his son married a Christian. Well, when he sees fit to acknowledge again that I'm his son, maybe then I'll write. . . .

Today was almost warm. The sun shone brightly, and a touch of spring was felt. Oh, to have summer here again! I'd even be willing to take the blistered faces, the sand in everything, of our first weeks in France. I'm glad that summer and not winter lies ahead.

I'm so glad that so much of our lives lies ahead of us. It's like fighting your way across a desert with the vision of an oasis always before you. The closer you get to that oasis, the stronger you seem to get—the harder you fight to get there.

And I think that you, my oasis, are seeming closer all the time. Somewhere on the horizon, the vision of you grows clearer, closer. I feel that you are really in sight now.

And I'm fighting to get to that vision—to you. And I'll get there soon. I *must*.

MARCH 19, 1945

It's hard to explain and harder to realize, but here we are in Germany, where the people are definitely Nazi, and to look at them, there's absolutely no inkling as to what must lie beneath. Yet these are the people who thought themselves "superpeople" . . . who up to a year or so ago were preparing to rule the entire world. This time it is *they* who are receiving a conquering army . . . this time *they* are feeling the fruits of warfare. They produced a Hitler, and now they are getting what Hitler meant for other peoples. . . .

Can it be? Is the sun just over the next hill? Is it too much to hope that finally the German collapse will be complete? Oh, my love, how I am hoping. . . .

APRIL 25, 1945

The news tonight is that Berlin is completely encircled. That's good. Perhaps the fall of Berlin will be the finishing touch. I hope.

While we were evacuating civilians for our quarters today, the women burst into tears. And because they had to move their children. Can you imagine? When their soldiers were killing children in Russia, Poland, France, I'll bet they were all smiles. But they cry because they have to move their kids from one house to another. I think we Americans are treating these people too nicely. But as I read what I've just written, I think *Perhaps I'm becoming quite a hardhearted guy.*

MAY 7, 1945

My beloved,

Well, we should be jubilant as hell—as of one minute past midnight tomorrow night, the war in Europe will be over. That means we did it. The day we've been dreaming about . . . it is upon us. Yet somehow there is no jubilation . . . I can see no hysterical celebration . . . the war is over, that's all.

I wonder about the scenes in the States tonight . . . I can picture the ecstatic people . . . the drunks . . . but for us the war has been over for some days, and this just makes it official. The Army goes on, war or no war.

All the things that were big a little while ago—large numbers of Germans surrendering, the lack of shells coming at us—have suddenly become uninteresting. I want you, and everything else just brings a yawn.

I'm surprised at the lack of interest we show in the end of the war. I guess that after all these months of fighting, it's just too much to grasp all at once. I really do not know the reason; all I do know is that I am tired.

I'm tired, and the company is tired, and the news of the end of hostilities was rather wasted . . . we're glad, of course, but we are tired and worried about the *other* war. . . .

We should know before too long just what our status will be about the war in the Pacific, but until then . . .

I suppose I really shouldn't be writing a letter tonight because I'm in a depressing mood . . . but I'm so tired of being away from you. I so want to get back to you . . . I guess that nothing else can mean much. . . .

The country here in Austria is beautiful. But nothing will be as beautiful to me as 127½ W. Williams St. in Michigan City. I wish I had something to drink . . . I'd get drunk as hell. . . .

I think I'm just in the mood to write a letter to my father that should singe all his senses . . . by golly, I think I'll do it.

I want to go to sleep in your arms. What else is there in this world that can mean as much as that?

COURTESY OF PAUL Q. LIPMAN

Sergeant Lipman receives the Bronze Star for his heroic service in France on August 23, 1944. On that day he led a boatful of soldiers across a river "with complete disregard for his own safety as bullets churned the water all around his craft," the Army record states.

I'm enclosing a photo of me handing a cigarette to what once was a man . . . taken in one of the nicer concentration camps.

In the other picture with skeletons, for that's all they are, they are trying to climb on top of the bus to get out of the camp—they couldn't wait for another one. We GIs had to point pistols at them to make them get down.

The couple with the blankets were still able to walk around. The negative of the kid in clothes shows his father lying under a tree dying and no hope possible . . . the kid was going nuts trying to get someone to do something.

There are two negatives of the crematory itself . . . we could still see bones in the oven. And there is one last negative of Lieutenant Spero and me (I'm closest to the fence), slightly blurred, showing the barbed, electrified wire of the camp and behind it the pretty scenery.

I finally got that letter off to my father. I do not think it was a kind letter, and I did not try to justify anything . . . I just told him a thing or two that happened during 10 months of front-line fighting, and after a bit I asked him just what in hell was I fighting for . . . if not the right to seek happiness . . . if not to crush the very sort of prejudice he harbors . . . and I did throw in a reason or two why you didn't have it any easier than I do . . . why you were the only one for me, and he could take it or leave it. I was quite blunt and made no effort to keep any of the horrors from him, and I let him know that there is still another war to be fought. I suspect that the letter will leave him angrier than he was before, and that's all right with me too. I've had more petty stuff thrown at me than I feel I want to handle, but the family kept asking me to write to him, and I did . . . though probably not the way they thought I would.

As yet there is no news. No nothing. We are still in the mountains, and the threatened May snowstorm eased up. The sun was out for a bit today, and it was warmer. Hmmm, such things to write about . . . weather!

If we have to stay up here much longer, we'll go batty—it's like being in jail. I guess that in other times people spent lots of money to come up to this forsaken place . . . money wasted, says I. The Austrians can take their mountains and shove 'em up their valleys as far as I'm concerned. Hmmm, such things to write about . . . scenery!

I dreamed of you last night. I dreamed we were out dancing, and Bing Crosby was singing and making eyes at you, and I became quite angry and said to myself, "Take it easy . . . after all, you just got back from a war, and you could still be in those Austrian Alps. . . ." And then I woke up and found I was still in these high hills. Never even had a chance to go home with you. But the dance was nice . . . you are so pretty, and your hair smelled so clean . . . hmmm . . . such nice things to write about . . . you. . . .

Lieutenant Spero just came by and asked me to send his regards to you—so here they are, regards from Lieutenant Spero.

And all the love in the world from your husband, who prays each night that he can be coming home to you soon. . . .

Forever, your Paul

Epilogue

Paul returned home in December 1945. The letter that he had written his father had an effect. Although his father had refused to open the letter, he stayed within earshot while Paul's brother read it aloud at a family gathering. Within a year Paul and his father were reconciled—just four weeks before the birth of Paul and Virginia's first child, Doug.

COURTESY OF PAUL Q. LIPMAN

Liberation, May 1945: Paul Lipman hands a starving concentration-camp survivor a cigarette.

Paul's letters and war photographs were kept in a cardboard box that was moved from one basement to another. When Doug became a professional storyteller, he opened the box, read scores of the letters, and turned them into this story.

On December 26, 1993, Paul and Virginia celebrated their 53rd wedding anniversary.

Lieutenant Spero spent the remainder of his tour of service as a victim of "battle fatigue," overcome by the stress and horrors of war.

A freelance musician, a storyteller, and a teacher since 1971, Doug Lipman is known nationally as a performer, a coach, a workshop leader, and a writer. His numerous publications include Parents' Choice Award–winning recordings, a regular column called "Tips From the Storytelling Coach," a critically acclaimed videotape, Coaching Storytellers *(Enchanters Press, 1993), and a forthcoming book from August House on the art of coaching. To promote peer-coaching among storytellers, he travels widely from his home in Winchester, Massachusetts, leading workshops on supportive coaching.*

The Garbage Story

Susan "Supe" O'Halloran

This story tells of my coming of age on the southwest side of Chicago. As a teenager in the 1960s I traveled from the protective circle of the neighborhood women gathered on the front porch into the wider world of race, politics, and personal protest. Although all of the story's events are true, some people and places have been combined. The story reveals how I discovered the limited view I had been given of the city and its people—and how white people also lose when racial injustice is allowed to exist.

SUMMER AFTERNOONS IN THE 1950S, YOU COULD ALWAYS FIND THE WOMEN ON my block sitting out on the front-porch steps. But it wasn't always the same front steps. The women were nomads; they moved from porch to porch. On my South Side of Chicago front porch it was like one big day-time pajama party. The women set each other's hair and did each other's nails and talked about what they had cleaned that day. We little kids sat there with them, acting bored—but I could have listened to their stories forever.

See, the ancient Greeks had creation myths, and the ancient Egyptians did too. Well, my neighborhood had creation myths, stories from when we kids were babies and our neighborhood was just being built. I lived by 87th and Kedzie, the far southwest corner of the city, and back then the edges of Chicago were still forest and farmland.

The women would say, "You kids hear the rat story?" We'd say yes, and then they'd tell it to us again. Apparently as each new block of our neighborhood was being carved out of the forest, the city wasn't doing a very good job of clearing away the debris, and there was a vermin problem. So my neighbors took it upon themselves to get rid of the fallen trees and piles of brush. They started setting fires all over the place. "And sure enough," the women told us, "out came rats—running, screeching, hollering, their coats red with flame." It was a delightful image with which to send young children off to their naps.

Then they'd say, "You kids hear the garbage story?" We'd say yes, and then they'd tell it to us again. When my family and my neighbors moved into their new homes, our block was a complete mudhole—no streets, no sidewalks. We didn't even have front porches. The garbage men refused to come into our block because their trucks kept getting stuck.

"So every morning," the women told us, "you would see this army of men marching down the street like zombies, holding these greasy, stained paper bags at arm's length so that their work clothes wouldn't get dirty, carrying the garbage to an open field three blocks away that everyone used as a dump."

There were no plastic Hefty bags back then. Finally we got streets, and the city said we could have alleys too. The garbage trucks could come in back there.

"But," the ladies said, "we knew how you kids liked to play out back. If there were cars and trucks back there, someone might get hurt. So we said, 'No—no alleys,' even though that meant each week we'd have to carry our garbage cans out front to the street to be picked up out there. But we did it."

And that was always the point of these stories: We did it. We care. We take care of our neighborhood.

I never argued with them. I just remember hanging on the railings of those front porches, looping my arms and legs through the curlicue ironwork, being held there day after day by the possibility of receiving adult attention.

In 1964, when I was 14, my mother died. My dad worked two jobs, and my grandparents who lived with us were getting old, so if I needed to be driven somewhere, the ladies drove me. A couple of times some of the ladies even went to my parent–teacher conferences. When we teenage girls would see the women sitting out on one of the front porches, we'd go and talk to them.

"How's the biz?" they'd ask. That was our code for "How's the boys? Who do you like this week?"

We'd tell the ladies whom we liked and who didn't like us back. Then one of the ladies would put an arm around us, give us a hug, and say, "Oh, those boys—they don't know what they're missing."

Sometimes the support we got from the ladies wasn't even asked for. Right before my eighth-grade graduation dance the women got in a big discussion about whether I should shave my legs. Now, the antishaving group argued that the hair on my legs was light and that if I shaved, it would grow in dark. But the proshaving group said, "Yeah, but what if her hair shows under her nylons and someone teases her? What if she gets embarrassed at the dance?" It was great because I didn't know what to do. I could just sit back and let this committee of mothers help decide the future of my legs.

Another day I came out, and the women were sitting on my front porch as usual. Mrs. McQuaid looked up at me and said, her voice dripping with sympathy, "Sue, you got your friend. Got your friend today, huh?" Now, I'd never heard the word used that way, but by the way she said it, I knew what it meant. I said yes, feeling happily betrayed by my grandmother, who must have told them. I beamed, the ladies beamed, and I knew I'd become part of that circle of women. There were days I think I would have sold my soul for one of the big woman-hugs you could get on the front porches of 84th Street.

Then we got to be older teens, some of us 16, 17, 18—and the tone on the front porch changed. We became more independent. We argued with the ladies about whether the Beatles' hair was too long, whether the hemlines on our skirts were too high, whether the curfews they imposed were too early. But even as we argued, the ladies looked at us with pride. It was a normal part of breaking away. They knew we were good kids. We weren't with the rough kids, smoking cigarettes on the benches of Ashburn Park. No, we were on the front porch; we were where we belonged. It was OK to argue there—about everything except . . . race, which the women did every single day.

Back then, in the 1960s, the southwest side of Chicago was all white, and people weren't shy about expressing their beliefs. The more racist-sounding ladies would say things such as, "They live 20 in a room. They have too many children." This from a staunch Catholic woman with 10 children of her own. Others would say, "Oh, it's just excuses. If we can do it, they can do it. We raised ourselves up." Then the ones on the porch who thought of themselves as more liberal-minded would say, "It's just poverty. They need to educate themselves. It'll take time."

The discussions really got heated up if the ladies had been watching the noon news that day and had seen pictures of civil-rights demonstrations down South. It never failed to amaze me that all of us could be looking at the same picture and some of us would see the billy clubs of the Southern sheriffs striking the people while others would see only the arms of the demonstrators reaching out to resist the police.

Now, John Kennedy had been one of my heroes. I mean, the first Irish Catholic president, for heaven's sake. When he was alive, he had been in favor of civil rights. But not most of the Irish Catholic women on my front porch. They'd say, "Demonstrators. Troublemakers. They're asking for it. Things can't change that fast." I'd listen to them and think, *Well, at least we're not the South.*

Sometimes those racial discussions would get so tense, they'd begin to threaten the unity on the front porches. So one of the ladies who was a peacemaker would signal "That's enough, now" by saying, "Oh well, there's good and bad in every race." The conversation would begin to dwindle down. The only thing left to discuss was how many good and how many bad.

Now, the more racist-sounding ladies knew "they" had more bad among them. The ladies had evidence—stories from their husbands who were policemen or stories from friends who had lost their homes in changing neighborhoods.

But the biggest evidence of all was how people kept up their homes, how much garbage was around their homes. Once or twice a year I'd take the el with some of the women to go shopping downtown at Marshall Field's. Back then the South Side el zoomed you behind the "three flats"—triplex houses with one flat stacked on top of another—and apartment buildings in all-black neighborhoods. You could see into people's back yards. The more prejudiced ladies were thinking, *I rest my case; just take a look.* You could see them looking down, mentally counting off, "Bad, bad, bad, bad, good—see, if she can do it, they can do it—bad, bad, bad." Sometimes they'd even whisper, "See, they're lazy. They don't take care of their homes." And the more liberal-sounding ladies would counter, "No—they just need someone to show them how."

The el jogged along the tracks, the door slid open and closed at each stop, and I searched for something to say to the more prejudiced ladies. But I didn't know what to say. Then one of the ladies would make a joke or put a protective arm around us girls, and I'd melt back in. I didn't want to lose them, I guess. And like I said, I didn't have any evidence. Then one day I had a chance to go and get some.

It was the fall of 1966, and lots of changes were taking place at my all-girl Catholic high school. The nuns had changed their habits from long to short—their hemlines came all the way up the calves of their legs! And the nuns were given permission to take back their original names. So one day you'd have all these Sister Theonillas and Sister Anastasias walking around, and the next day it'd be Sister Tony Kennelly.

Sister Tony was a modern nun. She thought the nuns should get out of the convent and more into the world. One afternoon she asked three of us girls if we'd like to go with her to observe a neighborhood residents' meeting. She'd been invited to a meeting of the Lawndale Association, an all-black group on the West Side of Chicago that met to improve conditions in their neighborhood.

The circumstances were a little strange. Usually when there was an outing, we needed permission slips. But I figured Sister Tony had probably gotten the invitation at the last minute herself, and more than that, I

It was the fall of 1966, and lots of changes were taking place at my all-girl Catholic high school. The nuns had changed their habits from long to short—their hemlines came all the way up the calves of their legs!

figured she needed us girls to come along so she could call it a school event and get the use of the convent station wagon. Either way, I didn't care. I thought it was great. I'd get some stories to tell to the ladies on the front porch. I felt open-minded, cool, adventurous—till we got there.

We drove into the West Side. This was just two months after the 1966 West Side riots. Whole city blocks had burned down around Madison Avenue; the fires had reached two miles into the sky. In that one summer alone, 21 other U.S. cities had gone up in flames. It was the equivalent of 22 L.A. riots in the space of just a few months. And we drove in.

We saw boarded-up storefronts with graffiti painted on the wood: KILL WHITE GESTAPOS! KILL HONKY SONS OF BITCHES! We drove past bombed-out buildings, vacant lots filled with garbage, alleys strewn with broken glass, men lounging on street corners, drinking out of brown paper bags, eyeing us, leaning up against rusted-out cars with no wheels and no doors. I felt so white and so vulnerable, and everywhere I looked, I saw stories of the wrong kind to bring back to the ladies on the block.

We drove to the rectory where the meeting was supposed to take place. A group of black people were sitting on the front steps. John, a large man with graying hair, the leader of the group and the one who had invited Sister Tony, walked up to us as we were getting out of the car and said, "We're locked out. But don't worry. Someone'll be here soon with the key."

And there we were—three white girls and one modern nun—standing, grinning, on this all-black street. Out of the corner of my eye, in a vacant lot next to where we'd parked the car, I saw two rats fighting over what looked like an empty box of crackers.

One of the women sitting on the front steps must have sensed how uncomfortable we were and said, "Child, come sit over here." I didn't know which one of us girls she was talking to, but I moved first. I went and sat down in the space she had cleared in front of her. She patted her knees for me to lean my back against her legs, and her friend, a heavyset woman, scooted in next to me. I felt protected, surrounded, just a little white head peeking out.

The woman I was leaning up against was Nona. Nona was so thin, it looked as if she were wearing her skeleton on the outside of her body. She was dressed in her Sunday best. She wore white gloves and carried a flowered purse, and atop her head sat a flowered hat that had a single paper rose rising into the air like a periscope. Her friend's name was May. May wore a mink stole with the dead head of the mink still on it.

After we'd introduced ourselves, I asked Nona, just to be polite, "Where do you live?" Nona leaned down, swatted May on the shoulder, and said, "With this old thang!" They laughed like schoolgirls and started fighting over the flowered purse.

"It's mine."

"Is not. I had it first. You know it's mine."

Nona finally stuffed the purse behind her legs for safekeeping and started playing with my hair, twirling it in ringlets the way my mother used to do. Sister and the other girls came and sat down, and John passed around a thermos of coffee. Everyone was joking and teasing, and I swear, if I had closed my eyes, I could have been on one of the front porches of 84th Street.

Eventually the man showed up with the key and lots of apologies, and we went downstairs and listened to the meeting. I was getting great evidence. The Lawndale people were doing lots of good things. They were starting what today we would call a neighborhood-watch patrol, and they were fighting to get a church with a gym to open at three o'clock so the kids had somewhere to go after school.

Throughout the meeting Nona kept patting my hand, giving me the background, explaining what was going on. I needed an explanation when they got to the last agenda item: a garbage demonstration at City Hall. All it triggered in my mind was memories of our front-porch conversations: "Demonstrators! Troublemakers! Asking for it." But everyone had made us feel so welcome that I felt comfortable enough to ask some questions. The next few minutes of conversation changed my life 180 degrees.

I asked, "What are you going to demonstrate about?"

Nona said, "They make us live in filth."

"How can anybody *make* you live in filth?" I asked.

Nona answered, "Our garbage doesn't get picked up."

John added, "The sanitation department says they come in here, but they don't. Someone's palming a few bucks."

"Wait a minute," I said. "How could they get away with that?"

John looked at me incredulously and said, "We don't have no clout. We're expendable."

All at once the view from this street was so different from our view from the el. My perspective was changing from people who "didn't care" or "needed to be shown how" to people carrying out their garbage every Tuesday night just like we did, only the garbage trucks never came. Then, remembering our own garbage story, the one about our fathers, I asked, "Well, can you carry the garbage out yourselves?"

"Well, sure," Nona said. "People take the garbage out of their house and put it in the vacant lots, but that don't look none too nice." And it came to me—of course! The vacant lots were the dumps!

May was saying, "I spend every last dime on cans 'cause the landlord won't."

"Don't got to," Nona joined in. "He knows if we complain and move out, he's got 15 more families ready to move in. With not enough places for Negroes to live, don't matter how many people he crams in there or how he keeps it up, he'll rent that building."

"You don't own your own homes?" I asked.

"Used to," Nona said. "I paid on my house for 15 years, then slipped on the ice, missed one payment, and *whoosh!*—out on the street."

May leaned over to me and explained, "Nona, she worked as a maid, but she broke her hip."

"They can't do that!" I said. "You get lots of chances to pay. It takes months before they can foreclose, right?" I knew something about these things because my father worked part time as a mortgage officer at Talman Bank.

"No," said Nona, "they can kick you out after only one month 'cause Negroes can't get no loan. We have to buy a contract for deed without the protections from a regular bank. And the white man, he knows it too. Sells to people he knows can't get no regular job. So he take their down payment, their life savings. They pay on the house for a year, maybe two, then miss one payment, and *whoosh!* He take the house back, keep their down payment, and sell it again. Take someone else's life savings. But I lasted more than one or two years. I paid on that house for 15 years. And I didn't take nothing with me neither when I left."

"What would you take?"

Nona and May looked at each other and started laughing. "People get mad when someone take all their money. I've seen people walk out of them houses with the plumbing."

I remembered being about 10 years old at Al's bar on Kedzie Avenue. We kids sat at the tables, drank Orange Nehi, and ate pretzels. Our parents sat up at the bar. One night there was a man at Al's who wasn't from the neighborhood. "A big shot" my dad called him because he owned property and was talking real loud so the whole bar could hear him. "They don't take care of our places," he shouted. "I've gone in there, and they've taken the lighting fixtures. Those people, they live like animals."

My mind came back to the meeting with what I thought might be a possible solution. I was young, but I was a Chicago kid. I knew something about the political ropes. Mr. Burke, our precinct captain, lived just a few doors away. "Well," I said, "could you talk to your alderman about this problem?"

There was silence. Then they burst into laughter. The Lawndale people could not talk, they were laughing so hard. Nona could see I was embarrassed. She was patting my hand, trying to gather herself together. Finally she said, "Our alderman is some white man lives next to the lake. We don't never see him."

So in one three-minute conversation I had learned that black people didn't have the same city services. They didn't have the same representation. They didn't have the same chance to buy things, and these houses we were always looking at to see if they were kept up were owned by a bunch of white guys! And the thought came to me, *Oh, my God. We are the South!*

Nona leaned over to me and said, "Want to go?"

"Go where?" I asked.

"To the garbage demonstration at City Hall. It's today."

"Oh, yeah," Sister Tony said. "That's on our way home."

Now, wait a minute, I thought. We were on the West Side. We lived on the southwest side. Since when was east to downtown on the way home? But then I figured Sister Tony was secretly disappointed that she never marched with Martin Luther King, and this was a way for her to get in on the action.

John was saying, "If they say it is illegal for us to dump our garbage, we'll say it's illegal for them not to pick it up."

And I thought, *Oh, my God! I'm going to an illegal demonstration!* If I thought I was scared when I arrived at the meeting, I left there a nervous wreck.

We followed behind in the convent station wagon. About a dozen people had gathered for this demonstration, and there were two pickup trucks filled with garbage. We got to City Hall and parked across the street with the blinkers on, but the Lawndale people backed the pickup trucks right over the sidewalk.

They started unloading greasy, stained paper bags, holding them at arm's length, and plopping them in front of the bronze entrance, and a mound of garbage began growing in front of City Hall. We went and stood over by the trucks, talking with the people. At first there was a carnival atmosphere, everyone joking and teasing. John was unloading the truck, handing garbage to people, saying things like, "Oh, this must be your garbage, Tom—got a Seagram's bottle in it!"

Then a white woman came up behind me. She must have thought I was just a spectator. She said to me, "These people, they live in filth. It's disgusting. And they wonder why we don't want to live with them?"

How could I explain all I'd just learned? I started stuttering. "No,

I figured Sister Tony was secretly disappointed that she never marched with Martin Luther King, and this was a way for her to get in on the action.

181

that's not the way to look at it. You think you have the evidence, but you're looking at it wrong." The woman walked away. Nona, who had heard the woman—and I think the woman wanted her to hear—said, "You know, child, Hitler built those concentration camps with no bathrooms. He'd be showing people around. They'd catch some of that smell, and Hitler would say, 'Jews stink.' He had his evidence too. Some people will just never see."

Nona reached out, pulled me close, and gave me a big woman-hug. As I rested my head on her shoulder, I wanted to say, "Yeah, but, Nona, I hadn't seen either. I mean, why are your view from the street and our view from the el so different? And why hadn't I known?"

May came up behind me, and she gave me a hug too. "Sister and the other girls gone across the street to make sure the car don't get towed. You go too," she said. "We'll wave to you from across the street."

"Yeah," Nona said. "We're going to be on TV."

I started across the street, got halfway, and saw squad cars speeding down Clark Street, coming right toward us, their blue lights flashing. John was getting ready to make a speech; reporters held microphones to his face. But all the time John kept twisting his head, checking out the squad cars. He said, "Thirty-three percent of the population is forced to live on less than 20 percent of the land." The TV crew finally got its lights adjusted, and John stood taller, his voice booming like that of a Southern preacher. All the time he kept his eye on the squad cars.

"The West Side is the forgotten stepchild of the city," he said. "We are charged $10,000 for our homes because there is nowhere else for us to go. We pay taxes, but we do not receive comparable city services. . . ."

The policemen got out of their cars. The Lawndale people continued to place their garbage on the sidewalk. I could see May and Nona and the other people unloading the paper bags as they looked at the police. Then I heard screeching static sounds between the squad-car radios and the walkie-talkies some of the policemen were carrying. The Lawndale people began to sing, "We shall overcome, we shall overcome."

Then I saw half a dozen policemen raise their billy clubs into the air.

"But they aren't doing anything!" I said to Sister. Next there was lots of confusion as if some of the policemen didn't know what to do either. Some of them began to write out tickets for loitering or littering—I don't know which. But other policemen began to push at the people with those billy sticks. So the Lawndale people started to get down the way Martin Luther King had taught people to go limp during nonviolent demonstrations.

I saw Nona grabbing for May's arm and trying to sit down, but she had that bad hip so she was moving too slow. They'd try to get down, but they'd have to be quick—duck!—as a policeman swung a club overhead. Then more police arrived, circled the people, and began moving in, harvesting their pick of limp bodies.

Sister's arms were outstretched, straining, holding us girls back. I felt so ashamed because although I was calling out, "Nona! May! Watch out! Get down!" no part of me wanted to cross that street. Sister looked around nervously. When I think of it now, that young nun was all of 27, maybe 28 years old. There we were—no permission slips; we weren't even where we were supposed to have gone. If anything had happened to us, she'd be in big trouble.

Finally she said, "I think we'd better leave." And then to make us feel better, she added, "Don't worry. The Lawndale group's really organized. They know what to do if people get arrested. We'll call John when we get back to the school."

I began to step into the car, but then I turned around just in time to see a policeman carrying off a limp body—with a dangling hand clutching a flowered purse.

"Susan," Sister Tony snapped at me, "get in the car. C'mon. We're going home." Home. It was like being caught in a kind of bubble, a time warp. Even then, on some level I knew that as soon as I took a step in either direction, I'd lost something. I'd never be able to sit on my front porch the same way again—I couldn't even tell the ladies where I had been. But I couldn't go sit on May and Nona's front porch either.

And I wondered then, as I wonder now, where is the porch for all of us to sit, where I can hold the best of both these worlds—the love of the woman-circle I grew up in and the courage and the experience of those two women with the flowered purse?

Susan "Supe" O'Halloran is the author of The Woman Who Found Her Voice *(LuraMedia), a forthcoming fairy tale for adults, and* The Hunt for Spring *(Riverbank Press, 1995), a children's picture book. While being a mom, O'Halloran has also worked as a dance teacher, a deejay, a TV host, a corporate scriptwriter, a standup comic, an antiracism trainer, and an instructional designer. In 1993 she performed at the Exchange Place at the National Storytelling Festival in Jonesborough, Tennessee. O'Halloran is one of the directors of Chicago's Wild Onion Storytelling Celebration. She lives in Evanston, Illinois.*

An Orange

Joel ben Izzy

It takes hunting, digging, and searching to find some stories. Others seem to wander around, looking for a teller who will pass them on. This story falls into the latter category. It found me on a bus in 1971, when I was 12. The story can be told on Holocaust Remembrance Day, which takes place each spring. But it is also appropriate near Thanksgiving, as it emphasizes the importance of appreciating the wonder of what nature offers. As the Talmud says, "Who is rich? The one who can appreciate what he has."

WHEN I WAS A KID GROWING UP IN LOS ANGELES, I USED TO RIDE THE BUSES. IF you've been to L.A., you know that buses are not the preferred mode of transport. I know they weren't my preferred mode of transport. I hated them. Like every other kid in L.A., I wanted a car. It didn't matter that I was only 12 and couldn't drive. I wanted a car.

But I had no choice. So I rode the buses. It took hours to get across town, stopping every 50 feet or so to let the passengers on and off while the cars zoomed by. An afternoon spent riding the bus was long and hot and boring.

I remember one time I was riding a bus through Fairfax, the Jewish neighborhood in L.A. I was sitting in one of the front seats, the ones with the legroom, that are marked reserved for the elderly and handicapped. I figured it didn't matter because no one else was on the bus. Then we stopped near the farmers' market, and a thin elderly man got on, walking with a cane and holding a shopping bag. Sure enough, he came right to my seat. So I scooted over and made a place for him.

He looked me up and down. Then he reached into his shopping bag and pulled out an orange. He showed it to me.

"What do you think?" he said.

I looked at him, and I looked at the orange, and I said, "I think it's an orange." But that wasn't really what I was thinking. What I was really thinking was that there were a lot of crazies in L.A., and I was sitting next to one.

He looked at the orange and then looked at me again. "But what do you think of it?"

I took the orange and examined it. "Well," I said, "it's kind of small, and it's a little green on one side, but it's probably orange inside. But even if it was all green, you'd still call it an orange—you'd never call it a green. But it's just an orange." I handed it back.

He looked at me for a while. Then he said, "You don't understand, do you."

There, he was completely right. I had no idea what he was talking about.

He sat there looking at the orange and then looked up at me.

"I'm not from around here," he said. I had gathered as much. He spoke with some kind of thick European accent. "I was born in Germany before the second world war. I spent the war in a place called Auschwitz. Have you heard of Auschwitz?"

I had heard about World War II and the Nazi prison camps. We'd studied them in school. I told him so.

"But did they tell you about Auschwitz? Did they tell you how cold it was? Did they tell you"—and here he paused and thought for a moment—"that it was a world in black and white?"

The concentration camp at Auschwitz, Poland

I didn't say anything, and he went on.

"Everything there was black or white—or gray. The SS guards wore black uniforms and black boots. When the snow fell, it was pure white. The barbed wire on the fence was black, and we prisoners wore uniforms with black and white stripes. Underneath, our skin was pale and white from lack of sun, but the numbers they tattooed on us, they were black.

"When snow fell, it turned to gray the next day from the ashes that fell from the smokestacks. And the food was gray. It was soup, always soup. But the soup was made from a big barrel of water, maybe 50 gallons, that had two or three potatoes cooked in it until there was nothing left. The water turned gray like water from dirty dishes. But this was our food. Each day we would stand in a long line, each of us holding a tin bowl, waiting to get soup. We got one bowl each day, and that was all. If you got a piece of the potato, you were lucky.

"What time I had, I spent trying to stay warm. Our clothes were thin cloth—nothing more—and I used to walk near the fence looking for newspapers so I could crumple them up and put them in my clothes to keep warm.

"I remember one very cold day I found a piece of newspaper. When I picked it up, there was something orange beneath it. I had not seen anything orange in three months. I thought it might be something good, but I knew that if I bent down to pick it up and it was something good, if a guard saw me, he would shoot me to take it away. So instead I fell. I pretended to stumble. I knew that when a Jew fell, the guards laughed and looked away.

"I scraped my elbow, but it didn't matter. There, lying next to me in the snow was an orange. I couldn't believe it. I grabbed it, hid it in my clothes, and took it back to the barracks. There I hid it in a hole in the wall and waited until night.

"In the middle of the night, with my hands shaking, I took it out. Understand how hungry I was. I wanted to devour that orange. I was starving. But I knew that if I did, I would have nothing left. So I took that orange and rolled it in my hands so I could feel it. And then I closed my eyes and scratched the peel and smelled it.

"What I smelled was California. I had a brother who had left Germany before the war and moved to California. He had written me that the hills near Pasadena were beautiful and sunny and dry. He said there were so many orange trees that you could reach out and pick an orange and eat it, anytime you wanted. Even in winter.

"I opened my eyes again, and I was back in Auschwitz, in the barracks. I put the orange back.

"After that I brought the orange out each night, to roll it in my hands and smell it. I decided that I would let myself eat a piece of it after a bad day. I did not have to wait long. Soon there was a selection day. The guards lined us all up in a long line, and an officer at the front held a gun with a bayonet. He pointed it to one side or the other, shouting, 'Right! Left! Right! Right! Right! Left!' Those who were sent to the right would go back to the barracks. Those who were sent to the left—the ones who seemed sick or old or weak—would go to the showers. No one ever returned from the showers.

"I was sick. I had a cold and a cough. I promised myself that if I survived, I would eat a piece of the orange.

"When I got to the front, the guard looked at me. He paused. Then he shouted 'Right!'

"That night I took out my orange. I peeled it very carefully, very slowly. I saved the peel. I pulled out a section and ate it.

"I will tell you, nothing before or since has tasted so sweet. What I tasted was the taste of pure freedom.

"After that I ate a section of the orange every few days. The weather was so cold that it kept the orange for a long time, and by the time I finished the orange, the snow started to melt. Spring came. There were flowers, even in Auschwitz. And with the spring came the end of the war. I was freed, and I came here.

"But, you see, that orange saved my life."

As he said those words, the bus came to a stop. He stood up and gave me the orange. Then he said the word "Remember," and he got off the bus.

I never saw him again.

Joel ben Izzy gathers and tells stories in Europe, Israel, Asia, and the United States. He specializes in finding and recounting stories that have traveled great distances, across borders and through time. He tells many tales from his Jewish heritage. His tapes, published by Old City Press, have received awards from the Parents' Choice Foundation and the American Library Association. He lives with his wife, Taly, and their son, Elijah, in Berkeley, California.

Snapshot, 1944

David Mas Masumoto

A writer finds a photograph buried in his grandmother's dresser drawer, and he begins to ask questions: Where did the photo come from? Who were those people with the dark and blurry faces? What does the American flag symbolize? This story describes a Sansei, a third-generation Japanese-American, trying to make sense of the past—his family's history and the evacuation and relocation of Japanese from the West Coast of the United States during World War II. The story focuses on two times—the late 1980s and 1944—and on two places: Del Rey, California, and the Gila River Relocation Center, just south of Phoenix, Arizona. The terms Jiichan *and* Baachan, *used in the story, mean Grandpa and Grandma, respectively.*

I STARE AT THE SILENT AND STILL FACES, EXPRESSIONS FROZEN IN A SNAPSHOT. My family stands to the right. *Jiichan* holds a flag; *Baachan* lifts a photograph of her dead son. The aunts and uncles gather to the side; they look uncomfortable, cramped next to one another, unsure about what to do with their hands. Dad remains in the back, his face blurred in the shadows, almost unrecognizable. It was my uncle's funeral in 1944 at a place called Gila River Relocation Center in Arizona.

Jiichan stands erect, his chin out, body stiff. He does not press the American flag to his chest. His hands are loosely folded around the flag. His son lies in the U.S. Army uniform and casket behind him.

I never met *Jiichan*. He died before I was born. All I know are the stories my dad told.

"I remember the hot summer nights and Pop's wooden platform. Fresno's hundred-degree days would beat down on the place we lived. That shack had a tin roof, and the inside took hours to cool off after sunset. We didn't have a cooler or a fan, but it didn't matter; out in the country we didn't have electricity," said Dad.

"Pop made a low wooden platform from old barn wood. It rose about two feet off the ground, with a top area big enough for all of us kids. In the evenings Pop led everyone outside, and the whole family would lie on the platform, side by side, almost touching. After a day's work and a hot dinner and *ofuro* [Japanese bath], we gathered—talking, relaxing, gazing upward at the night sky. The dirt yard was beneath us; the vineyards began a few feet away. If a little breeze came, we could hear the grape leaves shifting and rustling. It seemed to make us feel cooler.

"Every summer we'd do that until it was time to go inside and sleep. Sometimes us boys would sleep all night on the platform. It was quiet, sort of peaceful."

The platform is gone, but some of *Jiichan*'s other works survive. In the back of our house stands a wooden bench. Simply made, the bench was never painted or sanded, yet the wood has become smooth from wear. Dad and I used it to take off our shoes after work. It felt good to relax for a moment, with the afternoon heat dissipating, the dust and sweat drying on our backs. In black letters *Hikazo Masumoto* is painted on one leg.

Funeral for three soldiers, Gila River Relocation Center, near Phoenix, Arizona, 1944

"After the camps, Pop was getting old for work on the farms," explained Dad. "But he loved to sit and stare into the fields. He made himself this bench, and he'd sit silently on it for hours."

In the corner of our living room, in a special compartment recessed in the wall, is the *butsudan* [Buddhist altar]. "Pop made it during camp, from scraps of wood," said Dad. It measures about two and a half feet by two feet. The outside is painted black, the inside a flat gold, neither varnished nor finished. A series of hinged doors folds open; three small altars with pillars, railings, and steps fill the interior. Most of the joints are notched—only a few nails used. The hinges are wooden slots and pegs fitted together.

EVERY SO OFTEN MOM OPENED THE *BUTSUDAN*, LIT THE CANDLES AND INCENSE, and offered fresh rice or food. The *butsudan* seemed to stare out at us, the incense dancing in the air and the candle flickering with any movement.

A photograph of *Jiichan* is kept before the butsudan. He was standing in front of a peach orchard when they took the picture. His arms hang to his sides, and his body is slightly slouched. He's wearing a black suit and a clean, pressed white shirt with a tie. Yet peeking beneath the cuffs of

Jiichan's pants are his old work shoes.

I'd study the picture, wondering about the old man I had never met. I'd look up at the *butsudan* and watch the incense drift through the air.

BAACHAN CLUTCHES THE PHOTOGRAPH OF HER DEAD SON. SHE STANDS NEXT TO *Jiichan*, who is on her right, and at her left is Fumiko, now the oldest child. *Baachan* lifts the gold-framed picture, her dark hands curled around the edges as she elevates it slightly, trying to hold it steady between herself and *Jiichan*.

Baachan lives with us, usually trying to keep out of the way, almost hiding, melting into the furniture. She does a little gardening, but she forgets about the running water and often floods the back yard. Or she doesn't remember where she planted the tomatoes and begins digging a new area for more plants.

I try to talk to her, but the Japanese I learned isn't the same. With *Baachan*, *jitensha* [bicycle] becomes *bai-ku*; *hon* [book] is *buu-ku*; digging weeds around vine stumps becomes *sha-bu-rin*; and most weeds are *warui kusa* [bad grass], while Johnson grass is *abunai kusa* [dangerous grass].

Jiichan died more than 25 years ago. *Baachan* says she's just waiting to die and join him. We tell her not to talk like that. At 85 she should be happy to be healthy. She doesn't answer, just nods her head.

When the photo exhibit of Executive Order 9066 was displayed in San Francisco, my aunt took *Baachan* to see it. My aunt had to explain to *Baachan* that they were in the Gila River photograph of the funeral for three families with dead sons. "*Baachan* cried," said my aunt. When they returned to Fresno, we asked *Baachan* about the exhibit. She couldn't remember much and said only a little, mainly about the drive there.

Sometimes *Baachan* just sits and stares, talking to herself. The same thoughts keep turning over and over in her mind. If I'm with her, she asks me five or six times in an afternoon, "Are you going to school? What kind of work you going to do?" The same questions, over and over.

She does remember the years of work, *shaburin* the vines, picking grapes next to *Jiichan*. But *Jiichan* and she never got a farm. After the camps, Dad worked and bought a farm, but for some reason *Baachan* insists the farm belongs to her and *Jiichan*.

She argues, demanding her farm. Her face changes; the deep wrinkles shift their pattern, and her muscles tense. Her hands, the rough, callused hands that used to *momo* [massage] my back, become clenched into fists. Her talking grows louder, the Japanese spliced with some English. "No!"

pierces her phrases. Her fist hits the table. She stands and begins raving about the land. She worked hard all her life, in the fields, next to *Jiichan*. Something belongs to her. The years, clearing the *abunai kusa*, she and *Jiichan*. She threatens Mom: "You kicked me out of my home. I have no home." Then silence. *Baachan* cries—no sounds, only tears. Dad gets her a tissue, and they sit together. No one talks.

YOU CAN BARELY SEE DAD, THE BLURRED FIGURE STANDING AT THE EDGE OF THE snapshot. Between Dad and *Baachan* were Aunt Fumiko, Uncle Kenji, who left for Chicago as soon as they let the Japanese out of the camps, and Aunt Kimiko, the little sister in bobby socks. Dad doesn't say much about the snapshot. "Yeah, I remember it" is about all he'll say.

Following the camps and time in the Army, Dad returned to the valley and farming. He found the family living in an abandoned grocery store. He hired himself out in the fields and hunted up jobs for an aging *Jiichan* and *Baachan*. The family tried to stay and work together. If Dad pruned vines, he'd have the old folks *nakagiri* [cut the center wood of the vines off the trellis wire]. When Dad picked grapes, he'd have them spread the grapes out on the wooden trays. Eventually Dad told Aunt Kimiko to get a job in the city—housecleaning, anything—so she could support herself and get out of the fields.

Dad continued to hustle for more work and money, learning to farm by renting some land and then gambling on a place of his own. It was a gamble *Baachan* never approved of because she felt it was too risky. There were too many things they did not know about, and she never approved of the idea, even after the land had been paid for and the farm established.

Dad's over 60 now, and he retains a farmer's tan: a dark face and branded *V* on his chest where the work shirt opens, with hands and arms browned to the point just above the elbows where rolled shirtsleeves end. In the past few years he has begun to slow down. On winter mornings he stays inside an extra hour or two before going out to prune. We talk more about farming and economics and politics or about football and baseball.

But once a thought about the snapshot did escape—a slip, a momentary flash of emotions. It happened on a cold, wintry morning when a chilling fog hovered outside, the type of fog that seems to penetrate to your bones. Dad stared outside and began whispering to himself. He was lost in thought, and a trance seemed to come over his face.

"What was I supposed to say?" he mumbled. Then out came a story about the funeral, after Uncle died. Dad fell into the role of eldest son.

Suddenly he had to take charge—he had responsibility for the family. He had to have all the answers.

"And what could I say to Pop? And Mom had all those questions— what was going to happen? All those questions . . . and what was I supposed to say?"

He sat and stared outside as the fog hugged the ground and enveloped the vineyards. We could barely make out their silhouette.

SILENT EXPRESSIONS LOCKED IN A SNAPSHOT. *JIICHAN* AND *BAACHAN* CLUTCH THE remains of their dead son. Dad stands in the blurred background.

I do not and cannot know what they felt. I was born 10 years later, in a different time and place. But a silence penetrates such gaps, linking me with my past: a silence felt by my family and carried through the years; a silence that teaches, yet I do not fully understand; a silence captured for a moment in a snapshot, 1944.

David Mas Masumoto is a farmer and a writer in Del Rey, California. He farms 80 acres of peaches and grapes and writes stories about the family farm, rural America, and the Japanese-American experience. He has published an oral history, Country Voices *(Inaka Countryside Publications, 1987), and a collection of short stories,* Silent Strength *(New Currents International, 1984). His most recent book is* Epitaph for a Peach: Four Seasons on My Family Farm *(HarperCollins, 1995).*

This story was first published in the book *Country Voices: The Oral History of a Japanese American Family Farm Community* by David Mas Masumoto (Inaka Countryside Publications, 1987). It is reprinted by permission.

Precious Freedom

Hanna Bandes Geshelin _____

This story describes a party I attended in 1989 in Boston, at which almost all the guests were émigrés from the U.S.S.R. The Soviet government had bugged homes, factories, and offices so the secret police could listen to private conversations. The persecution of Jews was worse. They were kept out of many universities and occupations and were beaten or sent to prison or Siberia for teaching or studying Jewish culture and religion. This story's immigrants kept their homeland's customs but quickly learned to think like Americans. As the story shows, we need to learn some lessons about freedom and oppression from these immigrants before they forget. Except for a few details, the story is completely true.

FREEDOM. MOST OF THE WORLD DOESN'T HAVE IT; DESPOTS AND REVOLUTIONARIES can take it away overnight. Like most valuable things, it's fragile. Just how fragile, I learned at my friend's "10 years in America party."

Tanya and I had been friends for most of that 10 years. For a while we'd spent hours together every week, but recently we'd grown apart. Even so, I was delighted to hear her voice on the phone.

"I'm having a birthday party, a turning-50 party. But I don't want people to know how old I am, so it's also my '10 years in America party.' Please come!"

"I'd love to!" I said. "What can I bring?"

"Bring the story of how we met and became friends."

The sound of Russian was floating into the lobby on drifts of cigarette smoke when I arrived at her building. *Of course*, I thought, *most of the guests will be Russian.* Hoping there'd be some other Americans there too, I went upstairs, pushed open her door, and went in.

People were crowded together, standing closer than Americans usually stand. The strong smell of sweat mingled with flowery perfume and smoke, and for a moment I couldn't breathe. Gold teeth flashed; rhinestones sparkled. A plaintive violin—the real thing, not a recording—wailed Russian folk tunes, and a couple of voices joined it. This was not your typical American party. It was straight from a foreign film—or from Moscow.

A great shaggy bear of a man waved a vodka bottle at me and shouted something that must have meant, "Come in, come in!"

"Tanya?" I yelled back, and the bear pointed toward the kitchen, explaining volubly in Russian. I elbowed through the crowd.

Entering the kitchen, I immediately flattened myself against the kitchen wall to avoid two arguing men, arms waving, who pushed out into the living room. *If that's how people at a party act*, I thought, *no wonder we've had the Cold War!*

I took a deep breath and looked around the kitchen for Tanya. I remembered the kitchen well. We'd painted it together. And I'd been the first person in years to really clean the old gas range. I taught Tanya how to use that stove, about the pilot lights for the burners and using a match to light the oven. I explained about defrosting the old refrigerator too; now through the crowd I caught sight of a new one, probably frost-free. Tanya was leaning against the new refrigerator, talking.

When she caught sight of me, she waved and yelled something in Russian. Then she laughed and said, "I forgot—you don't speak Russian. Come, I have to introduce you to my friends!"

I chatted with some people for a while, until the wailing violin gave way to foot-stamping accordion music, and everyone joined in the song. I pushed through the crowd to the table of food. It held little resemblance to the chip-and-dip spread of the typical American party.

There were five or six kinds of smoked fish, olives ranging from green through reddish brown to black, paper-thin slices of rye bread, seeded crackers, dishes of I-don't-know-what. Many guests had brought food, each donation a work of art: a small black oval dish with radish flowers, carrot curls, slivers of green pepper, and bits of cheese arranged like an abstract painting; tiny fish filets rolled around bits of green onion and laid out in a spiral. I was amazed and enchanted at the effort that had gone into each plate.

Days later, when I was grocery shopping, I remembered something another Russian friend had once said: "The first time I went to the supermarket in America, I ran from aisle to aisle, grabbing things. I filled the wagon to overflowing and spent, I don't know, probably a couple of hundred dollars on meat, fish, vegetables, and fruit. Most of it rotted before I could eat it. In the Soviet Union, if the stores had something today, you knew they wouldn't have it tomorrow. I couldn't believe that the supermarket would really have all that food the next day or the next or the next. Food, all the food I wanted—that was the hardest thing to get used to in America." Was it that respect for food, borne of shortages and hunger, remaining long after the supermarket had become part of the daily routine, that those beautiful offerings showed?

A gray-haired woman, ramrod-straight, saw me standing by the food, listening to the singing. "Natasha," she said, introducing herself. "Formerly brain surgeon, now accounting clerk. And you are Tanya's American friend."

She spoke of her jobs—the members of the Kremlin on whom she had operated, the routine job she now held. "I'm too old to go back to school so I can practice medicine here," she said. "And I don't want to retrain as a nurse after being one of the most important doctors in Moscow. I and my children will always be immigrants. But my grandchildren—they're 100 percent American!"

Natasha stayed by me, drawing me into conversation with many others, translating when necessary. Then Tanya shouted something in Russian, and the crowd fell silent.

"People are going to tell stories about Tanya now," Natasha said. "I'll translate for you."

One after another the guests stood and talked. One woman said she'd been very homesick and had been walking down the street almost crying from loneliness, missing her lifelong friend, Marina, when whom should she see coming toward her but Marina's younger sister—Tanya. Others talked about the way Tanya, an early immigrant, had eased their more recent settlement in America.

Finally it was my turn. Natasha turned to the crowd and spoke, then turned back to me. "Now I'll translate from English to Russian."

"Tanya asked me to tell you how we met," I began. "We met at the bus stop on a cold autumn day. We lived on the same street and took the same bus to work each day, and since the buses were unreliable, we stood at the stop for 10 or 15 minutes every morning.

"I had just moved to the city and didn't know many people. I was used to a small town, where people spoke to—or at the very least smiled at—everyone else. I hated the big-city way of avoiding the eyes of those around you. And there at the bus stop was a woman who smiled back!

"Finally one drizzly day when we'd waited almost a half hour for the bus, I said—in the rapid-fire way of talking I'd picked up since moving to the city—"Terrible weather, isn't it?"

"The woman said, 'Yes?'

"Somewhat encouraged, I continued, 'It's a real drag to get soaked and chilled to the bone before the workday even starts, don't you agree?'

"She smiled and said again, 'Yes?'

"'Clearly our bus service is really deteriorating.'

"'Yes?'

"And suddenly I realized she didn't understand a word I had said! I was silent for a moment, thinking. Then, pronouncing each simple word slowly and carefully, I said, 'The bus is very late.'

"'Yes!'

"From then on, Tanya and I were friends, the new Russian immigrant and the newly arrived country kid. We both felt like strangers in a strange land. For all our differences, we had a lot in common.

"Tanya would come over to my apartment. We'd sit in the kitchen and drink herbal tea, speaking of the weather or something equally unimportant. When the tea was gone, Tanya would say, 'Let's go for a walk.'

"It didn't matter how cold it was, Tanya still wanted to go for a walk. It was a bitterly cold winter, with weeks when the temperature hovered around zero. No matter; we'd bundle up, and off we'd go. And it was there, on the cold and windy streets, that the real Tanya would surface, where she would talk about the things that were important to her.

"At first I thought it just took her time to be comfortable with me. Then I realized I was wrong: something very different was going on.

"I noticed that although the weather was terrible, the streets were filled with Russians . . ."

"We hadn't bought cars yet," shouted the bear who'd waved the vodka bottle, and everyone laughed.

"That's also true," I said. "I think it was something else, though. I think no one really believed it was safe to speak indoors. Everyone thought the walls in America had ears, the way the walls in the Soviet Union did."

Shocked silence filled the room. Then the Russians began whispering to one another. I watched and listened, bewildered. What had I said?

After what felt like an eternity, the bear of a man said in a subdued voice, "We forgot what it was like not to be free. Living under Communism was so terrible, we thought we'd never forget, but we forgot. We all forgot."

"It took an American to remind us," added the violinist. "We're ashamed." He picked up his violin and started a mournful, wailing melody. Several soft voices joined the song, but after a few bars he stopped playing and waved the violin bow at the crowd.

"We can't forget," he shouted in his heavily accented English. "We must remember what it was like to live in fear, and we must tell the Americans. Because if they don't know how terrible it is not to be free, why should they defend their freedoms?"

He jumped to his feet, tucked the violin back under his chin, waved his bow at the crowd and at me, and shouted, "Sing!"

He began to play. And with the newest arrivals humming along, the Russian-Americans began the song. I joined them as we sang, together, "Oh, say can you see by the dawn's early light . . ."

Hanna Bandes Geshelin of Boston has told and written stories since childhood. Her children's novel, Reb Aharon's Treasure *(Targum/Feldheim, 1993), won the 1991 Sydney Taylor Manuscript Prize. She specializes in stories that present the wonder and joy of life. Having worked many years in the helping professions, she believes that everything is a lesson from which we can learn and grow. Her favorite stories share those special moments when suddenly everything is different.*

Tellers' Products and Services

John L. Beach

Books Without Covers, 1315 Kimberly Ave., Rock Springs, Wyo. 82901, 307-362-7495

Audiotape: *Stretching the West*, Books Without Covers, 1995

Performances: Outlaws of Wyoming; Stretching the Truth—Tall Tales; The Mountain Man Experience; Family Stories (Seeing Yourself); others also available. • Workshops: Tying Families Together Through Stories; Research Techniques for Stories; writing workshops for all age levels; others also available.

Joel ben Izzy

1715 La Loma Ave., Berkeley, Calif. 94709, 510-883-0883, fax 510-883-0888

Audiotapes (from Old City Press; $10.95 each plus $.83 tax for California purchasers): *The Beggar King and Other Tales From Around the World*, 1993 • *Stories From Far Away*, 1991

Performances: Stories from around the world • Workshops on the art of storytelling

Judith Black

Tidal Wave Productions, 33 Prospect St., Marblehead, Mass. 01945

Audiotapes (from Tidal Wave Productions; $10 each except where noted): *Adult Children of . . . Parents*, 1993, $12 • *The Home Front*, 1993, $12 (offered with *The Home Front Teacher's Guide*, grades 5–12, $6; tape includes the story "Rosie the Riveter") • *Banned in the Western Suburbs*, two tapes, 1989, $18 • *Glad to Be Who I Am*, 1989 • *Waiting for Elijah*, 1987 • *Hell for a Picnic*, 1984

Courses and seminars for teachers, museum docents, and historians on bringing history alive through story • Available for commissions—will create stories for organizations or focus on a specific time and place in history.

Lucille Breneman

619-487-5361

Book: *Once Upon a Time: A Storytelling Handbook*, Nelson-Hall Publishers, 1983, $21.95

Jack Briggs

History Teller, 2114 Exton Dr., Wilmington, Del. 19810, 302-475-9442

Audiotape: *Peddler's Pack: Being an Entertainment of Tales From Revolutionary America*, self-published, 1988, $10 postpaid (includes the story "Lydia Darragh")

Workshops for teachers on history-based thematic education and storytelling in the classroom • Living history and story programs performed in period clothing with artifacts, demonstrations, and stories of and from the era; programs include the Colonial Peddler, Union Civil War Soldier, Medieval Knight, Mountain Men and the Frontier, Marco Polo in China, Orville Wright and the First Flight.

Joseph Bruchac

P.O. Box 308, Greenfield Center, N.Y. 12833, 518-584-1728

Call or write to request a free catalog of books and tapes by Native American authors (including Joseph Bruchac). Send a stamped self-addressed 9- by 12-inch envelope.

Michael Carney

P.O. Box 158, Point Reyes, Calif. 94956, 415-663-1312

Audiotapes (self-published; $10 each postpaid): *Sacagawea and the Corps of Discovery*, 1992 • *A Touch of Magic*, 1990

Available to tell stories at schools, community centers, libraries, churches, storytelling festivals, and other venues.

Charlie Chin

Book: *China's Bravest Girl: The Legend of Hua Mu Lan*, illustrated by Tomie Arai, Children's Book Press, 1993 (6400 Hollis St. #4, Emeryville, Calif. 94608, 510-655-3395, fax 510-655-1978)

Jim Cogan

Storyteller, 323 E. Matilija St., Suite 110-159, Ojai, Calif. 93023, 805-640-1364, fax 805-640-0165

Audiotapes (from Quijote Productions): *The Little People: Participation Stories for Children*, 1994 • *Spirits in the Wind: Timeless Myths and Legends*, 1994 • *Telling American Tales: History, Legend, and Lore*, 1994

Performances: Quijote-in-Concert; storytelling presentations for festivals, conferences, conventions, libraries, schools (kindergarten through college), and special programs (D.A.R.E./D.A.T.E., child abuse, etc.) • Workshops: History as Story, for educators and professionals; Storytelling in the Classroom, as in-service, for educators; Tale of the Tell: Storytelling Skills, for children and adults • Residency: Students as Storytellers, varied lengths

Sheila Dailey

Storytime Productions, 1326 E. Broadway, Mount Pleasant, Mich. 48858, 517-772-3956

Audiotapes (from Storytime Productions): *Stories of the Long Christmas*, 1987 • *Land of the Sky Blue Waters: Stories and Legends of the Great Lakes* with curriculum guide *Taking It Further*, 1986

Books: *Putting the World in a Nutshell: The Art of the Formula Tale*, H.W. Wilson, 1994 • *Storytelling: A Creative Teaching Strategy* with tape *The Extraordinary Cat and Other Stories*, Storytime Productions, 1985

Workshops: Storytelling: Pathway to Literacy; Discovering the Formula Tale: A Beginner's Workshop

Lucinda Flodin

The Storyweavers, Route 1, Box 726, Hampton, Tenn. 37658, 615-725-3506

Audiotapes (self-published): *Mountain Spirits*, 1991 • *Strawberries in the Snow*, 1989

Hanna Bandes Geshelin

12 Brookside Ave., Worcester, Mass. 01602

Books: *Reb Aharon's Treasure*, Targum/Phillip Feldheim, 1993 • *Sleepy River*, illustrated by Jeanette Winter, Philomel, 1993 • *Spinning Tales, Weaving Hope: Stories of Peace, Justice, and the Environment*, edited by Ed Brody, Jay Goldspinner, Katie Green, Rona Leventhal, and John Porcino (includes a story by Hanna Bandes Geshelin), New Society, 1992

Workshops and performances: What's the Message?; Telling Your Own Stories; Healing Stories; The Panorama of Jewish Lore; Wonderful Women; Just for Kids; Life, Love, and Laughter; Helping Others; Strong Women, Gentle Men; Healing Tales; also story programs of particular interest to Jewish audiences

Karen Golden

Golden Button Productions, 1165 S. Sierra Bonita Ave., Los Angeles, Calif. 90019, 213-933-4614

Audiotape: *Tales and Scales—Stories of Jewish Wisdom*, self-published, 1993, $12 postpaid

Performances: A Walk Around the World in Stories and Shoes; Stories of Jewish Wisdom; Breathing Biographies • Residencies and workshops: History Alive; Everyone Has a History to Tell, to Write, to Share

Martha Hamilton and Mitch Weiss

Beauty & the Beast Storytellers, P.O. Box 6624, Ithaca, N.Y. 14851, 607-277-0016

Audiotape: *Tales of Wonder, Magic, Mystery & Humor From Around the World*, self-published, 1985

Videotape: *Tell Me a Story*, Barr Entertainment, 1986

Books: *Spinning Tales, Weaving Hope: Stories of Peace, Justice, and the Environment*, edited by Ed Brody, Jay Goldspinner, Katie Green, Rona Leventhal, and John Porcino (includes a story by Martha Hamilton and Mitch Weiss), New Society, 1992 • *Children Tell Stories: A Teaching Guide*, Richard C. Owen, 1990 (800-336-5588)

Storytelling performances for all ages • Storytelling workshops and extended residencies for schools and organizations • Adult workshops: Teaching Children to Tell Stories; How to Choose, Learn, and Tell a Story; Tandem Storytelling: How to Tell With a Partner; Why Every Teacher Should Be a Storyteller (how to tell to preschoolers, middle-schoolers, and so on)

Annette Harrison

6370 Pershing Ave., St. Louis, Mo. 63130, 314-725-7767

Audiotapes (self-published): *Lilith's Cave*, 1989 • *Storytelling, American Style* by Annette Harrison and Perrin Stifel, 1989 • *A Dash of Seasoning*, 1988

Books: *Easy-to-Tell Stories for Young Children*, National Storytelling Press, 1992 (NSA, P.O. Box 309, Jonesborough, Tenn. 37659, 800-525-4514) • *Storytelling Activities Kit* by Annette Harrison and Jerilynn Changar, Prentice Hall, 1992 (order from Annette Harrison)

Workshops: Catch the Storytelling Bug! A Participatory Workshop for Beginners; Storytelling: A Teaching Technique That Works; Developing Students' Storytelling Skills; A Student Storytelling Troupe: A Workshop for Junior and Senior High School Students; Working It Out! The Storytelling Connection to Conflict Resolution • Programs: Folklore From Around the World; Peace and Justice Tales; Listen My Children and You Shall Hear; From One Generation to Another; Stories for the Little Folk; Pick a Holiday, Pick a Season; Her Story • Also available for performances and keynote addresses.

Kendall Haven

1155 Hart Lane, Fulton, Calif. 95439, 707-577-0259

Audiotapes: *The Adventures of Christina Valentine* (three-hour six-episode radio drama), Children's Television Resource and Education Center, 1992 • *Fathers and Sons*, StoryStreet USA, 1992 • *Neighborhood Magic*, StoryStreet USA, 1990 • *Dinosaur Tales*, StoryStreet USA, 1986 • *Reluctant Heroes*, StoryStreet USA, 1986

Books: *The Women's Share: Forty Marvels of American History*, Libraries Unlimited, 1995 (800-237-6124) • *Marvels of Science: 50 Fascinating Five-Minute Reads*, Libraries Unlimited, 1994 • *The Killer Brussel Sprouts*, JTG of Nashville, 1991 (800-222-2584)

Performances and workshops at school, universities, theaters, and libraries nationwide; conducts workshops, in-services, and extended courses on the effective in-class use of storytelling as a powerful teaching tool.

Sharon Y. Holley

31 St. Paul Mall, Buffalo, N.Y. 14209, 716-886-1399

Storytelling performances focusing on African-American stories • Workshops: Infusing African and African-American Materials Into the Curriculum; Family Storytelling; Kwanza

Jonathan Kruk

24½ Garden St., Cold Spring on Hudson, N.Y. 10516, 800-578-4859

Audiotape/CD: *The Rainbow Dragon & Other Tales*, Wizmak Productions, 1995, $11 for tape, $18 for CD

Workshops: Children Making Children's Books; Story Maps; Local Lore; Creative Dramatics; Storytelling in the Classroom • Performances: Participatory Fables for Young Children; East of the Sun, West of the Moon; stories for children from around the world; Medieval Myths; Imps & Indians, Pirates & Patriots of the Hudson River

Paul Leone

184 Lakeview Ave., Jamestown, N.Y. 14701, 716-664-2997

Book in preparation: *Chautauqua Ghosts*, the ghosts of Chautauqua County and vicinity in historical settings

Workshops: History Through Stories; Creating Your Own History

Doug Lipman

Enchanters Press, P.O. Box 441195, West Somerville, Mass. 02144, 617-391-3672

Audiotapes: *Grass Roots and Mountain Peaks: Vision for the Storytelling Movement*, Enchanters Press, 1993 • *Now We Are Free: Stories and Songs of Freedom, For Passover and Anytime*, Enchanters Press, 1992 • *The Amazing Teddy Bear: Stories With Songs for Parent and Child*, Enchanters Press, 1991 • *Hopping Freights: A Wild '60s Adventure*, Yellow Moon Press, 1990 (800-497-4385) • *One Little Candle: Participation Stories and Songs for Hanukkah*, Enchanters Press, 1990 • *The Forgotten Story: Tales of Wise Jewish Men*, Yellow Moon Press, 1988 • *Milk From the Bull's Horn: Tales and Songs of Nurturing Men*, Yellow Moon Press, 1986 • *Tell It With Me: More Participation Stories With Songs*, A Gentle Wind, 1985 • *Folktales of Strong Women*, Yellow Moon Press, 1983 • *Keep On Shaking: Participation Stories With Songs*, A Gentle Wind, 1982

Videotape: *Coaching Storytellers: A Demonstration Workshop for All Who Use Oral Communication*, Enchanters Press, 1993 (81-minute VHS format; includes user's guide)

Book–tape combination: *We All Go Together: Creative Activities for Children to Use With Multicultural Folksongs*, Oryx Press, 1994

Books: *Storytelling Games*, Oryx Press, 1995 • *Spinning Tales, Weaving Hope: Stories of Peace, Justice, and the Environment*, edited by Ed Brody, Jay Goldspinner, Katie Green, Rona Leventhal, and John Porcino (includes a story by Doug Lipman), New Society, 1992 • *The Ghost and I: Scary Stories for Participatory Telling*, edited by

Doug Lipman   *(continued from previous page)*

Jennifer Justice, Yellow Moon Press, 1992 • *Joining In: An Anthology of Audience Participation Stories and How to Tell Them* (includes a story by Doug Lipman), compiled by Teresa Miller, with assistance from Anne Pellowski, edited by Norma J. Livo, Yellow Moon Press, 1988

Periodical: *The Storytelling Coach Newsletter*, published twice a year; free from Enchanters Press

Performances: Story and song, with guitar, banjo, button accordion, and other instruments; multicultural participation stories with songs for young ones; stories from history, tradition, and original material; story theater for adults • Workshops for children and adults: how to tell stories; using story games; using music with children • Coaching for storytellers and oral communicators at all levels; multiday workshops or consultations in your locale; coaching and producing of your audiotape

David Massengill
179 E. Third St. #20, New York, N.Y. 10009, 212-533-6297

Audiotapes ($12 each postpaid): *The Return*, David Massengill Music, 1995 (includes the song "Rider on an Orphan Train") • *Coming Up for Air,* Flying Fish, 1992 (CD $17) • *The Kitchen Tape,* self-published, 1987 • *The Great American Bootleg Tape,* self-published, 1986

Performances: Concerts including original songs written for dulcimer and guitar • Available for workshops, seminars, and concerts involving story and song.

David Mas Masumoto
9336 E. Lincoln, Del Rey, Calif. 93616, 209-834-3648, e-mail: masumoto@aol.com

Books: *Epitaph for a Peach: Four Seasons on My Family Farm*, HarperCollins, 1995 • *Country Voices: The Oral History of a Japanese American Family Farm Community*, Inaka Countryside Publications, 1987 • *Silent Strength*, New Currents International, 1984

Marie Anne McLean
203 Tudor Lane, Edmonton, Alberta T6J 3T5, Canada, 403-476-7736 or 403-476-0366

Write or call for information about storytelling services.

Mike T. Mullen
P.O. Box 23574, Pleasant Hill, Calif. 94523, 510-685-1772

Audiotapes (self-published): *Hoppy the Frog*, 1994 • *Storytellin' Hat*, 1993

Concerts and workshops for children of all ages

Kay Negash
5445 White Place, Boulder, Colo. 80303, 303-447-8679

Audiotapes (self-published; $10 each plus $2 postage and handling): *Growing Up: Stories of Home*, 1992 • *Old Irish Tales*, 1990 • *Stories Under the Stars*, 1988 • *Two Families*, 1986 • *Two Colorado Women*, 1984

Performances for adults and children: History stories (Aztec, Old West, Great Depression, Holocaust); personal and family stories; folk tales of many cultures; wildlife and environmental stories • Workshops: Interactive and participatory program that guides adults in creating their own personal and family stories; program to help children structure and tell spontaneous and prepared stories in classroom or recreational settings

Bobby Norfolk
Folktale Productions, P.O. Box 9182, St. Louis, Mo. 63117, 314-968-2606 or 314-968-4303

Audiotapes (from Folktale Productions; $11 each plus $1.50 postage and handling except where noted): *Storyteller in a Groove*, 1993 (CD $16 plus $1.50 postage and handling) • *Norfolk Tales*, 1989 • *Why Mosquitoes Buzz in People's Ears*, 1987

Theater productions: Scott Joplin: From Rags to Riches; Telling Our Stories: The Life of Paul Laurence Dunbar; Drums of Africa; Folktales From Around the World • Programs for all ages: Straight Talk; Holiday/Seasonal Tales; Folktales and More; Environmental Stories; Anansi the Spider Stories; Family Stories • Programs for children: Dinosaur Tales (grades K–8); Literature, Poetry & Prose (grades 4–12) • Workshops for adults: One-, two-, and three-hour workshops on storytelling techniques, theater, creativity, imagination, writing, and mime • Workshops for children: Themes include writing, voice projection, body movements, role-playing, storytelling techniques, and overcoming shyness. Participation activities are included.

Jay O'Callahan

Artana Productions, P.O. Box 1054, Marshfield, Mass. 02050, 800-626-5356

Audiotapes (from Artana Productions): *Father Joe*, 1994 • *The Dance*, 1992 • *Jeremy: A Christmas Story*, 1991 • *Coming Home to Someplace New: Pill Hill Stories*, 1990 • *The Silver Stream*, with music by David Gay, 1990 • *The Gouda*, 1989 • *The Island*, with music by David Gay, 1988 • *Mostly Scary*, 1987 • *Petrukian*, 1986 • *Village Heroes*, 1986 • *Little Heroes*, 1985 • *The Strait of Magellan*, 1985 • *Earth Stories*, 1984 • *The Golden Drum*, with music by David Gay, 1984 • *The Minister of Others' Affairs*, 1984 • *The Herring Shed*, 1983 • *Raspberries*, 1983 • *The Little Dragon*, 1982 • CD: *Around the Year With Jay O'Callahan*, 1993

Videotapes: *Atlanta Story Fest: The Herring Shed*, WPBA Atlanta, 1991 • *Atlanta Story Fest: Politics and Others*, WPBA Atlanta, 1991 • *Six Stories About Little Heroes*, Vineyard Video Productions, 1986 • *Herman and Marguerite*, Vineyard Video Productions, 1986 • *A Master Class in Storytelling*, Vineyard Video Productions, 1984

Susan "Supe" O'Halloran

927 Noyes St., Evanston, Ill. 60201, 708-869-4081

Audiotapes (self-published): *Moments of Grace*, 1995 • *Too Tall*, 1995 • *Mothers and Other Wild Women*, stories told by Nancy Donoval, Beth Horner, and Supe O'Halloran, 1993 • *Growing Up in Chicago*, volumes 1 and 2, 1992 and 1993

Books: *The Woman Who Found Her Voice*, LuraMedia, 1996 (800-367-5872) • *The Hunt for Spring*, Riverbank Press, 1995 • *Storybook Marriage*, self-published, 1994 (a collection of tales written for *Marriage Magazine*) • *The Woman Who Lost Her Heart*, with co-author Susan Delattre, LuraMedia, 1992

Performances: Personal stories; original fables; audience participation • Workshops: The Garbage Story and Other Ways to Undo Racism; The We in the I: Personal Stories That Become Universal; What Kind of Funny Are You? Adding Humor to Your Stories; Road Warriors: Taking Care of Yourself on the Road and at Home; Getting Published and Living to Tell About It

Duncan Sings-Alone

800 Oak Dr., Mechanicsville, Md. 20659

Book: *The Fractured Mirror: Healing Multiple Personality Disorder* by C. W. Duncan, Health Communications Press, 1994

Performances: Contemporary and traditional Native American stories for a variety of audiences

Fran Stallings

Prairie-Fire Productions, 1406 Macklyn Lane, Bartlesville, Okla. 74006, 918-333-7390

Audiotapes (from Prairie-Fire Productions): *Cat o' Nine Tales: Stories and Songs About Cats*, 1994 • *Crane's Gratitude and Other Tales of Animal Wit & Wisdom*, 1992 • *Storytelling With Autoharp*, 1991

Stories in anthologies: *Best Stories From the Texas Storytelling Festival*, edited by Finley Stewart, August House, 1995 (800-284-8784) • *We Like Kids' Animal Stories* (book and audiotape set), edited by Jeff Brown, Scott Foresman/Goodyear Books, 1994 • *The Ghost and I: Scary Stories for Participatory Telling*, edited by Jennifer Justice, Yellow Moon Press, 1992 (800-497-4385) • *Joining In: An Anthology of Audience Participation Stories and How to Tell Them*, compiled by Teresa Miller, with assistance from Anne Pellowski, edited by Norma J. Livo, Yellow Moon Press, 1988

Workshops: Getting Started in Storytelling: Teacher as Village Storyteller; Teaching Students to Tell: Re-creating the Village Community; Telling Personal and Family Stories; Putting the Story Back Into History; Curriculum Integration Through Storytelling; Joining In: Audience-Participation Storytelling; Stories for a Green Earth: Teaching Ecology and Biology Through Traditional Stories; Oklahoma History • Concerts and residencies: Call for information.

John Stansfield

Storytelling by John Stansfield, Box 588, Monument, Colo. 80132, 719-481-3202 or 800-484-6963, ext. 8253

Audiotapes (self-published): *Song of the Mountains, Song of the Plains*, 1990 • *Stories for All Seasons*, 1985 • *Favorite Stories*, 1982

Programs for all ages: The Living History of the West; The World of Folklore; Literature Aloud! • Workshops for school-age children to adults: Reclaiming the West Through Storytelling; Storytelling—The Tell-Tale Art; Storytelling in the Classroom; others also available.

Ruth Stotter

Stotter Press, Box 726, Stinson Beach, Calif. 94970
(Note: California purchasers must add sales tax.)

Audiotapes (from Stotter Press): *Women of the West*,
1995, $10 postpaid • *True Tales From California History*,
two tapes, 1991, $20 postpaid

Books (from Stotter Press): *The Storyteller's Calendar*,
published annually since 1988; current edition is $10
plus $2 postage and handling; earlier editions are $5. •
*About Story: A Collection of Articles About Stories and
Storytelling*, 1994, $15 plus $2 postage and handling

Richard Alan Young and
Judy Dockrey Young

P.O. Box 1300, Kimberling City, Mo. 65686-1300

Audiotapes (from August House, 800-284-8784): *Head
on the High Road*, 1993 • *There's No Such Thing as Ghosts*,
1993 • *Ozark Ghost Stories*, 1992 • *Ozark Tall Tales*,
1992 • *Favorite Scary Stories*, volume 1 (grades K–3) and
volume 2 (grades 4–6), 1991

Books (from August House): *Ozark Ghost Stories*, 1995 •
Race With Buffalo, 1994 • *African-American Stories for
Young Readers*, 1993 • *The Scary Story Reader*, 1993 •
Outlaw Tales, 1992 • *Stories From the Days of Christopher
Columbus*, 1992 • *Ghost Stories From the American South-
west*, 1991 • *Favorite Scary Stories of American Children*,
1990 • *Ozark Tall Tales*, 1989

Workshops, performances, and speaking engagements
are offered throughout the Midwest.

Index of Stories

Index of Tellers